P9-BZT-524

GOD

Also by Alexander Waugh

Time

GOD

Alexander Waugh

Thomas Dunne Books
St. Martin's Press ⚜ New York

THOMAS DUNNE BOOKS.
An imprint of St. Martin's Press.

GOD. Copyright © 2002 by Alexander Waugh. All rights reserved.
Printed in the United States of America. No part of this book may
be used or reproduced in any manner whatsoever without written
permission except in the case of brief quotations embodied in critical
articles or reviews. For information, address St. Martin's Press, 175
Fifth Avenue, New York, N.Y. 10010.

Every effort has been made to fulfill requirements with regard to
reproducing copyright material. The author and publisher will be
glad to rectify any omissions at the earliest opportunity.

www.stmartins.com

ISBN 0-312-32905-9
EAN 978-0312-32905-1

First published in Great Britain by REVIEW,
an imprint of Headline Book Publishing

First U.S. Edition: May 2004

10 9 8 7 6 5 4 3 2 1

For Mary

GOD

Alexander Waugh

Thomas Dunne Books
St. Martin's Press New York

THOMAS DUNNE BOOKS.
An imprint of St. Martin's Press.

GOD. Copyright © 2002 by Alexander Waugh. All rights reserved.
Printed in the United States of America. No part of this book may
be used or reproduced in any manner whatsoever without written
permission except in the case of brief quotations embodied in critical
articles or reviews. For information, address St. Martin's Press, 175
Fifth Avenue, New York, N.Y. 10010.

Every effort has been made to fulfill requirements with regard to
reproducing copyright material. The author and publisher will be
glad to rectify any omissions at the earliest opportunity.

www.stmartins.com

ISBN 0-312-32905-9
EAN 978-0312-32905-1

First published in Great Britain by REVIEW,
an imprint of Headline Book Publishing

First U.S. Edition: May 2004

10 9 8 7 6 5 4 3 2 1

For Mary

CONTENTS

LIST OF ILLUSTRATIONS

Page 1. (top left) Isis nursing her son Horus from the necropolis of Ballana Qustul Nubia © The Art Archive/Egyptian Museum Cairo/Dagli Orti (A); (right) The god Atum Ra from the deceased priest Menkheperre's funerary papyrus book of the dead, late New Kingdom © The Art Archive/Egyptian Museum Cairo/Dagli Orti (A); (bottom left) Ceiling decorated with astronomical scenes in tomb of Ramses VI, 1156–1148 BC 20th dynasty Egyptian pharaoh, Valley of the Kings, Thebes, Egypt (detail) © The Art Archive/Dagli Orti

Page 2. (top) The Holy Trinity by Titian (Tiziano Vecellio) (*c.* 1488–1576) © Prado, Madrid, Spain/The Bridgeman Art Library; (bottom) Moses and the Burning Bush by William Blake (1757–1827) © The Art Archive/Victoria and Albert Museum London/Sally Chappell

Page 3. (top left) The Trinity by J. Baco (1410–61) and J. Rexach (1415–84) © Musee de Picardi, Amiens/The Bridgeman Art Library; (top right) *Sinopia*: Face of God the Creator, in San Francesco (Treasury), Assisi by Jacopo Torriti (13–14th century) © La Scala; (bottom left) The Holy Trinity by Anonimo Flamenco (16th Century) © Prado, Madrid, Spain/The Bridgeman Art Library; (bottom right) Father Major Jealous Divine, founder of the International Peace Movement in 1919 © Hulton Archive

Page 4. (top right) Moses holding the Ten Commandments © Hulton Archive; (bottom left) A lithograph of Joseph Smith (1805–1844) © Hulton Archive; (bottom right) Neale Donald Walsch © Elizabeth Hinshaw

Page 5. (top) Taken from Royaumont, *Histoire de l'Ancien et Nouveau Testament* (1724) © Mary Evans Picture Library; (bottom left) The Madonna del Parto, *c.*1460 by Piero della Francesca, (*c.* 1419/21–92) © Chapel of the Cemetery, Monterchi, Italy/The Bridgeman Art Library; (bottom right) Ecstasy of St Theresa, sculpture by Giovanni Lorenzo Bernini (1598–1680) © Santa Maria della Vittoria, Rome, Italy/The Bridgeman Art Library

Page 6. (top) Jews in prayer at the Western, or Wailing, Wall, in Jerusalem, Israel © Hulton Archive; (bottom) A Muslim man praying in front of a mosque. An engraving by Whymper after S Senior © Hulton Archive

Page 7. (top) American evangelist Oral Roberts sits on a platform and holds his hand over a man's forehead as the man clutches his waist on stage during a prayer tour © Hulton Archive; (bottom) A Christian family say morning prayers before their breakfast *c.* 1848 © Hulton Archive

Page 8. (top left) The Liebana Beatus commentary on the Apocalypse from Guadalupe 10th century © The Art Archive/Real biblioteca de lo Escorial/Dagli Orti (A); (top right) Adam and Eve by Lucas Cranach, the elder (1472–1553) © The Art Archive/National Museum of Prague/Dagli Orti; (bottom) Dante meeting the thieves; canto 24 of the Divine Comedy (Hell) by Dante Alighieri (1265–1321) Italian writer, in 14th-century Venetian manuscript © The Art Archive/Biblioteca Nazionale Marciana Venice/Dagli Orti

LIST OF ILLUSTRATIONS

Page 1. (top left) Isis nursing her son Horus from the necropolis of Ballana Qustul Nubia © The Art Archive/Egyptian Museum
Cairo/Dagli Orti (A); (right) The god Atum Ra from the deceased
priest Menkheperre's funerary papyrus book of the dead, late New
Kingdom © The Art Archive/Egyptian Museum Cairo/Dagli Orti
(A); (bottom left) Ceiling decorated with astronomical scenes in tomb
of Ramses VI, 1156–1148 BC 20th dynasty Egyptian pharaoh, Valley
of the Kings, Thebes, Egypt (detail) © The Art Archive/Dagli Orti

Page 2. (top) The Holy Trinity by Titian (Tiziano Vecellio)
(c. 1488–1576) © Prado, Madrid, Spain/The Bridgeman Art Library;
(bottom) Moses and the Burning Bush by William Blake (1757–1827)
© The Art Archive/Victoria and Albert Museum London/Sally
Chappell

Page 3. (top left) The Trinity by J. Baco (1410–61) and J. Rexach
(1415–84) © Musee de Picardi, Amiens/The Bridgeman Art Library;
(top right) *Sinopia*: Face of God the Creator, in San Francesco
(Treasury), Assisi by Jacopo Torriti (13–14th century) © La Scala;
(bottom left) The Holy Trinity by Anonimo Flamenco (16th Century)
© Prado, Madrid, Spain/The Bridgeman Art Library; (bottom right)
Father Major Jealous Divine, founder of the International Peace
Movement in 1919 © Hulton Archive

Page 4. (top right) Moses holding the Ten Commandments © Hulton Archive; (bottom left) A lithograph of Joseph Smith (1805–1844) © Hulton Archive; (bottom right) Neale Donald Walsch © Elizabeth Hinshaw

Page 5. (top) Taken from Royaumont, *Histoire de l'Ancien et Nouveau Testament* (1724) © Mary Evans Picture Library; (bottom left) The Madonna del Parto, *c.*1460 by Piero della Francesca, (*c.* 1419/21–92) © Chapel of the Cemetery, Monterchi, Italy/The Bridgeman Art Library; (bottom right) Ecstasy of St Theresa, sculpture by Giovanni Lorenzo Bernini (1598–1680) © Santa Maria della Vittoria, Rome, Italy/The Bridgeman Art Library

Page 6. (top) Jews in prayer at the Western, or Wailing, Wall, in Jerusalem, Israel © Hulton Archive; (bottom) A Muslim man praying in front of a mosque. An engraving by Whymper after S Senior © Hulton Archive

Page 7. (top) American evangelist Oral Roberts sits on a platform and holds his hand over a man's forehead as the man clutches his waist on stage during a prayer tour © Hulton Archive; (bottom) A Christian family say morning prayers before their breakfast *c.* 1848 © Hulton Archive

Page 8. (top left) The Liebana Beatus commentary on the Apocalypse from Guadalupe 10th century © The Art Archive/Real biblioteca de lo Escorial/Dagli Orti (A); (top right) Adam and Eve by Lucas Cranach, the elder (1472–1553) © The Art Archive/National Museum of Prague/Dagli Orti; (bottom) Dante meeting the thieves; canto 24 of the Divine Comedy (Hell) by Dante Alighieri (1265–1321) Italian writer, in 14th-century Venetian manuscript © The Art Archive/Biblioteca Nazionale Marciana Venice/Dagli Orti

FOREWORD

Discussions about God were not encouraged at home. My father was reticent about his own religious views and shortly before his death offered me, chequebook in hand, the grand sum of my advance, so that I might withdraw this book from publication. He never asked what line the book was taking nor had he read a word of it – it was just finished – and I never learned what lay behind his eccentric gesture. 'When I am occasionally asked by a lunatic in the train if I believe in God,' he once wrote, 'I answer, "Sometimes." This is not because I sometimes also disbelieve in Him but because at other times I am reading a book, brooding about a famous actress or whatever.' God, for him, was a matter for discussion not with a lunatic, not in a train, not with his sons, not even perhaps with a priest, for 'Man's relationship to God,' he wrote, 'is an intensely private affair, the most intimate and personal of all his relationships.'

I tried to satisfy my own curiosity about the Divine Being at school; but my earnest questions were shunned by the school's chaplain who thought me perverse – 'presumptuous arrogance' he once called it in an end-of-term report. At Christmas the whole school was required to sing 'O come all ye faithful', 'God of God, light of light, lo, he abhors not the virgin's womb.' This line struck me as extremely odd, so afterwards I asked the chaplain why it was that God had decided to gestate inside the womb of Mary who was a married woman. Could he not have appeared magically as a fully grown saviour without having to be an embryo first? For which question I was required to write a thousand-word detention essay on the title

'Education is all that is left behind when you have forgotten what you have learned'.

Rather than waste any more time in this way I decided to pursue my own lines of enquiry. I read the Bible, the Apocrypha and later went on to discover the Qur'an, the wonderful pseudepigraphical texts of Nag Hammadi, Qumran and an abundance of ancient Jewish apocalyptic and mystic literature.

This then is the fruit of a long and at times 'perverse' investigation into the nature and being of God. It is a book not just about any old god, but about the God who created Adam and Eve, the God of Abraham, the God of the Jews and the Christians, that is also the God of Mormon and the God of Islam – without a doubt, the most influential figure in the history of human civilisation. For thousands of years, he has shaped the way the whole world looks, thinks and breathes. Yet, finding out anything about him – anything concrete, that is – is surprisingly difficult; for God is the slipperiest of all slippery fish.

Millions of words of scripture and theology have been published but only a tiny fraction of it describes God himself. In the Bible, for instance, God is arguably not even the central character. Jesus nabs that role in the Christian New Testament, while elsewhere others (Abraham, Jacob, Saul and David, for instance) are more to the fore than God is. In the Old Testament and the nearly identical Jewish scriptures, the *Tanakh* (henceforth referred to as the Hebrew Bible), God is not even mentioned throughout several books, while for huge chunks he is sidelined by political histories, squabbles, descriptions of primitive rites, long lists of obscure laws, genealogical surveys, sordid rapes, and other matters which are implicitly of greater interest to the Bible authors than God. Likewise the Qur'an (a book which Muslims believe to have been dictated by God himself through the agency of Gabriel to the illiterate seventh-century prophet, Muhammad) is not an autobiography. The Qur'an is a book of laws, guidelines for good living, a call to moral and religious obedience, all these things and more, but it is not a book *about* God.

Why is it then, that so little appears to have been written about God himself, the central *raison d'être* of it all? The reason, according to some, is that there is nothing to say about him; nothing, at any rate that could possibly make any sense. In *Denis Hid Divinity*, an anonymous fourteenth-century English mystical author suggests that any attempt to write about God will end in certain failure:

> Nor is he virtue, nor light, nor he liveth, nor he is life, nor he is substance, nor age, nor time, nor there is any understandable touching of him, nor he is knowledge, nor truth, nor kingdom, nor wisdom, nor one, nor unity, nor Godhead, nor goodness, nor is he spirit, as we understand spirit; nor sonhood, nor fatherhood, nor any other thing known by us or by any that be; nor he is anything of not-being things, nor anything of being things; nor any of those that be, know him as he is, nor he knoweth those things that be as they be in themselves, but as they be in him.

Not a promising start! The attitude, exemplified here, that no one can know what God is (only what he is not), is known to Christian theologians as the *via negativa* (the Negative Way) and to the Cabbalistic religions as Ein-Sof (an 'understanding' of God as 'that which cannot be conceived by thought'). According to Thomas Aquinas, a philosopher of the *via negativa*, in order to understand God at all 'we must consider the ways in which He is not rather than the ways in which He is'.

But there is no difference between the proposition 'God is *not* finite' and the statement 'God *is* infinite'. So that 'considering the ways in which he is not' must be just as futile as considering the ways in which he is. Even if it were true that God is infinite, what does this actually mean? Does he carry on expanding in time and space for ever? Or does he already encompass all of time and space (past, present and future) united without boundary?

Since human brains are *finite*, they should not be expected to understand the *infinitude* of God, for the whole (that is to say God,

3

the universe and everything in it) cannot be explained with the use of a single part (a finite human brain). If this is so and infinity really is impossible for human beings to comprehend, then to say that God is 'infinite' adds nothing to our understanding of him that is not already contained in the statement 'God is impossible to understand'. Nor is it any more helpful than statements like 'God is One', 'God is Truth', 'God is Wisdom', 'God is Beauty' – which, from a philosophical perspective, are all meaningless.

Not everyone will agree of course. Many believers will argue that such statements bear witness to a truth, a transcendental truth maybe, but a truth nonetheless which is pregnant with *mystical* significance – and here lies the rub, as the philosopher A. J. Ayer pointed out:

> If a mystic admits that the object of his vision is something which cannot be described, then he must also admit that he is bound to talk nonsense when he describes it. In describing his vision the mystic does not give us any information about the external world; he merely gives us indirect information about the condition of his own mind. (*What I Believe*)

Be that as it may, theists continue to assert that God cannot be understood without subscribing – at least in part – to a language of mystical explanations; a view, which irritates rational thinkers. 'Why must we be *irrational* in order to understand God?' Or, as that arch-critic of the Christian religion, Friedrich Nietzsche, bluntly put it, 'Mystical explanations are regarded as profound; the truth is that they do not even go the length of being superficial.' If that is accepted, what is left? Something worse than superficiality, or what? Nothing, perhaps.

Is there really nothing that can be known about God that will stand the test of reason? Even a seemingly obvious statement like 'God is God' can be pedantically refuted, for 'God', it would appear, means something completely different to everybody. To the writer (or writers) of Genesis, God was a deity of extraordinary powers, creator

I

Mewling and Puking

Why is it then, that so little appears to have been written about God himself, the central *raison d'être* of it all? The reason, according to some, is that there is nothing to say about him; nothing, at any rate that could possibly make any sense. In *Denis Hid Divinity*, an anonymous fourteenth-century English mystical author suggests that any attempt to write about God will end in certain failure:

Nor is he virtue, nor light, nor he liveth, nor he is life, nor he is substance, nor age, nor time, nor there is any understandable touching of him, nor he is knowledge, nor truth, nor kingdom, nor wisdom, nor one, nor unity, nor Godhead, nor goodness, nor is he spirit, as we understand spirit; nor sonhood, nor fatherhood, nor any other thing known by us or by any that be; nor he is anything of not-being things, nor anything of being things; nor any of those that be, know him as he is, nor he knoweth those things that be as they be in themselves, but as they be in him.

Not a promising start! The attitude, exemplified here, that no one can know what God is (only what he is not), is known to Christian theologians as the *via negativa* (the Negative Way) and to the Cabbalistic religions as Ein-Sof (an 'understanding' of God as 'that which cannot be conceived by thought'). According to Thomas Aquinas, a philosopher of the *via negativa*, in order to understand God at all 'we must consider the ways in which He is not rather than the ways in which He is'.

But there is no difference between the proposition 'God is *not* finite' and the statement 'God *is* infinite'. So that 'considering the ways in which he is not' must be just as futile as considering the ways in which he is. Even if it were true that God is infinite, what does this actually mean? Does he carry on expanding in time and space for ever? Or does he already encompass all of time and space (past, present and future) united without boundary?

Since human brains are *finite*, they should not be expected to understand the *infinitude* of God, for the whole (that is to say God, the universe and everything in it) cannot be explained with the use of a single part (a finite human brain). If this is so and infinity really is impossible for human beings to comprehend, then to say that God is 'infinite' adds nothing to our understanding of him that is not already contained in the statement 'God is impossible to understand'. Nor is it any more helpful than statements like 'God is One', 'God is Truth', 'God is Wisdom', 'God is Beauty' – which, from a philosophical perspective, are all meaningless.

Not everyone will agree of course. Many believers will argue that such statements bear witness to a truth, a transcendental truth maybe, but a truth nonetheless which is pregnant with *mystical* significance – and here lies the rub, as the philosopher A. J. Ayer pointed out:

> If a mystic admits that the object of his vision is something which cannot be described, then he must also admit that he is bound to talk nonsense when he describes it. In describing his vision the mystic does not give us any information about the external world; he merely gives us indirect information about the condition of his own mind. (*What I Believe*)

Be that as it may, theists continue to assert that God cannot be understood without subscribing – at least in part – to a language of mystical explanations; a view, which irritates rational thinkers. 'Why must we be *irrational* in order to understand God?' Or, as that arch-critic of the Christian religion, Friedrich Nietzsche, bluntly put it, 'Mystical explanations are regarded as profound; the truth is that they do not even go the length of being superficial.' If that is accepted, what is left? Something worse than superficiality, or what? Nothing, perhaps.

Is there really nothing that can be known about God that will stand the test of reason? Even a seemingly obvious statement like 'God is God' can be pedantically refuted, for 'God', it would appear, means something completely different to everybody. To the writer (or writers) of Genesis, God was a deity of extraordinary powers, creator of the world, who set 'the firmament of the heaven to give light upon the earth', and yet this same God is described, only a few pages on, as a mundane human figure, strolling in the garden at cool of day, a traveller with dirty, tired feet, supping with Abram at Mamre or wrestling without success against Jacob at Jabbok. To Job, God was the inexplicable cause of all human suffering and of all human joy; to Blake he was the odious Nobodaddy, to others he was, and still is, the immortal, invisible, transcendent oneness that cannot be described in any sensible form, while 'to the lexicographer,' wrote Samuel Butler, '*God* is simply the word that comes next to go-cart.'

What a headache! 'If a misanthrope intended to make the human race unhappy,' proffered the French philosopher, Diderot, 'what better way could he have thought up than the belief in an incomprehensible being about which men would never have been able to agree, and to which they would have attached more importance than their own lives?' To ask the question, 'What or who is God?' is to hope for a response that cannot possibly be given through an eternity of years. Likewise the related query 'Does God exist?' cannot be asked in the expectation of a sensible answer. Yet these questions *have* been asked again and again for thousands of years, and they are still being asked today. They ought to be treated with respect at the very least, for they are questions of the utmost historical significance.

But the acceptance of questions as historically significant does not, alas, solve the deeper problem. If God cannot be perceived at all, why bother? The fact is that *Denis Hid Divinity* has put forward one view, the *via negativa*, which is predictably contradicted by hundreds of alternative sources. While any single opinion about God can be shown to be wrong, the totality of all human opinion about him must, necessarily, be right. For, as the brave atheist would declare: 'Without human beings, God would cease to exist.' If God principally exists in the minds of millions of people both dead and alive, then the best thing for it is to seek him out from all sides at once, to blitz him, if you like, from every conceivable angle, from the broadest range of thought, vision, opinion, sudden intuition – it really doesn't matter.

For a hundred years, at least, theologians, historians and Biblical scholars have attempted to break God down into different historical components – there is Yahweh, for instance, bossy father of the Israelites; El-Elyon, detached high God of the pre-exilic priesthood; the Islamic Allah who employed Muhammad to reveal the Qur'an to the world, and then there is the merciful, loving, pitying God of the modern Christian church. To separate these strands is not to study God so much as to examine the history of changing *human* beliefs and evolving *human* attitudes towards him. Such a story has already been skilfully told by Karen Armstrong in her book *A History of God* (1993).

This book is not intended as a history of belief so much as a retrogressive quest for God. I have peeled away the layers of scholarship that had once disunited God from himself and have stuck him back together, as 'One' again. The God of the second book of Kings (who sends wild bears to tear forty-two joyful children limb from limb) and the God of Julian of Norwich (who is 'the Essence of Pure Love') are, after all, one and the same. If there is a problem reconciling them, it is a problem that lies elsewhere, for the focus here is on God himself, the great Lord of monotheism, who, for better or worse, is, and always was, 'one God'.

And so I have written a book of shifting premises, preached from several pulpits at once and have resisted the temptation to believe or to disbelieve any particular sources. That a violent and disagreeable get-together of bishops at the Council of Ephesus in the fourth century decided that some books should be incorporated into the canon of the Christian Bible while others should not, is neither here nor there. Moses, Muhammad the Prophet, Joseph Smith, Mechthild of Hackborn and the modern American author Neale Donald Walsch are just a few among many who claim to have received the written word of God. It is not the purpose here to give credence to some or to deny others, nor is it to judge the Bible as being more 'correct' than any of the apocryphal or pseudepigraphical texts which the debauched bishops of Ephesus rejected so many years ago. In this spirit, a line of argument constructed on the basis of a certainty in God's existence might be used, a few pages on, to point the atheist's ridicule. What is held to be a fact here might be treated as symbolic, figurative or allegorical there. I make no apology for this patchwork approach; the method is intended to serve a purpose.

What I have tried to show is that, seen from as many angles as possible, God is the most perplexing and yet most compelling figure in human history, revealed by a myriad of diverse sources, to be mighty, jealous, rude, babyish, deluded, omniscient, vicious, ratty, benign, merciful, duplicitous, mysterious, wise, ignorant, grand, humorous, cruel, loud, racist, just, unjust, both mutable and immutable, visible and invisible, oafish, fragrant, anarchic and so on and forth – there is probably not an adjective in the dictionary that couldn't be made to fit somewhere.

False start. – Why should anyone need to find God?

To this question the Roman Catholic Church has a ready answer of sorts: 'The desire for God is written in the human heart,' it says, 'because man is created by God and for God; and God never ceases to draw man to himself. Only in God will he find the truth and happiness he never stops searching for' (*Catechism of the Catholic Church*, 27).

Fair enough! Perhaps this is even true, but what does it tell us about God himself? Put in other words the Catholic answer may be rewritten thus:

> Human beings want to find God, because they are compelled to do so by God himself. Since they were made in the first place 'by God and for God', God must have created them exactly *as he wanted them to be* – i.e., suffering from a chronic deficiency of truth and happiness. This deficiency causes them to *need* their creator, for he alone can provide the truth and happiness that they must have in order to escape the misery of their condition.

If the Catholic answer is to be believed, human beings must all be junkies; they were made to be junkies by their creator, a dope pedlar with a monopolistic grip on all the dope who (worst of all) is invisible and practically impossible to find. In which case, searching for God is best resisted. 'Impossible,' says David Hume; questions about God are 'so interesting, that we cannot restrain our restless enquiry with regard to them even though nothing but doubt, uncertainty and contradiction have, as yet, been the result of our most accurate researches' (*Dialogues Concerning Natural Religion*, I).

— 2 —

Another false start. – Why does anyone *want* to find God? Why does anybody *want* to find anything? 'That which I want to find, when found, will satisfy my need.' That's the rule.

Two questions then:

1. What need do people suppose that finding God will satisfy?
2. Why do people assume that finding God will satisfy that need?

Let us take a believer's answer first. It might go something like this:

God will satisfy my need for ultimate happiness and truth. The happiness will be caused by God's *Love* shining down upon me and the *Truth* will be revealed by my unity with him and by my understanding of the unity of all things. And in answer to your second question: I can only assume that these, my needs, will be satisfied because this is what I have been told will happen, since I was a wee thing, fresh from m' nappies. I was told it by my parents, by the teachers at my school and by the priests of my church.

More or less what eleventh-century Archbishop Anselm had in mind when he wrote: 'I do not try to understand in order to believe, I believe so that I may understand.' Believers have been told, by people they trust, that God will satisfy their need for truth and happiness, that is why they want to find God.

But what of the others? What of those who want to find God but have no grounds to believe in him in the first place? What *needs* do *they* believe will be satisfied by finding God? In Voltaire's view, 'If God did not exist we would have to invent him.' Why? Because people have a *need*. Here we go again. What need?

'The need to satisfy my curiosity, that is all,' the agnostic might say. 'So much has been said and written about God, that I am curious to find whether any of it is true. If it is, I would be delighted to discover if he is capable of satisfying all or any of my needs. That is why I *want* to find God.'

It seems that everyone would like to find God, be it from an impulse of love, an uncertain belief or just idle curiosity. But how does that help us to understand him?

Answer: Not a jot!

—— 3 ——

Two more false starts. – To those who ask 'What was God doing before he made heaven and earth?' comes the stock reply: 'He was preparing hell for people who ask silly questions.' Even Augustine knew this old chestnut in the fourth century and dismissed it as 'facetious', but others may yet wish to pursue the question. What exactly *was* God up to before he made heaven and earth?

In the scriptures there are two 'In the beginnings'. The first is the famous opening to the book of Genesis: 'In the beginning God created the heaven and earth. And the earth was without form and void; and darkness was upon the face of the deep.' The second 'In the beginning' (which appears only in the Christian Bible) comes from the Gospel of John: 'In the beginning was the Word, and the Word was with God, and the Word was God. The same was in the beginning with God.'

For the sake of chronology, the second 'In the beginning' (John's version) is the better place to start, for it seems to be referring to an earlier event than the one described in Genesis. For Genesis describes only as far back as the beginning of the world. God, it says, creates in the first instance a dark, formless, void earth. Nothing is mentioned as to how God gathered the materials for his task, or what, if anything, he was doing *before* that point.

John's beginning, on the other hand, seems to refer to a different moment at which God and the Word (whoever or whatever that may be) are enjoined in a mystical union. Heaven and earth have not yet been created. So what is John's 'beginning' precisely supposed to be the beginning of? Perhaps it is the beginning of the whole universe, something bigger and older than mere heaven and earth. Modern scientists believe the earth to be at least 5 billion years younger than the universe. But even if John's beginning starts 5 billion years before the beginning described in Genesis, there remains the same unfathomable puzzle: what was God doing before the creation of the universe? John and Genesis are equally unhelpful.

— 4 —

Blind idler. – In the mid-nineteenth century Kersey Graves, a 'weak atheist' from Richmond, Indiana, attempted to figure what God was doing before the creation of heaven and earth by digging for clues in the Genesis story itself. This, a process of extrapolation, bore pleasantly ludicrous fruit. He wrote:

> We are told that God created the light (Gen. 1:3), the conclusion is forced upon us that, prior to that period, he had spent an eternity in darkness. And it has been discovered that all beings originating in a state of darkness, or living in that condition, were formed without eyes, as is proved by blind fishes being found in dark caves. Hence the thought is suggested, that God, prior to the era of creation was perfectly blind.

And on he goes, taking each verse at the opening of Genesis to its logical conclusion:

> 'God saw the light that it was good' (Gen. 1:4). Hence we must infer that God had just recovered his blindness, and that he had never before discovered that light was good. Of course it was

good to be delivered from eternal darkness; 'And God called the light Day, and the darkness he called Night' (Gen. 1:5). And to whom did he call them? as no living being was in existence until several days afterwards. Hence there was no need of calling them anything; and, as we are told Adam named everything, he could as easily have found names for these as for other things. (*The Bible of Bibles*, 15:5–7)

So God was blind before he created the world, was he? But what was this blind God doing? Freethinkers have an answer for that too: if Christianity taught that God created the whole universe *ex nihilo* (out of nothing) then 'there was nothing for God to do, and nothing for him to do it with, hence he must have spent an eternity in idleness, a blind, solitary monarch without a kingdom' (*ibid.*).

— 5 —

The answer is revealed to God. – Augustine hated the idea that God was loafing about in idleness before the creation. The mere suggestion was repugnant to his creed, since idleness has never been a good thing to Christians and God is by definition the very essence of all that is good. One day, Augustine told God the truth about what was happening before the creation, revealing to him in an extraordinary book called *Confessions*, that there was no beginning *before* the creation of heaven and earth since time itself did not exist. The argument ran like this:

Those who cannot understand why You were idle through countless ages should wake up and pay attention, because the thing they cannot understand is a fiction. How would countless ages have passed if You had not made them, since You are the author and creator of all ages? What times would there have been if they had not been created by You? How could they have passed without ever having been? Therefore, since all times are Your work, if there was any time before You made heaven and earth, why is it said that You were idle, not at work? Since You had made time itself; times would not pass before You had made them. (*Confessions*, 11:12)

— 6 —

Small time correction. – How could Augustine be so sure that God had not created time long before he created anything else? This would have allowed him to loll around for eons before bothering himself with the problems of a created heaven and earth.

Such a scenario did not occur to Augustine who predictably failed to understand the nature of time when he argued that God, 'author and creator of all ages', had made it. *Predictably?* Yes, because Augustine admitted himself that time confused him terribly. 'What is time?' he pondered:

Who can explain it easily and briefly, or even when he wants to speak of it, comprehend it in his thought? Yet is there anything we mention in our talking that is so well known and familiar? So what then is time? If no one asks me, I know, if they ask and I try to explain, I do not know. (*Confessions*, 11:14)

Augustine, wake up and pay attention! Time can be easily explained as an effect caused by the existence of things. If things exist, so by necessity, does time, it is a symptom of the existence of things. If only one thing existed in the whole universe (a cosmological singularity, let's say) then time would not exist, for in such a condition, there would be no sense of 'before and after' or 'duration' (the only ways by which time can be measured). As soon as more than one thing comes into being, so does time.

If God (as Augustine maintained) created time, he must have done so *inadvertently*, as time would have been the unavoidable by-product of the things he created. However, if God (as is so often stated) is 'One' there is a possibility that, if he alone existed before the creation, time did not. So Augustine might have got it right – by accident!

— 7 —

Walk on the wild side. – 'In the beginning was the Word, and the Word was with God, and the Word was God. The same was in the beginning with God. All things were made by him; and without him was not anything made that was made' (John 1:1–3). Any reader who is not too mesmerised by the music of these words might be wondering what this famous passage really means. Why should God, right at the beginning of things, be with a word? And what exactly is it, this word? Is it spoken? Is it written? How could a mere word have 'made all things'? John goes on to explain: 'He was in the world, and the world was made by him and the world knew him not . . . And the Word was made flesh and dwelt among us, and we beheld his glory, the glory as of the only begotten of the Father, full of grace and truth' (John 1:10, 14). So John is talking about Jesus, is he? Jesus is the Word. Why then does he insist on calling him the Word?

The answer is not as complicated as it might seem. Ancient Israelites, like many ancient peoples, were obsessed with names, believing that they conferred power on those who held them, divine names especially so. God's name was so powerful that it could be used to invoke magic. This is how one Gnostic name for God, *Abracadabra*, came to be used centuries later to pull rabbits out of hats. Whether or not the Word was the same as God's secret name is not certain, though it may well have been. What is certain is that God was believed to have created the world by the power of this Word alone, a word which became so important to ancient minds that, before long, it had gained an independence from God, somehow without violating the central tenet of Jewish monotheism that God was 'One and all alone'. When the Christians decided that Jesus was divine they had to find 'natural' ways of explaining his divinity that would fit comfortably within existing monotheistic dogma. Being divine entailed immortality for one thing. The resurrection might help to explain how Jesus lives for ever, but it was also necessary to show that Jesus, like God, had always existed from the beginning of time and did not simply spring into being, *ex nihilo*, on Christmas day in the year 1.

The gospel master-stroke was to identify Jesus with the Word. It was a daring, indeed brilliant, manoeuvre, for by making Jesus and the Word one and the same, Jesus' divinity was settled without compromising God's essential unity.

There was only one small problem though, which, by sweeping under the carpet, John hoped would disappear. What John does not reveal to his readers is that the Word already has a name. It is not Jesus, Christ, Immanuel, or anything like that; the Word is not even a male, for he is a she, and her name is Sophia.

— 8 —

Choosing her name. – In Greek, *sophia* means wisdom and, yes, God's eponymous friend was wise – by some accounts at least. English translations of the Bible call her Wisdom with a capital W, but this is not a becoming name. In French her name would be *Sagesse*, *Hokma* in Hebrew, *Klokhet* in Swedish and *Weisheit* in German. Not one of these is pretty. We shall stick with Sophia.

— 9 —

Who is Sophia? What is she? – The relationship between God and Sophia has never been entirely clear. She asks to be called a 'sister' (Prov. 7:4), a term which bizarrely can be used in the Bible to denote sister, wife *or* lover; she is described as the perfect wife (Prov. 31:10), God's helper (Prov. 3:19), and more worthy of desire than precious jewels (Prov. 8:11). In the book of Proverbs Sophia reveals that God 'possessed her' and compares herself 'as one brought up with him', implying a simultaneous relationship of mistress *and* sister. She says:

> God possessed me when his purpose first unfolded. I was set up from everlasting, from the beginning, before the earth came into being. When there were no depths I was brought forth; before the mountains were settled, before the hills was I born. When he prepared the heavens I was there. When he established the clouds above, when he strengthened the fountains of the deep. When he assigned the boundaries of the sea, when he laid the foundations of the earth, I was by his side, the master craftsman, as one brought up with him. And I was his daily delight rejoicing always before him. (Prov. 8:22–31)

Did God create her, then, or did she come into being *with* God at the same time?

There seem to be a hundred answers to this. Once she claimed to have 'issued forth from the mouth of the Most High and covered the earth like a mist.' (Sir. 24:3). Coming forth from someone's mouth suggests gestation and birth, however irregular. Was Sophia God's daughter then? The apocryphal Wisdom of Solomon describes her as a filial puff from the divine lungs:

> For she is the breath of the power of God, and a pure influence flowing from the glory of the Almighty: therefore can no defiled thing fall into her. For she is the brightness of the everlasting light, the unspotted mirror of the power of God, and the image of his goodness. (Wisd. of Sol. 7:25–6)

In the *Hellenistic Synagogal Prayers* of the second to third century CE Sophia is emphatically described as God's daughter (*Hell. Syn. Pr.* 4:38) who plays a major part in the process of creation, confirming that she was also 'the Word' by which God ordered the creation in the first place. 'How magnified are your works, O Lord! You made everything with Sophia, for just as she was not exhausted in the bringing forth of different races, neither has she neglected to make for each a different providence' (*Hell. Syn. Pr.* 3:16). In Jesus ben Sirach's book of Ecclesiasticus (Sir.) Sophia describes her throne as a 'a pillar of cloud', the very same form into which God transformed himself when appearing to Moses (Exod. 13.21). Was God impersonating Sophia's throne? Or is Sophia's enigmatic relationship to God that of a cat to its master's lap? God and Sophia are extremely close yet their relationship remains frustratingly opaque. Let us call them 'companions' and leave it at that.

— 10 —

Sophia's profession. – Sophia wanted to be a teacher, she wanted to act as an intermediary between God and all people on earth. Her chosen subject was 'the knowledge of things divine and human, and of their causes' (4 Macc. 1:15). Previously she had worked as a prophet (Prov. 1:20–33) but it is to the teaching profession that her heart naturally inclined. Failing to find employment in a regular school, she tried to muster pupils for herself by shouting at passers-by from the roadside:

Is she not calling you? Is Sophia not raising her voice? On the heights overlooking the road, at the crossways, she takes her stand: by the gates at the entrance to the city, on the access-roads she cries out 'I am calling to you all people, my words are addressed to all humanity. Simpletons learn how to behave. Fools come to your senses. Listen, I have something important to tell you, when I speak I am always right. My mouth speaks only the truth for evil is abhorrent to my lips.' (Prov. 8:1–7)

Sophia's aggressive methods did not always find favour and when she

20

saw that her message was not getting through she turned abusive: 'Since you have ignored my advice, I, for my part, shall laugh at your distress, I shall jeer as terror overtakes you, when your misery rushes in like a whirlwind, when strife and anguish bear down on you. Then you will call me, but I shall not answer, you will look for me desperately, but you won't find me,' Sophia once shouted, at no one in particular.

— 11 —

Sophie's choice. – To what extent God loved, admired or, at any rate, wished to be with Sophia remains a mystery. In the book of Proverbs, Sophia is rich, she is also charitable, but God is not around to help and she cuts a lonely figure: 'Sophia has built herself a large house with seven pillars, she has slaughtered her beasts, drawn her wine, laid her table and dismissed her servants' (Prov. 9:1–3a). What she was doing building herself a mansion is never explained; for God had ordained her a humbler abode: 'Pitch your tent in Jacob,' he said, 'and make Israel your inheritance' (Sir. 24:10). Elsewhere Sophia is found to be sharing a flat with Prudence (Prov. 8:12), but Enoch testified that when she came down to earth and was unable to find a suitable dwelling she returned, displeased, to heaven where she remains to this day: 'Sophia could not find a place in which she could dwell,' he said, 'but a place was found for her in the heavens. Then she went out to dwell with the children of the people, but she found no dwelling place and so she returned to settle permanently among the angels' (*1 En.* 42:1). Her decision to leave the earth was greatly mourned: 'Who hath gone up into heaven, and taken her, and brought her down from the clouds? Who hath gone over the sea, and found her, and will buy her for pure gold?' wailed Baruch (3:30). But Sophia had made her choice and was adamantly sticking by it.

— 12 —

Self-portrait. –

I, Sophia, share a house with Prudence. I am mistress of witty inventions. I hate arrogance and pride, wicked behaviour and a lying mouth. I have sound advice, common sense, I understand everything and I have strength. It is through me that monarchs rule and princes decree what is right. I love those who love me; whoever searches eagerly for me finds me. With me are riches and honour, great lasting wealth and saving justice. The fruit I give is better than even the finest gold, the return I make is far better than the purest silver. I walk in the way of uprightness, in the path of justice, to endow my friends with my wealth and to fill their treasuries. (Prov. 8:12–21)

— 13 —

What God calls himself. – God is fussy about names. In the book of Genesis he tells Abram, Sarai, Jacob and several others to change theirs, often by adjusting a single letter for purposes which are now obscure. He is equally peculiar about his own name. 'Why ask my name, it is a mystery,' he wrily informed the inquisitive Manoah (Judg. 13:18).

Indeed it is a mystery, as one of the patriarchs (Jacob) knew only too well. At Jabbok God flatly refused to reveal his name to Jacob (Gen. 32:29) but, a short while later at Paddan Aram, he told him his name was El Shaddai (Gen. 35:11). Later still, while Jacob was preparing for his trip to Egypt, God introduced himself as El (Gen. 46:3). But Jacob ignored all of these and prayed to God using a different set of names altogether: Abaoth, Abrathiaoth, Sabaoth, Adonai, Astra (*Pr. Jac.* 15). Jacob may have been talking to more than one god, of course.

Many generations later God entered into a similarly furtive discussion with Moses, first insisting his name was I AM, changing it to 'I am Yahweh', and explaining later that 'to Abraham, Isaac and Jacob I appeared as El Shaddai, but I did not make my name Yahweh known to them' (Exod. 6:2). That ought to have cleared things up, but having assured Moses that 'this [Yahweh] is my name for ever, and this is my memorial to all generations', he could not resist a tiny adjustment; 'Yahweh's name is the Jealous One' (Exod. 34:15), God let slip to Moses.

To Hosea he declared, 'You will call me Ishi, no more will you call me Baali' (Hos. 2:16).

—— 14 ——

A philosophical moment. – It came to pass one day that God wished to be served on Mount Sinai by the Israelites, his chosen people. But there was a problem; they were stuck in Egypt (held in bondage, by a snobbish Pharaoh) and the mountain where God wished to be served was a good 600 miles distant. To add to these difficulties God knew that if his people ever managed to escape from Egypt they would head, first and foremost, for Canaan, the land, dripping with milk and honey, that he had promised them many years before, and Canaan, as it happened, was in diametrically the opposite direction from Mount Sinai.

Never mind, he would cross that bridge when he came to it. First he needed to find a good leader among the Israelites. There has been much debate about who it was that God eventually chose. Some (like Strabo, Apion and Freud) say he was a disaffected Egyptian priest from Heliopolis, others that he was a Midianite. In either case he bore the Egyptian name of Moses and could not speak Hebrew at all well. God's chosen people, supposedly descendants of Abraham, may have been *hapiru*, non-Egyptian itinerant labourers, that were forbidden from owning property and forced to work on the construction of palaces for Rameses II (1304–1237 BCE). If *hapiru* and Hebrew were not quite the same thing God did not seem to mind. What was important was to get these people out so that they could worship him at Sinai. To this end God hid himself in a burning bush and when Moses passed by flickered like fire appealing to Moses from within the bush: 'You must go to Pharaoh and tell him you want to lead the people out. When you have brought the people out of Egypt you shall serve God upon his mountain.' Fine by Moses, for at that stage he had no idea that God's mountain was so far in the wrong direction from Canaan. But whose voice was this calling him? Moses needed to know:

'When I tell the other *hapirus* – er, I mean Hebrews – that the God of their fathers has sent me to them and they ask your name. What shall I tell them it is?'

And God replied 'EHYEH ASHER EHYEH' (which is translated in the King James Bible as 'I AM THAT I AM'). And God said to Moses, 'Tell the children of Israel that I AM has sent me to you.'

Moses must have thought he was joking, or at least, giving him the brush off, along the lines of:

'Why should I tell you my name. What is it to you or to them? Just tell them that I am who I am.'

'But who exactly is it that YOU ARE?'

'My name is Yahweh.'

'Ah, but *Yahweh* means HE WHO IS in a forgotten Hebrew dialect (at least some people think it does). So what are you saying? Is your name I AM or is it HE WHO IS? There is a big difference, you know.'

'I first told you I AM THAT I AM; it is only twentieth-century scholars who have speculated that my name is actually HE WHO IS, but I am telling you now. My name is Yahweh, now get along and stop wasting time.'

'You say your name is Yahweh, yet I am to tell the Israelites that I AM sent me to them. I think, therefore YOU ARE . . . um . . . yes, indeed, Yahweh.'

— 15 —

Gnostic name hunting. – Gnostics that spent their lives in pursuit of *gnosis*, or divine knowledge, believed that God's name was a secret, but to those who knew it and could shout it out, he would appear, genii-like from a bottle, and grant requests 'at once' to those who had summoned him. Whoever could discover God's secret name would thus be in possession of great power, and so, not unnaturally, many gnostic sects devoted their lives to the search of the hidden name. 'We have waited for You eagerly, says Isaiah, 'Your name, even Your memory, is the desire of our souls' (Isa. 26:8).

The technical method which the gnostic employed to discover God's name was called *gematria*. It relied, in the first instance, on believing that some numbers were sacred and others were not, so the first part of the game required the gnostic to find a sacred number. The reasons why any number was sacred were usually shallow. The number 40 was revered because God had spent 40 days with Moses writing the law on Mount Sinai. The African Christian bishop, Cyprien, declared that 31 was sacred, for that was the age he believed that Jesus had reached at the time of the crucifixion. He also made claims for other numbers: 16 – because the crucifixion happened in the sixteenth year of the reign of Tiberius; and 300 – because someone had told him that this number was represented by the letter T which, in his view, resembled a crucifix.

The art of *gematria* relied on ascribing to every letter of the alphabet a numerical value. Suppose a gnostic looking for God's name had chosen 7 as his sacred number (because of the 7-day creation in Genesis, let's say); if he were using the Roman alphabet and had numbered the letters A as 1, B as 2, C as 3, D as 4 and E as 5, then any combination of these letters which added up to 7 (and sounded good) would be regarded as a possible name for God. In this case BE, EB, DAB and, ironically, BAD would all be suitable candidates.

Once he had sorted the letters the gnostic would shout each name twice in succession, at the top of his voice. 'DAB, DAB!' If God failed to appear he would not be deterred. He would simply classify the name as 'expressible' and file it neatly away, while his hunt for the ultimate secret name (the one that would conjure all the power) would continue, using other numbers and letter combinations.

In a pseudepigraphical prayer, Jacob attempted to conjure God with a string of mystical names: 'God *Abaoth, Abrathiaoth, Sabaoth, Adonai, Astra,* the Lord of all things. I summon you. You who give power to those above and those below and those under the earth. Lord God of the Hebrews *Epagael,* of whom is the everlasting power, *Eloel, Souel.* He who has the secret name *Sabaoth* God of Gods, amen, amen' (*Pr. Jac.* 9–15).

Shout them as loud as you wish; nothing seems to happen. Using gematriaic systems many stupendously silly names have been ascribed to God: Abraxas, Ababib, Belbot and Taptapiron are among the 'expressible' ones.

— 16 —

The unsolved riddle of God's secret name. –

I am the one who is, but you consider in your heart. I am robed with heaven, draped around with sea, the earth is the support of my feet, around my body is poured the air, the entire chorus of stars revolves around me. I have nine letters, I am of four syllables. Consider me. The first three have two letters each. The last has the rest and five are consonants. The entire number is twice eight plus three hundred, three tens and seven. If you know who I am you will not be uninitiated in my wisdom. (*Sib. Or.* 1:137–46)

—— 17 ——

A neat file of seventy expressible names. –

The Holy One blessed be he, has seventy names, which may be expressed, and the rest, which may not be expressed, are unsearchable and without number. These are the names which may be expressed:
1. Hadiriron YHWH of Hosts, Holy, Holy, Holy; 2. Meromiron; 3. Beroradin; 4. Ne'uriron; 5. Gebiriron; 6. Kebiriron; 7. Dorriron; 8. Sebiroron; 9. Zehiroron; 10. Hadidron; 11. Webidriron; 12. Wediriron; 13. Peruriron; 14. Hisiridon; 15. Ledoriron; 16. Ṭaṭbiron; 17. Ṣaṭriron; 18. 'Adiriron; 19. Dekiriron; 20. Lediriron; 21. Šeririron; 22. Tebiriron; 23. Taptapiron; 24. 'Ap'apiron; 25. Šapšapiron; 26. Ṣapṣapiron; 27. Gapgapiron; 28. Raprapiron; 29. Dapdapiron; 30. Qapqapuron; 31. Haphapiron; 32. Wapwapiron; 33. Pappapiron; 34. Zapzapiron; 35. Ṭapṭapiron; 36. 'Ap'apiron; 37. Mapmapiron; 38. Sapsapiron; 39. Napnapiron; 40. Laplapiron; 41. Wapwapiron; 42. Kapkapiron; 43. Ḥapḥapiron; 44. Tabtabib, that is Yah the greater YHWH; 45. 'Ab'abib; 46. Qabqabib; 47. Šabšabib; 48. Babbabib; 49. Ṣabṣabib; 50. Gabgabib; 51. Rabrabib; 52. Ḥarabrabib; 53. Pabpabib; 54. Habhabib; 55. 'Ab'abib; 56. Zabzabib; 57. Sabsabib; 58. Ḥashasib; 59. Ṭabṭabib; 60. Wesisib; 61. Pabpabib; 62. Basbasib; 63. Papnabib; 64. Lablabib; 65. Mabmabib; 66. Nupkabib; 67. Mammambib; 68. Nupnubib; 69. Paspabib; 70. Ṣaṣṣib.

These are the names of the Holy one which go forth adorned with many crowns of flame. (*Alphabet of Aqiba*, first to second century CE)

— 18 —

Name medicine. – According to the first century Greek *Testament of Solomon* many afflictions can be healed by shouting out God's mystical names. This extraordinary book opens with the story of Solomon's favourite builder, a nice young boy 'much loved' by the king, who was working on the construction of the Temple in Jerusalem, but every evening the boy was having his thumb sucked by an evil demon called Ornias. 'When I, Solomon, heard these things,' recalled the Semitic king, 'I went into the Temple of God and, praising him day and night, begged with all my soul that the demon might be delivered into my hands, and that I might have authority over him.' God obliged by giving Solomon a magic ring with which to thwart the evil thumb-sucker and several other demons besides. Using the power of his new ring Solomon was able to coerce destructive spirits into revealing the antidotes to their evil. Thus he learned from Rhyx Ichthuon, for instance, the demon responsible for detached tendons, that by yelling the holy name '*Adonai malthe*' the demon would retreat; Rhyx Hapax, the spirit of insomnia, is ousted by writing '*Kok Phedismos*' on bits of paper and dangling them from one's temples; colic is cured by shouting '*Iaoth, imprison Kourtael*', while 'terrible farts that burn right up into the bowels' will disappear in a puff of smoke at the mere whisper of the words '*Arara! Arare!*'

— 19 —

Plumbing for Yahweh. – Yahweh may, or may not, have been the name used by the ancient Hebrews to denote their God, the Lord of Israel. There have been many attempts to trace the origins of this name. Perhaps it comes from the Graeco-Egyptian divine name Iao; if not, its etymology may lie in the third person singular of a rare Hebrew version of the verb 'to be', *hawa*. Others have claimed that *Yahweh* is related to the divine name of Jove, the god who was worshipped by the Etruscans and by the Romans as Jupiter. Digging deeper still some scholars have attempted to link *Yahweh* to an etymological compound of Jah (Iao) and Hawah (the Hebraic name for Eve) implying perhaps that *Jahawah* was once a plural androgynous godhead.

In this game people may believe whatever they wish to believe, and indeed they do, but as one dictionary entry on God's name tartly concedes: 'What is important is not the origin of the name, but the nature of the God who bore it in the Bible' (*Oxford Companion to the Bible*, 1993). Be that as it may, nobody knows the origin of this name for certain nor, surprisingly, have they any idea how it should be pronounced.

— 20 —

How to say it. – Where the word *Yahweh* appears in the Hebrew Bible it was originally written as a symbol YHWH (known as the sacred Tetragrammaton) but pronounced *adonay* (meaning 'Lord' in Hebrew). For ages, God's name was regarded as ineffable, far too holy to be uttered by human lips, and so, after centuries of reading YHWH as *adonay*, everyone forgot how the name was originally supposed to be pronounced. Was it *Yohiweh*, *Yahewoh*, *Yihowih*, *Yihiwih* or *Yohowoh*? The combinations were legion, but as fear of the perils of speaking God's name diminished, so, sooner or later, an official decision on how YHWH ought be pronounced needed to be made.

In about 1000 CE someone – we know not who – tried to solve the problem by adding the vowels of *adonay* to the consonants of the Tetragrammaton. A simple task, but he managed to screw it up. Instead of getting *Yahowah* he arrived at *Jehovah*, a name which has been used (gingerly) in some Protestant circles ever since. Meanwhile Catholics and many Jews, after years of hesitation, having rejected *Jahoh* and *Jao* (two close contenders), plumbed for *Yahweh* instead.

29

— 21 —

El-Al. – El, supreme God, throughout much of the Middle East, was once known as Al to the Muslims. The origin of these names probably stretches back to the 'Ali' of ancient Egypt who were, in effect, spin-off gods – the limbs, lips, joints etc. of Amon, high god of the Egyptian deities. To Islam, Allah or *al-Lah* means simply 'the God', but this is not the only name he is given. The Qur'an contains ninety-nine sacred names which are regularly chanted in prayer: *al-Qahtar* (he who overpowers), *al-Halim* (he who acquiesces); *al-Ghani* (abundant and infinite); *al-Muhyi* (giver of life); *al-Kalimah* (giver of speech); *al-Basit* (the generous giver); *al-Qabid* (the taker awayer) and so on and so forth. As Arab legend has it there are one hundred names in all but Muhammad (in gratitude to a camel that once shaded him from the heat of the sun) whispered the hundredth name into the camel's ear. It was probably *al-something* but nobody knows what. That is why camels are able to look so conceited to this day.

— 22 —

Elohim. – The word *elohim*, strictly speaking, means 'gods' (it is a plural word) and most specifically refers to the heavenly assembly of the sons and daughters of El which, at one time, ruled over the ancient Canaanite and Israelite religions. The word has caused no end of embarrassment in Jewish and Christian circles since it occurs over 1500 times in the first 15 books of the Bible (the most sacred manifesto of both Jewish and Christian monotheism) in which only *one* god is *supposed* to exist. To solve the problem *Elohim* has been mistranslated as God (with a capital G) such as we find at Genesis 1:26: 'And God said, Let *us* make man in *our* image, after *our* likeness' – whoops!

—— 23 ——

Big El, little El: what begins with El? – The supreme god of the *elohim* is El himself, father and master of all the heavens. He is the 'el' of Israel, the 'el' of Bethel and the 'el' of Ishmael; the 'el' of Gabriel, Michael and Uriel. His divine name is omnipresent throughout the history of most Middle Eastern religions; it is Babylonian, Phoenician, Aramaic, Canaanite, Arabic and Hebrew. God introduces himself to Abraham as *El Shaddai* (Gen. 17:1) meaning 'God of the Mountain', and elsewhere in the Bible he is *El Elyon* (Most High God), *El roi* (God of Vision), *El Sabaoth* (God of the Heavenly Hosts), *El Chay* (Living God), *El Neqamah* (God of Vengeance), *El Ma'al* (God above), *El Qanna* (Jealous God) and *El Bethel* (God of the Covenant). Do all these names belong to just one god? If not, who, in heaven's name, are all the others?

—— 24 ——

Putsch plot. – By the beginning of the First Millennium BCE, Yahweh, once the lucky-mascot battle God of a little group of itinerant Israelites, had become a unique symbol of Israelite supremacy over neighbouring tribes. 'Yahweh is indubitably the cause of our success on the battle-field,' they would cry, 'Without Yahweh we shall be defeated.'

Loyalty to Yahweh thus became the single most important creed in the battle-torn tribe of ancient Israel. As victory followed victory so the mascot of Yahweh was vaunted on ever higher poles, while the rival mascots of their tribal enemies, Dagon and Ba'al, were smashed and trampled in the mud. How long would it be before the Yahwist Israelites proscribed the worship of any god but Yahweh?

'We must worship Yahweh and Yahweh alone. We must call him God and have no other gods besides him.'

31

'But what about El? We cannot stop worshipping him. He created heaven and earth, he is the chief of all our gods. He is father of all the *elohim* including Yahweh. You do not intend us to give up the worship of El, do you?

'But El is not only *our* god, he is the god of our enemies, the Canaanites, too. We can do without him. All we need is Yahweh. He is the special god of our people now not El.

'But who can we say created heaven and earth if it wasn't El?'

'Yahweh, of course.'

'But it says in the scriptures that El and all the *elohim* did it, not Yahweh.'

'Ah yes, but they are one and the same, don't you see?'

'No. I don't understand.'

'There is only one God of Israel, don't you agree?'

'Yes but . . .'

'And Israel is superior to all the other nations, is she not?'

'Yes but . . .'

'Then Yahweh the God of Israel must be the supreme God of all the gods; he must be El.'

'Ah I get you, a putsch. You mean we'll get Yahweh to take over the *elohim*?'

'I would not put it as indelicately as that, but let's just say that El was Yahweh all along.'

'But what about the rest of the *elohim*?'

'God *is* the *elohim*, you fool, he is El Elyon, he is El Shaddai, El Bethel and El Qanna, the whole ruddy lot of them. Take this down: "Listen, Israel! Yahweh is our *elohim*, Yahweh alone! You shall love Yahweh with all your heart, with all your soul, with all your strength. Let these words I urge upon you today be written on your heart" (Deut. 6: 4–6).'

'That's clever.'

'Very clever. Let's use it in our book.'

—— 25 ——

Dysfunctional family. – When a peasant farmer happened to pass his plough over an artificial mound at Ras Shamra on the Mediterranean coast of northern Libya in the late summer of 1929, he heard a funny noise. What was that his plough had faltered against? He looked bewildered. 'Perhaps I better get the police.' A few days later experts agreed that the plough had struck a tiny corner of the long lost Canaanite city of Ugarit. This was to prove the most important archaeological discovery of the twentieth century. Thousands of interesting things were unearthed at Ugarit, among them a mythological tale, etched onto stone tablets in 1380 BCE. In the story, El, high God of Canaan reveals that 'the name of my son is Yaw'. Some scholars believe, as many had long suspected, that God's (Yahweh's) father was none other than the Canaanite supreme deity, El, and that God was once, like Ba'al and Dagon, simply one of the *elohim*.

In the book of Deuteronomy God (Yahweh) is granted Israel at a carve-up of family property presided over by El: 'When the Most High (El Elyon) gave the nations their heritage he partitioned out the human race by assigning boundaries according to the number of the sons of God (the *elohim*). Yahweh's portion was the house of Israel' (Deut. 32:8).

According to this passage God must be El's son, but the monotheistic defence interprets it differently. 'No, no, what the deuteronomist is really saying is that God (El Elyon) divided the lands among the "sons of God" (for which read "angels") and that he kept the House of Israel for Yahweh (i.e., for himself).' This argument fails to convince most modern scholars.

If God (Yahweh) really was one of the sons of El, he can lay claim not just to a father but to a whole squabbling family of Middle Eastern gods. His mother would be Athiru or Asherah, the fertility goddess; and his siblings are Ba'al, the god of fertility (a much hated figure in the Hebrew Bible), who spends most of his time fighting his other brothers, Mot (god of drought, infertility and death) and Yam (the many-headed monster god of the waters, who is also the god of chaos). Their sister is Anat, a feisty battle-axe who, when not being raped by Ba'al, enjoys fighting at his side against Mot. On one occasion she fought for three days in a lake of blood which rose to her breasts with dismembered heads and hands adorning her wrists like jewellery.

— 26 —

God's father and mother. – El was a benign and majestic figure who kept himself to himself living in a tent-like shrine somewhere in the Amanus mountains which, to those who worshipped him, were located then at the centre of the universe. Like his Egyptian and Assyrian counterparts, Ra and Asher, El was represented by the sun, his wife, by the moon and his sons and daughters, the *elohim*, by the stars. El was the divine creator of all things. He was also the procreator who helped mortal human beings in their struggles to conceive and give birth. The Canaanites at Ugarit depicted him as an old man with a long white beard, sometimes with an erect penis, which earned him the affectionate sobriquet, Bull-El. At his own banquets he would often drink too much, yet he was revered as 'Father of Years' and as 'Kindly One, Merciful El'. His wife on the other hand was more problematic.

Asherah was beautiful (not according to modern taste) but she must have once been thought attractive as surviving images depict her naked at Ugarit, being fought over by unnamed rival gods. She is sometimes represented as a bricklayer or builder, a reference to the palace which she built for her power-maniacal son, Ba'al. There is a story preserved on a late Hittite tablet in which she tries to seduce Ba'al, but is rejected and bravely takes her complaint to her husband, El, who puts Ba'al into her power. That she briefly married her other son, God (Yahweh), is dimly remembered as an undignified episode in the early history of Yahwism.

— 27 —

The wife that was hidden in a grove. – In the religions of Assyria and Canaan fertility was ruled by two deities, Asher (El), god of the sun, and Asherah, goddess of the moon. When not being symbolised by sun and moon, Asher was occasionally represented by a penis and Asherah by an iconic vulva. The ancient Canaanites believed Asherah to be the female consort of their supreme deity, El, and when El was usurped by the Jewish Yahweh who became the one and only god of all the universe, the goddess Asherah was, for a while at least, dragged along to be his consort.

Yet there was a problem, the priests of the new religion were trying to assert that Yahweh-God was the one and only god. It would not do to worship any other, not even his wife. But how could the priests get rid of Asherah? She was popular with the people. Infertility was despised by society and, in order to avoid the opprobrium of childlessness, couples felt duty bound to make sacrifices to Asherah. What help was Yahweh, a deity without a phallus? How could he possibly help them to conceive? If they wanted babies there was only one thing for it. Phallic effigies (also called *asherah*) were set up in sacred places and danced around in a naked frenzy, the dancers hoping all the while that Asherah, goddess of fecundity, would look favourably upon the scene and multiply their off-spring.

Phallic *asherahs* were duly erected all over the place, on hills and dales, in woods and copses, even in God's sacred Temple at Jerusalem (2 Kings 18:4; 21:7; 23:6) and by his holy shrine at Bethel (2 Kings 23:15). Inscriptions, recently discovered, describe sanctuary dedications to 'Yahweh and his Asherah' but, for all this, God did not have his wife for long, as the powerful Yahwist prophets were hell-bent on divorce. Later, in an effort to obscure the polytheistic phallicism of the Hebrew Bible, the word *asherah* was translated into Greek as *alsos* meaning 'groves' (or bunch of trees) and, because of this, the word 'groves' has inappropriately been entered into many English translations of the Bible where 'phallic effigies' would have been a more correct rendering.

When Yahwist prophets rail against the fertility cult of Asherah, Bible translators, in their embarrassment, have thus reduced the prophets' rage to comic nonsense: 'The children of Israel did secretly those things that were not right against the Lord their God, they set them up images and groves [!] on every hill and under every green tree' (1 Kings 14:23); 'And he brought out the groves [!] from the house of the Lord, without Jerusalem, unto the brook at Kidron, and burned them at the brook at Kidron, and stamped them small into powder, and cast the powder thereof upon the graves of the children of the people' (2 Kings 23:6). King Asa, deposed his mother (Queen Maachah) for making an obscene grove (1 Kings 15:13); women knitted garments for groves (2 Kings 23:7) and sacred vessels in the Temple were made for 'Ba'al, for the grove [!], and for the Host of Heaven' (2 Kings 23:4).

And thus it was, that God's wife, the great porn goddess Asherah, was wrenched from her consort and mischievously hidden in a grove.

— 28 —

Marriage made in heaven. – The name of God's wife, Asherah, is derived from her longer Ugaritic name, *Rabbatu 'athiratu yammi*, meaning 'The Lady who Treads on *Yam*'. *Yam* was the seven-headed sea dragon of Canaanite religion, whose destruction paved the way for the creation of the world. In the Bible, God is also described as 'treading on the back of *Yam*' (Job 9:8) and 'breaking the heads of the dragon in the waters' (Ps. 74:14). Perhaps it was this risky aquatic sport that drew them together in the first place.

—— 29 ——

Two lovely big trees. – The difficulty for ancient Israelites in having to abandon all female goddesses in order to worship the one invisible God of Israel is hard to conceive. They complained bitterly to Jeremiah about this: 'We wish to carry on doing what we have always done,' they pleaded, 'burning incense to the Queen of Heaven, pouring out drink offerings to her, as we have always done, we, and our fathers, our kings, and our princes in the cities of Judah, and in the streets of Jerusalem' (Jer. 44:17).

'Very well,' said God, 'I shall destroy Judah completely; they shall perish; they shall fall to the sword or die of famine, from least to greatest they will expire and be an object of execration and horror, a curse and a laughing stock' (Jer. 44:12).

In such a manner was Asherah thrown out; her worship constantly attacked as an evil and an outrage by the prophets of Yahweh; her worshippers threatened with capital punishment. Inevitably Sophia (whose province was wisdom not sex) had a longer innings. But as long as the need for a fertility goddess prevailed, Sophia, as the predominant female spirit of Jewish religion, was under pressure to take over Asherah's mantle in the fertility department.

Solomon was so enamoured of Sophia's beauty that he desired to take her for his bride (Wisd. of Sol. 8:2), but to other, cruder folk, the phallic symbolism that had worked so well for Asherah, might just as easily be transferred to Sophia. Asherah was symbolised by vulvas and tall trees, and thus Sophia too came to be known as the 'tree of life' (Prov. 3:18), even comparing herself, on one occasion, to the most inviting, scented, sensual grove:

> I have grown tall as a cedar on Lebanon, as a cypress on Mount Hermon; I have grown tall as a palm in En'Gedi, as the rose bushes of Jericho, as a fine olive in the plain, as a plane tree I

have grown tall. Like cinnamon and acanthus, I have yielded a perfume, like choice myrrh, I have breathed out a scent, like galbanum, onycha, labdanum, like the smoke of incense in the temple. I have spread my branches like a teberinth, and my branches are glorious with graceful shoots, my blossoms bear the fruit of glory. I am the mother of pure love. Approach me, you who desire me, and take your fill of my fruits, for memories of me are sweeter than honey, inheriting me is sweeter than the honeycomb. Those who eat me will hunger for more. No one who obeys me will ever have to blush, no one who acts as I dictate will ever have to sin. (Sir. 24:17–30)

— 30 —

Isaiah's punishment for loving trees. –

Yes you will be ashamed of the trees which give you such pleasure; you will blush for the gardens that charm you. Since you will be like a tree with faded leaves, like a garden without water. The man of high estate will be tinder, his handiwork a spark. Both will burn together and no one will put them out. (Isa. 1:29–31)

— 31 —

Father–son relationship. – El's family was an unruly bunch. Four of his sons, Ba'al, Mot, Yam and God were constantly pitching for his job, squabbling and fighting with one another to increase their own dominions. Anat had incestuous yearnings for Ba'al, while Asherah, whose sexual advances were rejected by Ba'al (though some say she married him) eventually, if briefly, married God.

God was disgusted by all of his brothers and sisters, finding them callous, amoral and shameful in the extreme. In a brave speech to the heavenly assembly, God attacked them all, telling them that they would die, like mortal human beings, if they could not get their act together. It was a carefully aimed address, delivered at one of his father's divine council meetings. This was God's first step in his own bid for supreme power. The event is dutifully recorded in the 82nd Psalm:

God takes his stand at the Council of El, surrounded by all the other gods, he delivers his judgements. 'How much longer do you intend to continue with your injustices, to uphold the prestige of the wicked? Let the weak and the orphan have justice too. Be fair to the wretched and the destitute. Rescue the weak and the needy, save them from the clutches of the wicked. Ignorant and uncomprehending they wander in darkness, while the foundations of the world are shaking. I ask you now: Are you not gods, are you not all the sons of El, the Most High? No! Then you will die as human beings do, as one man, you shall fall together as gods. Arise! Judge the world, for all nations belong to you. (Ps. 82)

In this one speech, God comes close to usurping El's position. El is present (we presume), but remains stony silent, presiding, watching, waiting perhaps as Yahweh, his moralising son, rails against all the other deities. And why is the mighty El so *piano* tonight? Is he aware that his days are numbered?

—— 32 ——

Little sister Anat. – Anat is no help to God but of tremendous assistance to her favourite brother Ba'al. When she is not standing naked on a lion holding a bunch of flowers (as she is frequently depicted) she fights with galling ferocity at her brother's side, leaping to his defence against Mot, 'with a sword she split him, with a sieve she winnowed him, with a fire she burnt him, with mill-stones she ground him, in a field she scattered him and fed his flesh to the birds'.

Why she was so fond of Ba'al remains a mystery for he was vile to her. One day, while she was wandering around disguised as a heifer, Ba'al raped her '77 – even 88 times'. In an Egyptian twist to the tale, Anat was bathing by the sea at Hamkat when Ba'al (Seth) 'leapt on her as the sacred ram leaps, forcing her to the sand'. The rape hurt Ba'al's penis so badly that he felt ill for days. Anat 'the Victorious, a man-like woman' informed her father what had happened. El's judgement was that 'It is punishment for his folly, since he had intercourse with her in fire and raped her with a chisel.'

One reason why Anat was so grateful for her brother's chisel rape might be explained by a recently discovered Canaanite script which reveals that 'the mouth of the womb of Anat was closed by the god Horan so she could become pregnant but could not bear, and was opened by Ba'al.' When told of Ba'al's death Anat went into a deep and bitter mourning: 'Like the longing of a wild cow for her calf, like the longing of a wild ewe for her lamb, so was the longing of Anat for Ba'al.' And on another ancient Ugaritic tablet it is written: 'Anat walked along lamenting the beauty of her brother; how fair! The charm of her brother; how seemly! Then she devoured his flesh without a knife and drank his blood without a cup.'

— 33 —

Big brother Ba'al. – On the the face of it Ba'al is about as obnoxious as a brother can be. He is El's Regent, conceited, bumptious, noisy, violent and inconsiderate. He was the warrior god of the Canaanites, often depicted carrying a spear, a mace or a sword, who was held aloft on high poles and encouraged to smash God for six in frequent battles against the Israelites. But God was a local issue for Ba'al, he was the small fry, known to the Israelites as Yahweh. Ba'al had greater problems to contend with than the petty disputes between the Canaanites and their ambitious neighbours, for it was Ba'al's job to subdue the forces of chaos which constantly threatened to destroy the ordered universe.

Ba'al was worshipped by the Canaanites because he (like Asherah) kept Yam (the sea monster and representation of chaos) in check and was thus revered as a provider and maintainer of natural and civil order.

The Canaanites also believed that Ba'al was the only god strong enough to subdue and control Mot whose passions for aridity, sterility and scorching heat, constantly threatened to destroy the land of Canaan by drought. Ba'al, the storm god, rode the clouds and provided rain. His pitched battle with Mot is recorded on tablets at Ugarit: 'They eyed each other like burning coals: Mot was strong, Ba'al was strong. They bit like serpents; Mot was strong, Ba'al was strong. They tugged like greyhounds; Mot fell down, Ba'al fell down on top of him.'

Ba'al's victory over Mot was more pleasurable to the Canaanites than their Ugaritic words could say. They promoted Ba'al with a quasi monotheistic zeal, just as the Israelites were promoting God to the same ends. Ba'al, like Yahweh, had set his sights on a takeover of the *elohim*, and he declared: 'I alone am he that shall be king over the gods. It is I alone who fattens gods and men and who satisfies the multitudes of the earth.' (*Canaanite Myths and Legends*, p. 43) What could El do now but sit and watch? The fight was on – *Yahweh vs Ba'al*. It was a battle to the death, simulated on earth by Israel against Canaan, a little local squabble to determine who would be heavyweight champion of the heavens.

—— 34 ——

Great gods think alike. – At the Council of El, God wanted to protect the poor and wretched from the heartless gods of the *elohim*. Ba'al, it is true, was not so bothered with protecting the poor, but in other ways he and God were remarkably alike. If Ba'al could claim to have subdued the chaotic sea monster Yam, so too could God who divided the sea with his enormous strength and cracked the skulls of the twelve-headed sea monster Leviathan (Ps. 74:13–14). If Ba'al was able to parade himself as the great provider of rain, so too was God.

In the beautiful 65th Psalm of David God surpassed even Ba'al in the magnificence of his bountiful deeds:

Who stills the roaring of the seas, the roaring of their waves and the tumult of the peoples? They who dwell in the ends of the earth stand in awe of your signs; you make the dawn and the sunset shout for joy. You visit the earth and cause it to overflow; you greatly enrich it. The stream of God is full of water; you prepare their grain, for thus you prepare the earth. You water its furrows abundantly, you settle its ridges and soften it with showers, you bless its growth and have crowned the year with your bounty so that your paths drip with fatness. The pastures of the wilderness drip and the hills gird themselves with rejoicing. The meadows are clothed with flocks and the valleys are covered with grain; they shout for joy, yes, they sing.

Not only can God provide a better quality of rain and fertility than Ba'al, but he too is a storm God, and a better one at that: 'When you set out from Seir,' sang Deborah and Barak in what is possibly the oldest passage of the Hebrew Bible, 'when you marched from the field of Edom the earth trembled and the heavens dropped and the clouds pelted down water. The mountains melted before Yahweh, God of Israel' (Judg. 5:4–5). It seems that whatever Ba'al could do, God could do it better.

The Canaanites boasted that Ba'al could ride upon the clouds so the Israelites put God to ride on a whirling tornado; Ba'al could increase fertility among Canaanite couples, God could magic a barren, 90-year-old Israelite woman to conceive. To the Israelites Ba'al would cease to be revered by anyone; in time even his name would be be changed to *boshet*, meaning shame. One of Saul's sons who had proudly born the name of *Ishbaal* was later known as *Ishboshet* (2 Sam. 2:8).

—— 35 ——

God takes charge. – The assertion that God has taken over the position of El and is now running the *elohim* is implicit in the name *Yahweh Sabaoth* (God, Lord of Hosts), first given to him at the beginning of the first book of Samuel. The Hosts are, of course, the heavenly armies, the sub-gods represented by the stars. *El Sabaoth* became *Yahweh Sabaoth* for 'the Lord of Hosts is the God of Israel' (1 Chron. 17:24); 'O Lord of Hosts, God of Israel, that lives between the cherubs, you are God, you alone. You are God of all the kingdoms of the earth, you have made heaven and earth' (Isa. 37:16).

By the time Isaiah was writing his first chapters in the seventh century BCE God reigned supreme, at least in the hearts of a few Yahwist Israelites. To these men and women the God who ruled the starry *elohim*, was not El, but Yahweh. For the new God of Israel 'came from the midst of a myriad of holy ones. In his hand they were. At his feet they fell. Under his guidance they went swiftly on' (Deut. 33.2). And so God was able to employ the stars to fight against the Canaanite commander Sisera (Judg. 5:20) and to sing his own praises (Job 38:7).

By the middle of the first millennium El was gone and soon the *elohim* would be banished for ever too. The sun, even as a symbol, would cease to be worshipped, for God was now alone and ineffable, too holy to be represented by anything at all, as a late addition to the book of Deuteronomy makes clear. Moses says:

Take great care what you do. See that you do not act perversely, making yourselves a carved image in the shape of anything at all: whether it be the likeness of a man or woman, or of any beast on the earth, or any bird that flies in the heavens. When you raise your eyes to heaven, when you see the sun, the moon, the stars, and all the array of heaven do not be tempted to worship them and serve them, for God has allotted them to all people. But God has taken you, and brought you out of Egypt, to be a people all of his own as you still are today.' (Deut. 4:15–20)

Victory then for Yahweh – on the surface at least.

II

Shining Face

Creative recipe. – When God created heaven and earth, he had never done anything quite like it before, the difficulty perhaps was in knowing where to start. Do you make the water first and then place the land on top, or do you start the other way round, laying down the land and pouring the water around it? What about the heavens, where do they fit into the scheme things? And what of the off-shoots? Sound and colour for instance – do they need to be separately created or will they just come about naturally? Fortunately for God, there was already a good recipe to follow. He found it in a book called *Enuma elish* (named after its first words which mean 'when on high'). It is a Babylonian creation myth written over a thousand years before the book of Genesis.

The *Enuma elish* contained a formula which God was able to follow more or less to the letter. This is it:

First take your desolate formless waters which you will find covered in darkness (you may have to create these, otherwise use ones which were prepared earlier), and before doing anything with them, create some light.

And so God said his very first words, *'yhi or'* (which in Hebrew means 'Let there be light!' or simply 'Light!'). As he said it, light appeared. 'God saw the light, that it was good.' But there must be more to it than that. What next?

Step two: Make a firmament, that is to say, a dome-like structure onto which you can, in due course, stick your stars. That seemed easy enough. When God had done that, he called it *heaven*, a nice word which is still in use. The third phase, according to the *Enuma elish*, involves making some dry land. God did that without the slightest difficulty, placing it into the waters which he had gathered together and coming up with two more smashing good names, 'the Sea' and 'the Earth'. Again God 'saw that it was good'.

Back to the Babylonian cook book. What's next? Luminaries! Yes, indeed:

> And God said let there be lights in the firmament of the heaven to divide the day from the night; and let them be for signs and for seasons and for days and years. And let them be for lights in the firmament of the heaven to give light upon the earth. And God made two great lights, the greater to rule the day, and the lesser light to rule the night: he made the stars also.

And he 'saw that it was good'.

Now the path was clear to create the most exciting thing of all: Man. 'Not yet,' thought God and, delaying his pleasure for an instant, deviated for the first time from the Babylonian schema by creating a few animals. Few is perhaps an understatement – in fact he created 'every living creature that moveth, which the waters brought forth abundantly, after their kind and every winged fowl after his kind. And God saw that it was good' (Gen. 1:21).

At last, it was time for the crowning glory, the icing on the cake: God put down his copy of *Enuma elish*, for he knew instinctively what had to be done. Picking up a small cluster of dust, he sculpted it into an image that resembled his own, and breathing into its nostrils, Hey Presto! God created Man. But, wait a minute, something was wrong. What could it be? Perhaps God was getting tired after six days' arduous work. He needed rest and so, for the first time, did not bother to 'see that it was good'.

— 37 —

Making angels. – Not all angels were created at the same instant. New ones are endlessly being formed by a heavenly prince called Radweri'el

YHWH, described by Enoch as 'more exalted than all princes, more wonderful than all ministers'. From his position above the *Seraphim*, Radweri'el talks and 'from every utterance that issues from his mouth an angel is formed, and it joins in the songs of the ministering angels and recites the prayer before the Holy One' (*3 En.* 27:3). In one ancient text discovered at the Egyptian library of Nag Hammadi in 1945 the Angel of Life advanced on a foolish prophet, crying and shouting, 'You are wrong, you idiot! She breathed into his face, and her breath became a fiery angel; and that angel bound him and cast him down into Tartyros below the abyss' (*Hyp. Arch.* 91:11).

Elsewhere Enoch relates that God too is capable of performing the same trick. In the proper order of things, angels are supposed to sing 'Holy!' for which they receive three crowns; 'Holy! Holy!' for which they are given one more crown, followed by 'Holy! Holy! Holy! YHWH of Hosts!' for a fifth. But if they sing any of this out of order, even by mistake, they will be blasted to smithereens by a 'devouring fire which goes out from the little finger of the Holy One. Then the Holy One, blessed be he, opens his mouth and, with one word, creates new ones like them to take their place. Each of them stands in song before his throne of glory and recites "Holy!" as it is written' (*3 En.* 40:4). According to Islamic tradition the *cherubim* were made from tears blubbed from the eyes of the archangel, Michael, caused by his grieving at the pitiful state of humanity.

—— 38 ——

The making of Adam. – The traditions of Islam have preserved more details about how God made Adam than are found in the Book of Genesis. Originally he sent three angels, Gabriel, Michael and Israfil, down to earth to collect up various samples of mud from different geological strata. This he hoped would allow him to colour man according to the different shades of mud that were presented to him. But when the three angels arrived on earth, Earth herself started to fret: 'If you take that mud back,' she said, 'God will create a rebellious creature with it, and out of exasperation with that creature, he will surely curse the earth.' The angels took her point and returned empty-handed to God. So God sent another angel, Azrael, to get the mud. Azrael did not give a damn about hurting Earth's feelings, grabbing in his hands as much mud as was needed, and returning it without hesitation, to God. God was so pleased with Azrael that he named him 'Angel of Death' and gave him the task, thereafter, of separating peoples' bodies from their souls.

Once he had approved the mud, God ordered angels to take it all to Arabia (to a place between Mecca and Tayef) and to knead it like dough until it was soft enough for him to swoop down from heaven and fashion it into something interesting. In the event God made a statuette, probably of himself, and left it to dry in the baking-hot wind for forty years, during which time many of the angels regularly came to inspect it. One of God's favourites, the angel Iblis, kicked the little statuette until it started to ring out like a bell. When it was dry God animated it with a soul and carried it proudly back to paradise.

— 39 —

All about Eve. – In the book of Genesis chapter two it is said that God created Eve out of Adam's rib as he slept. The reason for her existence was to assist Adam, probably in his gardening duties. She was meant to be his 'help mate' but the first thing she did was to lead him astray. It was a fatal error. But Genesis may have got the story wrong. In *2 Enoch* God admitted another reason for creating Eve: 'I imposed sleep on Adam,' he said, 'And I created for him a wife so that death might come to him by his wife' (*2 En.* 30:17). If Eve was born with a pre-ordained mission to kill Adam the traditional view of her as a sinful, weak and destructive woman needs to be reviewed.

—— 40 ——

Iblis declares himself. – God was so pleased and impressed by the man he had made that he desired all of his angels, even the most important of them, to bow in reverence to Adam. Unsurprisingly Iblis (who had kicked Adam as a maquette when he was drying in the wind) objected: 'I am better than he is,' he whinged, 'You created me out of fire and you created him only out of clay.' God said (according to Arberry's translation of the Qur'an):

'Get down out of it;
it is not for thee to wax proud here,
so go thou forth; surely thou art among the humbled.'
Said he, 'Respite me till the day they shall be raised.'
Said He, 'Thou art among the ones that are respited.'
Said he, 'Now, for Thy perverting me,
I shall surely sit in ambush for them on Thy straight path;
then I shall come on them from before them
and from behind them, from their right hands
and their left hands; Thou wilt not find most of them thankful.'
Said He, 'Go thou forth from it, despised
and banished. Those of them that follow thee – I shall assuredly
    fill Gehenna [Hell] with all of you.'
                                        (Qur'an 7:11–17)

—— 41 ——

Duff toys. – If God created Man for his own amusement then it must be admitted his idea of entertainment is very remote from our own. Adam and Eve were no good. They were neither witty, nor were they wise. At no time did they demonstrate physical or mental prowess,

51

they had no sense of honour, no sense of humour, not much by way of courage, a propensity to disobedience, a dismally narrow outlook on life and both of them, to their eternal shame, were easily led by the nose. In short, Adam and Eve were dull dogs. That is, according to Genesis.

To Milton, however, Adam and Eve were fascinating creatures. He was attractive, inquisitive and noble of both mind and frame; she was comely, alluring and a delight to the eye. When Satan first saw them in the garden at Eden even he was struck by their magnificence:

> Godlike erect, with native honour clad,
> In naked majesty seemed lords of all.
> Though not equal, as their sex not equal seemed;
> For contemplation he, and valour formed;
> For softness she and sweet attractive grace;
> He for God only, she for God in him.
> His fair large front and eye sublime declared
> Absolute rule; and hyacinthine locks
> Round from his parted forelock manly hung,
> Clustering, but not beneath his shoulders broad.
> She as a veil down to the slender waist
> Her unadorned golden tresses wore dishevelled,
> But in wanton ringlets waved,
> As the vine curls her tendrils, which implied
> Subjection, but required with gentle sway,
> And by her yielded, by him best received,
> Yielded with coy submission, modest pride,
> And sweet, reluctant, amorous delay.
> Nor those mysterious parts were then concealed.
>
> (*Paradise Lost*, IV)

God told Enoch that Adam and Eve had only lasted five and a half hours in Paradise, before they were booted out (*2 En.* 32:1). Had he not read Milton? Like a child rejecting a brand new toy because he can't get his head round the instructions, God acted in haste, and may have made a mistake.

— 42 —

The Tree of Knowledge. – God made Adam somewhere (we are not told where) and moved him thence into the Garden of Eden 'to dress it and keep it up'. In the middle of this garden he had already planted two trees, one the Tree of Life, the other (with delicious looking fruit upon it) the Tree of Knowledge of Good and Evil. The first thing God said to Adam was this: 'Do not take the fruit from the Tree of Knowledge or you will die.' Then God created Eve, as a helper, for Adam, out of Adam's spare rib.

A serpent, popularly held to be Satan in disguise, persuaded Eve to ignore God's injunction and eat the fruit. From this act of disobedience, it is taught that the whole of humanity will continue to suffer by the inheritance of original sin until the Day of Judgement. The traditional view of God as creator of all things, as all-good, all-knowing and all-powerful, runs into grave difficulties at this point. A short list of major theological hiccups might include the following:

- Why, if God is perfectly good, did he create a tree that gave knowledge of evil?
- Why did he ask Adam to tend the exact same garden in which this pernicious tree had been planted?
- Why did he allow the tree to grow fruit that would whet the appetites of man?
- Why did God instruct Adam not to eat the fruit when knowledge of good and evil is surely a helpful and useful thing to acquire?
- If God is all-knowing and he knows in advance that Adam and Eve will eat the fruit, why does he bother to tell them not to?
- If the fault lies with the serpent-devil for persuading Eve to eat

53

the forbidden fruit, why did God, 'creator of all things', create the serpent-devil?

- If creating the serpent-devil was somehow outside of God's control could he not at least have prevented it entering the Garden of Eden in the first place?
- If Adam was ignorant of the difference between right and wrong before he ate the apple, why should he be punished for disobedience?
- God created Eve as a helper to Adam but what sort of helper is it that damns her husband and their descendants for ever? Is God not able to create better helpers than that?
- God told Adam and Eve not to eat the fruit invoking death as a penalty, but the devil-serpent told them they should eat it in order to receive revelation and knowledge. Why should Adam and Eve in their ignorant state trust God any more than the Devil on this issue?
- Why, if God is all-powerful, is he less able to persuade Adam and Eve than the devil?
- God said Adam would die on the day he ate the fruit, but he lived for 930 years, the serpent-devil, on the other hand, assured Eve that they would not die by eating the fruit. Who should Adam and Eve trust more thereafter, God or the Devil?

For thousands of years theologians have offered varying responses to these questions, attempting to harmonise this ancient fable with their newer concept of an all-good, all-loving, all-knowing, all-creating, omnipotent father. To all but the most wilful theologian, however, God cannot come out of the Eden story smelling of roses. If the downfall of man was caused by Adam eating an apple, then God must take the rap, as Jesus was bluntly told by his neighbour on the cross:

You can blame it on Adam
You can blame it on Eve
You can blame it on the apple

But that I can't believe
It was God that made the Devil
And the woman and the man
And there wouldn't be an apple
If it wasn't in the plan.
It's God they ought to crucify
Instead of you and me
I said to the carpenter
A-hanging on the tree.

('It was on a Friday Morning' by Sydney Carter)

— 43 —

Mirror image. – The *elohim* said, 'Let us make man in our own image, after our likeness' so it would be useful to know in what way Adam was created in the image of the gods. We might start by asking what sex Adam was, or would that be too obvious? Adam is after all a boy's name signifying the male half of the first human couple, but is there any chance that Adam might have been a girl? 'Adam' has *become* a boy's name but cannot have been such when the first human was given it.

In the Assyrian language *adamu* means 'to produce'. Adam may have got his name because he was 'produced' by God or because he (or she) was the producer of the rest of mankind. The word is also used to denote redness, the *Adamah* of Joshua (Josh. 19:36) are the red lands, suggesting perhaps that God created Adam with a red face (like his own) or fashioned him from a variety of reddish clays. A more sober etymology suggests a link with a Hebrew word for 'earth'. In any case there is no suggestion of sex in these derivations, with the possible exception of the last (earth) which is usually mythologised as feminine. One suggestion is that God created Adam as an androgynous being like himself, for in the day that God created man it is written, 'male and female created he them; and blessed them and called their name Adam' (Gen. 5:2).

Some myths have it that the serpent seduced Eve and was the father of her children, but since Adam had sexual intercourse with her (Gen. 4:1) and since all the biblical genealogies point to Adam as a father, it is better to stick with the traditional line that man is descended from Adam who was made by God *in his own image.*

Nor is it helpful to suggest, as many theologians do, that the connection between the image of God and the image of man is purely spiritual; that man's *spirit* or *soul* contains his only resemblance to God and not his body. That is not what 'image' means. Moreover spirits, as the same theologians all agree, do not have *images.* If Adam was made in the *image* of God there must have been a *physical* resemblance between them, otherwise scripture would have recorded that he was made in the 'spirit of God' or 'in the spiritual likeness of God'.

In order to know what God looks like we need to gather all that we can about the physical image of Adam and Eve. Unfortunately scriptural testimony here is scant. Abraham caught a glimpse of them in an apocalyptic vision: 'I looked to the picture', he said, 'and my eyes ran to the side of the garden of Eden. And I saw there a man, very great in height and terrible in breadth, incomparable in aspect, entwined with a woman who was also equal to the man in aspect and size' (*Apoc. Abr.* 22:5). According to Mormon tradition Adam was the spit and image of Jesus Christ, for 'God made man in his image' means to the Mormons that Jesus Christ (the *Logos*) made Adam in *his* (Jesus') image.

The best physical description of Adam and Eve is found in Milton's *Paradise Lost.* If God really looks like Milton's Adam he must have broad shoulders, curly locks, parted hair and mysterious nether regions, but no modern religion will stand for that.

—— 44 ——

Cain and Abel. – Of Adam and Eve's two sons God marginally preferred the younger, Abel. No reason is given for this but it was usual for God to favour younger sons above their older brothers. He liked Isaac more than Ishmael; Jacob more than Esau, and, in the apocryphal Psalm 151, God preferred David to all of his taller and handsomer older brothers. Even so, when Cain slaughtered his little brother Abel by knocking his brains out with a stone, God protected the elder 'to prevent whoever might come across him from striking him down' (Gen. 4:15).

According to Islamic tradition (in which the brothers are known as Kabil and Habil) Cain carried Abel's corpse around on his shoulders until it stank, when God, with the help of a raven, taught him how the dead should be buried. After that Cain ran to the land of Nod where he had a baby and built a city. It is common to ask several questions at this point. How, if Adam and Eve had only two sons, was it possible for Cain to have a baby and for whom did he build the city? Moreover, who did God suppose Cain might come across to strike him down apart from Adam and Eve? The Bible says that another son was born to Adam and Eve called Seth, but only after Cain had killed Abel. Baby Seth was neither a threat to Cain nor, while still in the cradle, worth building a city for.

In the second-century BCE *Book of Jubilees*, sometimes called *The Little Genesis*, it is explained that Adam and Eve had two daughters, Awan, who married Cain, and Azura, who married Seth, but that still leaves the other questions unanswered. It must have always been a part of God's grand scheme that the human race should descend from two incestuous couples. Among the sexual laws which God dictated to Moses, incest between a brother and sister is not proscribed, though a man is specifically forbidden from sleeping with his mother, stepmother, half-sister, granddaughter, stepsister, aunt, wife of an uncle, daughter-in-law, stepdaughter, step-granddaughter (Lev. 18:6–18) and mother-in-law (Deut. 27:23). Cain and Seth did none of these things. Building a city entirely for oneself and one's family is not an abomination according to the law, but possibly a sign of madness.

— 45 —

The next man. – The Bible suggests that God took little or no interest in human affairs from the time of the death of Adam until the old age of Noah which was ten generations later, but this is not quite true. His favourite, perhaps among all the people that ever lived, was Enoch, not to be confused with Cain's boy of the same name but the son of Jared, descended from Adam in the line of Seth and Noah's great-grandfather. This wonderful man is only fleetingly mentioned in Genesis: 'In all Enoch lived for 365 years. Enoch walked with God. Then he vanished because God took him' (Gen. 5:24).

The idea that Enoch did not exactly die but was *translated* into another life set imaginations aflame. Jewish tradition proclaims him the inventor of mathematics and astronomy as well as the first author. Books containing his visions and prophecies were said to have been carried by Noah onto the ark and preserved, with countless pairs of animals, for the posterity of the world. Three of these books survive, albeit in fragmentary form. *1 Enoch*, or *Ethiopic Enoch*, is the most complete and dates from 100–200 BCE. Apart from the Ethiopic text other fragments have been found in Greek and Latin, as well as Aramaic and Hebrew fragments among the Dead Sea Scrolls at Qumran. The book of *2 Enoch* was probably written in the second century CE and survives in an Old Church Slavonic manuscript first seen by Western scholars at the end of the nineteenth century, while the third book, known as the *Hebrew Apocalypse of Enoch*, once attributed to a Palestinian scholar called Rabbi Ishmael who died *c.* 132 CE is now believed to have older Aramaic origins.

God's love for Enoch is made quite clear from all three books. In the third he is transformed into the Angel Metraton and stands (second only to God) in the great hierarchy of heaven, affectionately known to all as the 'lesser YHWH'.

— 46 —

Drowning by numbers. – In the days of Noah, God had still not murdered many people – later he would prove a pastmaster, employing swords, arrows, hailstones, rocks, plagues, hernias and earthquakes as pesticides against the human race. But for his first big kill, God needed to be certain of success. Luckily, having created man himself, he was ken to the weaknesses of Man's design – he knew, for instance, that the wretched creature needs a constant supply of fresh air to keep it alive. There are various ways in which God could deprive the whole human race of air: he could vacuum the atmosphere; send packets of irresistible biscuits that explode in the oesophagus and block the wind pipe, but, in the end, he found an easier option – rain.

He had sent rain many times before, and although its effects had been positive in the past, he realised that a major deluge, big enough to cover the whole earth, right to the tops of its mountains, would lead to hypoxia in every human being; and God knew from his vast medical knowledge that hypoxia led to death. But why should he wish to kill these people?

'He regretted having made human beings on earth and was grieved at heart' (Gen. 6:6), but this in itself was not enough, he needed something to charge them with, however trumped up.

'Corruption! That's it. I shall accuse them all of corruption.'

'What about the other things that will surely die in this flood?' Noah might have asked, 'What of the charming giraffe and the cute bunny rabbit? What have they done wrong to deserve death by hypoxia?'

'I shall rid the surface of the earth of the human beings that I created

– human and animal, the creeping things and the birds of heaven – for I regret having made them' (Gen. 6:7).

'But wait a minute, what about nasty sharks, stingrays, jellyfish and things like that; just because they can swim, why should they get off scot free?'

But it was too late, for God had made up his mind and there was no going back. He had resolved to kill all people and all non-aquatic animals and that was that. Over the next forty days millions of lives were lost, but God must have regretted the terrible stench that fumed up from the rotting dead, for when the flood subsided and Noah sacrificed a few of the flood survivors on his altar, 'God smelt the pleasing smell and said to Noah "Never again shall all living things be destroyed by the waters of a flood, nor shall there ever again be a flood to devastate the earth"' (Gen. 8:20–9:11).

From then on, floods were out; they smelled like rotting drains and what God liked best was burning flesh. For his next great holocaust, the destruction of the cities of Sodom and Gomorrah, he did not have to think long or hard before choosing his weapons – fire and brimstone would do the trick.

— 47 —

Errant wisdom. – The French thinker and aristocratic *bon viveur* Montesquieu probably thought he was being clever when he observed that 'if triangles had a god, he would have three sides'. As it happens, this same point was made 2,200 years earlier by the Greek philosopher Xenophanes. 'If cattle or horses had hands,' he claimed, 'or were able to draw with their feet and produce the works which men do, horses would draw the forms of gods like horses, and cattle like cattle, and they would make the gods' bodies the same shape as their own.' What about all those ancient Egyptian gods and goddesses? Amon with his head of a ram? Vulture-faced Nekhebet? Or the lovable Set, brother of Osiris, whose composite form incorporated a greyhound's body, slit eyes, squared-off ears and a long forked tail? What about them? In the past, when Egyptologists have unwrapped ancient mummies, they have invariably found preserved within, small, but perfectly normal human beings.

—— 48 ——

Now you see him; now you don't. – Has anyone actually seen God? The question should be easy enough to answer but the scriptures offer a bewildering swarm of contradictions. Jesus, for example, is on record as saying that 'no man has seen God at any time' (John 1:18), but Micaiah hotly denied this: 'I saw the Lord standing upon the throne,' he said (1 Kings 22:19).

God warned Moses: 'Thou canst not see my face, for there shall no man see me and live' (Exod. 33:20); but only a few biblical pages back Jacob declared: 'I have seen God face to face and my life has been preserved' (Gen. 32:30). Jesus had insisted that it is not just the Lord's face which cannot be seen but his whole 'shape' (John 5:37), yet this too is contradicted many times over, not least in the book of Exodus where 'Moses, Aaron, Nadab, Abihu and seventy elders of Israel saw the God of Israel beneath whose feet there was what looked like a sapphire pavement pure as the heavens themselves, but he did no harm to the Israelite notables; they gazed on God and then they ate and drank' (Exod. 24:9–11).

Elsewhere God is described as talking to Moses 'mouth to mouth' conversing 'face to face, as a man speaks to his friend' (Exod. 33:11; Deut. 34:10), even though on rare occasions God is prickly about Moses seeing his face, allowing the holy man a view only of his mighty hind quarters: 'Place yourself on the rock,' he once said to him, 'and, as my presence passes by, I shall put you in a cleft of the rock and shield you with my hand until I have passed by. Then I shall take my hand away and you will see my back but my face must not be seen' (Exod. 33:21–3).

The Bible freely admits that many besides Moses have at one time or another been privy to the sight of God: Amos, Job, Micaiah, Isaiah, Ezekiel and Daniel are among them.

So why should there be any confusion? Is God visible or not? The Bible enters the theological debate not as a single document with one clear theology but as a set of books written by a great many people at different times with contrary views. The debate as to whether God could or could not be seen in anthropomorphic form was more alive in biblical times than it is today. Nowadays, among modern believers, seeing God (in the image of man), standing in any one place at any one time, contradicts the dogma of divine immortality, invisibility, immutability and omnipresence. In order to uphold these beliefs the doctrines of Judaism and Christianity have needed to argue that all anthropomorphic sightings of God are allegorical, symbolic or visionary – a bright light will do, they say, nothing more than that. Any hands, feet, nostrils, arms or legs will spoil everything.

— 49 —

Deathly sight. – The notion, oft repeated, that to see God necessitates certain death (see Exod. 19:21; 33:20; 1 Sam. 6:19, and elsewhere) needs some explaining. Why should God wish anyone who sees him to die? If a human being causes other peoples' deaths in this way it would be assumed that there was something so shameful or repellent about his appearance that urgent measures were needed to conceal it. But this is unlikely to be the case for God. In any event, as an omnipotent being, he could, if he wished, make his image safe and palatable to the human gaze. A doctrine of the 'beatific vision' encourages Christians to believe that they will be able to see God in the afterlife if they have properly followed the ways of Christ during their time on earth. But this is a doctrine of the Middle Ages, neither Moses nor the authors of the Pentateuch nursed any hope of seeing God after their deaths. In life the sight of God meant certain death, even, on occasion, for

angels (*1 En.* 14:19), and certainly for mortals: 'If a man should look
he will melt like wax before the face of God' (*Ques. Ezra* A 26).

—— 50 ——

Cunning defence. – Moses and his clever brother, Aaron, were struggling to maintain control over 600,000 recalcitrant Israelites as they
wandered through the desert from Egypt in the wrong direction for
the Promised Land. The only means of keeping such a rabble in order
was to threaten it with the wrath of God. 'Obey us or—' (a long list of
punishments can be found at Lev. 26:14–40). The greatest threat to
Moses' and Aaron's control was the possibility that some rebel might
stand before the crowd and claim: 'I too have a special relationship with
God. Moses and Aaron are frauds. You must follow me instead.'

Now Moses protected himself from this eventuality by imposing
the death penalty on false prophets (Deut. 18:20) and by further
declaring that 'anybody who catches sight of God, will die'. These
two pieces of legislation gave Moses and Aaron all the authority they
needed to despatch pretenders: 'If you say you have seen God,' they
could argue, 'then you must be dead. But since you are patently
still alive, you must be lying. Therefore you are a false prophet
and must be executed right away!' In the meantime Moses side-
stepped the problem in his own case by declaring: 'All I ever saw
was God's back and that, by special dispensation from the Lord
himself.'

—— 51 ——

God shoots Nicholas a loving glance. – Nicholas of Cusa (1401–64),
a German cardinal and philosopher, was twinkled upon by God. Far
from dying, the cardinal had a wonderful time, concluding that God's
long stare revealed his special love:

Lord, thy glance is love. And just as thy gaze beholdeth me so attentively that it never turneth aside from me, even so is it with thy love. And since 'tis deathless, it abideth ever with me, and thy love, Lord, is naught but thy very Self, who lovest me. (*De Visione Dei*, 1453)

— 52 —

Isaiah's vision. – Although Isaiah claimed to have seen God his first instinct was to give nothing away, revealing only that 'Mine eyes have seen the King, the Lord of Hosts' (Isa. 6:1–5), with no physical description forthcoming. He saw him 'sitting upon a throne high and lifted up, and his train filled the temple'. There was a terrible noise caused by angels shouting: 'Holy, holy, holy is the Lord of Hosts. His glory fills the whole earth.' So loud they were that the door-posts shook. The Temple was full of smoke but Isaiah was able to make something out, even through the smoke, for immediately he started to panic fearing that what he had seen would cause him to perish. 'Woe is me! for I am undone,' he cried, but in an instant his iniquity was washed away by an angel sweeping down from on high and pushing white-hot coals onto Isaiah's lips as a means of purifying him for a life of prophecy.

Isaiah's description of his vision of God is not illuminating. From the fact that God was wearing a train it might be deduced that a human form was lurking underneath it, but even this is flimsy, speculative evidence.

— 53 —

Elijah and the vision that got away. – Elijah, a Tishbite prophet and formidable worker of miracles, escaped death when he was snatched up to heaven in a mighty wind by a chariot with horses of fire. Some

years earlier he had been fleeing his enemies and was lying under a juniper tree in the wilderness wishing he were dead. He fell asleep to be woken by an angel that had baked some bread for him. The bread gave Elijah strength to travel for another forty days, all the way to Horeb, God's own mountain. It was in a cave at Horeb that a voice said to him: 'Go out and stand on the mountain before God,' for at that moment God passed by:

There was a great strong wind which smashed the mountain and broke the rocks by the power of God. But God was not in the wind. After the wind, an earthquake, but God was not in the earthquake. After the earthquake, fire; but God was not in the fire. And after the fire a light murmuring sound. When Elijah heard this he covered his face with his cloak and went out to the entrance of the cave. (1 Kings 19:1–13)

Elijah's inability to see God anywhere in all this hubbub was undoubtedly due to the reluctance of the authors of the first book of Kings to admit that God could be seen at all. The same determination to stop people imagining God as a visible form is also evident in the warning that Moses gave to the children of Israel who had seen God at Horeb: 'Be careful, for your own sakes,' he told them, 'for you saw no shape that day at Horeb when God spoke to you from the heart of the fire, see that you do not corrupt yourselves by making an image in the shape of anything whatever: be it statue of a man or of a woman, or of any animal on the earth' (Deut. 4:15–17).

— 54 —

Confirmation of Genesis? – Philosopher, mathematician and Christian apologist, Blaise Pascal (1623–62) had a mystical experience on 23 November 1654 in which he may or may not have seen God. To his credit he reached for a pen as soon as the incident was over in order to record what it was that he had seen and felt. The experience, which affected him for the rest of his life, was jotted on a small scrap of paper. This is what it said:

> From about half past ten in the evening to about half an hour after midnight.
> Fire.
> 'God of Abraham, God of Isaac, God of Jacob,' not of philosophers and scholars.
> Certainty, certainty, Beyond reason. Heart-felt joy, peace.
> My God and Your God.
> 'Thy God shall be my God.'
> Forgetfulness of the world and everything except God.
> The world has not known thee, but I have known thee.
> Joy! joy! joy! tears of joy!

In this short note Pascal seems to be claiming that he came into the presence of the God of Genesis, the self same anthropomorphic figure who dined with Abraham, chose a wife for Isaac and wrestled with Jacob. This Genesis God is the true God of Pascal's vision, not the immutable, transcendent, eternal, omnipotent God-concept of the philosophers. Some may feel that the words as Pascal wrote them were gibberish; nothing more than tired or drunken jottings, but to the man himself they were of colossal significance, for when he had finished writing he folded the paper and carefully sewed it into the lining of his doublet where it was discovered many years after his death.

— 55 —

Ezekiel's vision. – Ezekiel was a Jewish priest's son among the Babylonian exiles, known to God by the honorific title 'son of man'. Many of his visions and prophecies are perverse, some pornographic, others comic. Ezekiel relates how God one day commanded him to swallow an enormous scroll of parchment inscribed with 'Lamentations, dirges and cries of grief' (Ezek. 2:8–10) and describes how God tied him down on his left side for 390 days and forced him to eat barley bread baked with human faeces (Ezek. 4:4–13). Elsewhere God lifts Ezekiel by his hair and sweeps him distances of up to eight miles at a time.

Should Ezekiel's one and only vision of God be trusted on the basis of these bizarre goings on? His famous description comes at the end of a vivid encounter with God's horrifying charioteers, but Ezekiel, usually a robust writer, was on this occasion careful to stress that what he saw in this vision was not exactly God himself but only the 'appearance of the semblance' of the Lord:

Beyond the solid surface, above the heads of these creatures, there was what seemed like a sapphire, in the form of a throne. High above on the form of a throne was the semblance of form with the appearance of a human being. And I saw from what appeared to be his loins upwards the gleam of amber, what looked like fire with radiance all about it. Like the appearance of a bow that is in the cloud on a day of rain, such was the appearance of the semblance of the presence of the Lord. When I beheld it, I flung myself down on my face and I heard the voice of someone speaking. (Ezek. 1:26–8)

—— 56 ——

What Daniel saw. – With Daniel, as with Isaiah, the emphasis of his description of God lies not so much on the beatific vision itself but on the strange things that were going on around him. In this case fearful monsters: a lion with eagles' wings, then a bear with three ribs in its mouth, a leopard with four wings on its back and, most galling of all, an iron-jawed ghoul which devoured every creature it saw and

67

crushed the remnants underfoot, before sprouting horns with human eyes and boastful grinning mouths:

> While I was watching, thrones were set in place and The Ancient of Days took his seat. His robe was white as snow and the hair of his head as pure as wool. His throne was a blaze of flames, its wheels were a burning fire. A stream of fire poured out issuing from his presence. A thousand thousand waited on him, ten thousand times ten thousand stood before him. The court was in session and the books lay open. (Dan. 7:9–10)

Daniel's vision offers several features of interest. First of all, it is obvious that Daniel has seen God in the image of a man, he has white hair on his head and a robe. It is curious that God should make his entrance as all these bizarre monsters are showing off to Daniel instead of concerning themselves in the praise or service of God. God's throne is also noteworthy. It has wheels on it, suggesting, not that God is disabled – he took his seat, unaided – but that he uses his throne as a vehicle sometimes, to get himself from A to B.

— 57 —

Shome mishtake. – The prophet Micaiah saw God 'sitting on his throne, and all the host of heaven standing by him on his right hand and on his left' (1 Kings 22:19). Amos saw him 'standing upon the altar' (Amos 9:1) while Habakkuk claimed that 'His glory covered the heavens and the earth was full of his praise. And his brightness was as the light; and he had horns coming out of his hand' (Hab. 3:4). Even if (as some biblical translations assert) Habakkuk did not mean 'horns' but 'rays of brightness', the vision remains maudlin and bizarre.

It may be that all of the prophets were pathological liars, for lying was a mark of their trade. Four hundred lied at once to the King of

Israel (1 Kings 22:5–11) and Jeremiah, though a prophet himself, was scandalised: 'They are all greedy for gain,' he complained, 'prophet no less than priest, all of them practise fraud' (Jer. 6:13). God railed against them too: 'Do not listen to what those prophets that prophesy to you are saying; they are deluding and cheating you with false visions' (Jer. 23:16).

Isaiah was convinced that many of the prophets were not only liars but alcoholics as well: 'The priest and the prophet have erred through strong drink,' he lamented, 'they are swallowed up of wine, they are out of their minds with strong drink, they have become confused in their visions and stumble in judgement. For all the tables are covered with vomit and filthiness, not one of them is clean' (Isa. 28:7–8). When alcohol is attributed the cause of hallucination the hallucinations happen not while drunk but during the period of 'drying out' after a heavy binge. In which case Habakkuk probably saw horns on God's hands while Isaiah was cleaning the sick off the tables.

—— 58 ——

A sighting in the woods. – In 1820 a 15-year-old American youth from Sharon, Vermont set out into the woods to find God. He had been disturbed by his neighbours (Methodists, Baptists and Presbyterians, religious to the last) each of them claiming for a different denomination. The youth (whose name was Joseph Smith), inspired by the Epistle of James, which says 'If any of you lack wisdom, let him ask of God, that giveth to all men liberally, and upbraideth not; and it shall be given him' (Jas. 1:5), set off with the express purpose of asking God which Christian denomination he should join.

At a suitable spot in the woods Smith started to pray out loud. It was a pleasant, clear day, but to his horror a thick darkness suddenly surrounded him and he was overcome with despair and a nasty feeling he was doomed. Let the youth himself take up the story from here:

It no sooner appeared than I found myself delivered from the enemy which held me bound. When the light rested upon me I saw two Personages, whose brightness and glory defy all description, standing above me in the air. One of them spake unto me, calling me by name and said, pointing to the other – 'This is My Beloved Son. Hear Him!' My object in going to inquire of the Lord was to know which of all the sects was right, that I might know which to join. No sooner, therefore, did I get possession of myself, so as to be able to speak, than I asked the Personages who stood above me in the light, which of all the sects was right (for at this time it had never entered into my head that all were wrong) – and which I should join. I was answered that I must join none of them, for they were all wrong; and the Personage who addressed me said that all their creeds were an abomination in his sight; that those professors were all corrupt; that: 'they draw near to me with their lips, but their hearts are far from me, they teach for doctrines the commandments of men, having a form of godliness, but they deny the power thereof.'

He again forbade me to join with any of them; and many other things did he say unto me, which I cannot write at this time. When I came to myself again, I found myself lying on my back, looking up into heaven. When the light had departed, I had no strength; but soon recovering in some degree, I went home. And as I leaned up to the fireplace, mother inquired what the matter was. I replied, 'Never mind, all is well – I am well enough off.'

I then said to my mother, 'I have learned for myself that Presbyterianism is not true.'

It seems as though the adversary was aware, at a very early period of my life, that I was destined to prove a disturber and an annoyer of his kingdom; else why should the powers of darkness combine against me? Why the opposition and persecution that arose against me, almost in my infancy? (*Joseph Smith History*, pp. 17–20)

— 59 —

Enoch's vision. – Of all the written descriptions of God's physical appearance Enoch's is the most generous. What did he see? First a vision from *1 Enoch*, disarmingly similar to Daniel's:

> And I observed a lofty throne, and from beneath the throne were issuing streams of flaming fire. It was difficult to look at it. And the Great Glory was sitting upon it – as for his gown which was shining more brightly than the sun, it was whiter than any snow. None of the angels was able to come in and see the face of the Excellent and the Glorious One and no one of the flesh can see him – the flaming fire was round about him, and a great fire stood before him. (*1 En.* 14:19–22)

If Enoch was unable to see God clearly in his first-century Ethiopic text, he managed to make up for it a century later in the Slavonic Apocalypse. In this ancient scripture Enoch is first lead by the Archangel Michael through various heavens, not until he reaches the tenth is he brought face to face with God:

> And on the 10th heaven, Aravoth, I saw the view of the face of the Lord, like iron made burning hot in a fire; it emits sparks and is incandescent. Thus even I saw the Lord in the face. But the face of the Lord is not to be talked about, it is so very strong and very glorious, marvellous and supremely frightening, terrible and horrifying. Who am I to give an account of the incomprehensible being of his beautiful appearance, never changing and indescribable, of his multiple voice and his great Glory. (*2 En.* 22:1–5)

Some time after this vision Enoch called together his sons in order to explain to them what he had seen:

71

Oh my children, my beloved ones! Listen, my children, it is not from my lips that I am reporting to you today, but from the lips of the Lord I have been sent to you. For you hear my words, out of my lips, a human being created equal to yourselves; but I have heard from the fiery lips of the Lord. For the lips of the Lord are a furnace of fire, and his angels are the flames which come out. You my children, see my face, a human being created just like yourselves, but I am one who has seen the face of the Lord, like iron made burning by a fire, and it is brought out and it emits sparks and it is incandescent. But you gaze into my eyes, a human being equal in significance to yourselves; but I have gazed into the eyes of the Lord, shining like rays of the sun and terrifying the eyes of a human being. But you my children see the right hand of one who helps you, a human being created identical to yourselves; but I have seen the right hand of the Lord helping me and filling heaven. But you see the scope of my activity, the same as your own but I have seen the scope of the Lord, without limit and without analogy, and to which there is no end. (*2 En.* 39)

— 60 —

Dante's theophany. – In *The Divine Comedy* Dante went in search of God. Like Moses looking for the Promised Land, he went first of all in the wrong direction – down, instead of up. In hell he met Virgil who led him through a conical funnel of bowges where, at each stage, if not impeded by ferocious demons, the two poets were able to gaze on the punishment and despair of others. Having thoroughly examined every chamber of hell Dante clambered up into purgatory, a mountain of circular ledges containing all the sinners who had repented but were not yet deemed good enough for heaven. Finally he reached heaven (*Paradiso*) where he entrusted himself to the guidance of Beatrice Portinari (*c.* 1265–90), the girl he had fallen in love with during a church service when she was only nine years old. Since then Beatrice had married a man by the name of de Bardi and died.

In heaven Beatrice guided Dante well enough, but at the last hurdle, just as they were about to see God, she turned away leaving him in the hands of St Bernard of Clairvaux. Bernard, who is and always was, obsessed with the Virgin Mary, found the 'Mother of Our Lord' lurking among the myriad petals of a rose and prayed that she might intercede with God on behalf of Dante so that the great Florentine might have a chance to enjoy the Beatific Vision. Mary did her bit. God was prepared to show himself to Dante. Bernard smiled and signalled to Dante to look up; but he was already looking up. He did not need Bernard's help at that final moment.

Anyone who reads what Horace Walpole called that 'extravagant, absurd, disgusting' *Divine Comedy* from its beginning in hell is, by this stage, at a fever pitch of tense anticipation, for by the end of the third and final book, the author is at last about to see what he had been searching for all this time – a vision of God. But, damn it all, at this riveting climactic moment Dante, one of the greatest descriptive writers of world literature, is suddenly at a loss for words:

> Bernard conveyed to me what I should do
> By sign and smile. Already on my own
> I had looked upwards, as he wished me to.

> For now my sight clear and yet clearer grown,
> Pierced through the ray of that exalted light,
> Wherein, as in itself, the truth is known.

> Henceforth my vision mounted to a height
> Where speech is vanquished and must lag behind
> And memory surrenders in such plight.

> As from a dream one may awake to find
> Its passion yet imprinted on the heart,
> Although all else is cancelled from the mind,

73

So in my vision now but little part
Remains; yet in my inmost soul I know
The sweet instilling which it did impart.
(*Paradiso,* XXXIII)

What a rip off! Is that it?

Not quite – in the few lines remaining to this epic poem Dante tried
to clarify. He wrote that he had seen a supreme light and that he beheld
all things in heaven and earth as one spatial and temporal unity; the
universe being inside God. The creator himself appeared before him
as three differently coloured circles of one dimension (a trinity). As
he stared at these circles he noticed a human form within them and
just as he was wondering how the relation between the human form
and the circles worked, a ray of divine light flooded his mind, putting
an end to his vision, evaporating his will to knowledge and leaving a
great many questions unanswered:

I wished to see how the image to the circle
Conformed itself, and how it there finds place;

But my own wings were not enough for this,
Had it not been that then my mind there smote
A flash of lightning, wherein came its wish.

Here vigour failed the lofty fantasy:
But now was turning my desire and will,
Even as a wheel that equally is moved,

The Love which moves the sun and the other stars.
(*Paradiso,* XXXIII)

—— 61 ——

Does God have a body? (Issue resolved). – Most religions deny that God has a corporeal nature. If it appears that way in the early books of the Bible, it is not so in fact. References to his arms, hands and feet are supposed to be read as analogous or symbolic. His 'arm' means his 'strength', his 'eyes' are representative of his 'omniscience', his 'wings' his 'protectiveness', and so on and so forth. But God does not treat his own body as analogous, far from it. Time and again he implies that he *does* have a real body. *Implying* though is not the same as *stating* and the ambiguity of the Hebrew Bible has allowed the argument to swell out of all proportion.

Realising this petty human squabble could not go on for ever God approached his old friend the prophet Joseph Smith at Ramus, Illinois, on 2 April 1843, where he told him: 'The father has a body, a body of flesh and bones as tangible as man's; the Son also; but the Holy Ghost has not a body of flesh and bones, but is a personage of Spirit. Were it not so, the Holy Ghost could not dwell in us' (*Doctrine and Covenants*, 130:22). That settles the matter for once and for all – does it not?

—— 62 ——

A checklist of body parts. – The following is a list of the anatomical limbs and organs of God's body as they have been revealed in scripture, in ancient texts and in the findings of archaeology:

Arms. – Isaiah believes that God will 'show the weight of his arm' (Isa. 30:30) when he is angry. Daniel who saw God's arms described them as of polished brass (Dan. 10:6). There are many examples where God's arm is a symbol of strength and protective kindness, for as the psalmist sings: 'You have a strong arm; Your hand is mighty, Your right hand is exalted' (Ps. 89:13).

Bowels. – When God laments the destruction of Moab he says, 'my bowels shall sound like a harp over Moab as my inward parts shall quiver for Kir-haresh' (Isa. 16:11), but the twanging sound of God's bowels is not always so easy to hear. In the silence Isaiah feels forsaken and calls up to heaven: 'Where is thy zeal and thy strength, the sounding of thy bowels . . . are they restrained?' (Isa. 63:15). God tells Jeremiah that his bowels are indeed troubled (Jer. 31:20). Elsewhere he desires his divine bowels to be understood as some kind of incubating womb, admitting to Isaiah that Israel was once 'carried by my bowels' (Isa. 46:3).

Breasts. – God's breasts are only mentioned on rare occasions and there is only the faintest of allusion to his having breasts in the Hebrew Bible (Num. 11:11–13). However, they are fully exposed in the cryptic, pseudepigraphical *Odes of Solomon*, in which book they are milked by the Holy Spirit whose own bosom is subsequently used, like a cocktail shaker, to blend God's milk, as at the conception of Christ:

The Father is he who was milked, and the Holy Spirit is she who milked him; Because his breasts were full, and it was not desirable that his milk should be released without purpose. The Holy Spirit opened her bosom, and mixed the milk of the two breasts of the Father. The womb of the Virgin took it, and she received conception and gave birth. (*Odes Sol.* 19:2–6)

John of Patmos reveals that he once saw God 'girt about the paps with a golden girdle' (Rev. 1:13). Whether he means female-style breasts when he says 'paps' or whether even he is talking about God, or some other divine apparition, are issues which are still hotly debated today.

Eyes. – 'I have gazed into the eyes of the Lord, shining like the rays of the sun and terrifying the eyes of a human being' (*2 En.* 39:5). Peter describes God's eyes as focused only on the righteous (1 Pet. 3:12), while Abraham, who knew God well enough to serve him dinner, describes him as 'many eyed' (*Apoc. Abr.* 17:15).

Fingers. – God uses his fingers for writing. The two tables of stone that he gave to Moses on Mount Sinai were 'written with the finger of God' (Deut. 9:10). Though at Belshazzar's banquet (Dan. 5) God 'sent' some fingers (possibly not his own) to write a cryptic message on the wall. Elsewhere God's finger is a symbol of his power or involvement, as, for instance, when the Egyptians blamed the finger of God for producing a plague of lice (Exod. 8:19) or when Jesus claimed to cast out devils with the finger of God (Luke 11:20). According to *3 Enoch* God's little finger is able to shoot fire in order to attack 'angels and the ministers' who fail to say their prayers properly. 'Whenever they do not recite the "Holy" according to its proper order, devouring fire goes out from the little finger of the Holy One, blessed be he. It falls on their ranks, and splits into 496,000 myriads and devours them at a stroke' (*3 En.* 40:3). Immediately afterwards a storm wind blasts the hapless frazzles into an even hotter River of Fire where 'they are deduced to mountains of burning coal'.

Face. – In the Bible, God's face is a metaphor for his Divine Presence and references throughout to 'seeing God's face' or 'appearing before God's face' should be interpreted in this way. However, when God is described as talking 'face to face' and 'mouth to mouth', and when God's tongue, nose, eyes and lips are described, it is safe to presume that the early biblical writers envisaged God as having an anthropomorphic human face. Enoch described God's face as 'like iron made burning hot by a fire, and it is brought out and it emits sparks and is incandescent' (*2 En.* 39:5), later proclaiming that it is so hot and bedazzling as to be able to melt mortals like wax. When God's face is veiled (Deut. 31:17; Isa. 8:17, and elsewhere) he has metaphorically turned his presence away (usually as a gesture of disgust at the depravity of the Israelites) but in the *Hebrew Apocalypse of Enoch*, God veils his face because he is worried what it might do to the heavens: 'otherwise the heaven of Arabot would burst open in the middle, because of the glorious brilliance, beautiful brightness, lovely splendour, and radiant praises of the appearance of the Holy One, blessed be he' (*3 En* 17:3). John of Patmos agrees that his face is 'like the sun shining with all its force' (Rev. 1:16), but Jacob, who saw God 'face to face' at Jabbok and was not burnt, later declared him multi-faced, addressing God in prayer as the 'twelve-topped, twelve-faced, many-named fiery one' (*Lad. Jac.* 1:17).

Feet. – In the book of Genesis Abraham offers to wash God's feet (Gen. 18:4). The washing of feet in the Bible is a symbolic ritual of servitude, as when Jesus strips naked, girds a towel around his middle and cleans the disciples' feet with it (John 13:4–5). The Bible does not reveal if Abraham stripped off or not, nor does it say if God's feet were dirty or just tired. A suggestion of tired feet is perhaps reinforced by descriptions of the Temple of Solomon as God's footstool (Lam. 2:1; 1 Chron. 28:2; Ps. 99:5; 132:7). To Isaiah, God declared that 'heaven is my throne, and the earth is my footstool' (Isa. 66:1), while to Ezekiel, God warned against defiling 'the place of my throne and the place of the soles of my feet' (Ezek. 43:7). Elsewhere God's feet are mentioned as hovering over darkness or thick cloud (2 Sam. 22:10; Ps. 18:9) and the prophet Nahum suggests that the clouds we see from earth are 'the dust of his feet' (Nah. 1:3). In the book of Psalms David implores God to lift up his feet as a rebuke against the outrages in the sanctuary (Ps. 74:3). The symbolic or metaphorical definition of God's feet in these passages is not clear. A more anthropomorphic foot testimony is given in the Revelation of St John where it is written that God's feet are 'like unto fine brass as if they burned in a furnace' (Rev. 1:15); Habakkuk too attests that 'burning coals went forth at his feet' (Hab. 3:5).

Flesh and bones. – 'The father has a body of flesh and bones as tangible as man's,' God told Joseph Smith in 1843 (*Doctrine and Covenants*, 130:22)

Hair. – 'His head and his hairs were white like wool, as white as snow' (Rev. 1:14); 'and the hair of his head like the pure wool' (Dan. 7:9).

Hands. – Moses says that God brought his people out of bondage 'by strength of hand' (Exod. 13:3), a reference which is obviously figurative as elsewhere, but Enoch saw tears flooding from God's right hand: 'Then the right hand of the Omnipresent One wept, the five rivers of tears flowed from its five fingers, and, falling into the Great Sea, made the whole world quake' (*3 En.* 48a:4).

Heart. – 'And it repented the Lord that he had made man on the earth, and it grieved him at his heart' (Gen. 6:6). To Isaiah, God says 'the day of vengeance is in mine heart' (Isa. 63:4).

Lips. – God's lips are often mentioned, usually, like so many of his bodily organs, as dangerously hot (Isa. 11:4). Isaiah observed that they were 'full of indignation' (Isa. 30:27).

Mouth. – God's mouth is fearfully hot. 'A devouring fire shot from his mouth' (Ps. 18) and in the book of Revelation a double-edged sword shot out of it too (Rev. 1:16). God describes his mouth as delivering words of justice (Isa. 45:23) and his breath like 'an overflowing stream' (Isa. 30:28).

Nose. – Samuel said he saw smoke billowing out of God's nostrils (2 Sam. 22:9) and this idea is duplicated in the Psalms. God is particularly partial to the smell of burnt meat, a pleasant odour which the Israelites purposely waft towards him for appeasement (Gen. 8:21; Lev. 1:9), but refuses to enjoy the smell when he is angry with them. He loves sniffing incense but only if it is properly made by a good perfumier (Exod. 30:34–37). In the book of Job it is stated that the 'glory of his nostrils is terrible' (Job 39:20). God admits to having a nose (Isa. 65:5).

Phallus. – Given that it is never mentioned in the Bible if God has a phallus or not, an extraordinary amount of research has gone into the subject. Post-Freudian, feminist scholarship, particularly in America, has searched and searched for the divine penis and scores of books have covered the issue – *Behind the Sex of God* by Carol Ochs, *God and the Rhetoric of Sexuality* by Phyllis Trible, 'God's Body' by Naomi Janowitz, *God's Phallus* by Howard Eilberg-Schwartz – to name but a few. All have hoped to unveil the divine penis, but none has yet been found. The Mosaic prohibition on images of God has not helped either, but a few have survived. In Montfaucon's *Antiquity Explained* (1721) there is a drawing of an ancient talisman that was found in Egypt. It is described as part of the collection 'from the cabinet of M. Foucault', made of basalt, measuring 5 inches by 3 inches. On it is a picture of an ithyphallic deity with the names 'Iao' and 'Abraxas' inscribed above and below. Both of these names are used of the monotheistic, Semitic God, Yahweh. This singular item seems to provide the only evidence that in early times at least, God may have had a penis.

Tongue. – 'His tongue is like a devouring fire' (Isa. 30:28).

Wings. – God's wings are mentioned in two of the Psalms (36:7 and 57:1) in the book of Ruth (2:12) and the second book of Baruch (2 Bar. 41:5). In each case they are described as protecting wings. There is no known scriptural source which describes him actually using them to fly.

Womb. – The people of Israel are brought forth from God's womb as the Lord himself declares they are 'borne up by my womb' (Isa. 46:3). When asked by his people why he had forsaken them God compared himself to a mother with breasts and a womb: 'Will a woman give up the child at her breast, will she be without pity for the child of her womb? Yes, these may, but I will not let you go out of my memory' (Isa. 49:15). To Job, God suggested that his womb was the place where ice and frost are made (Job 38:29).

— 63 —

Vital statistics. – The question of whether God is infinite or not might have been settled as early as the third century of the Common Era, if only people had been prepared to listen to those Jewish mystics whose writings have been preserved in ancient scrolls known as the *Hekhalot* (Palace) texts. In one of them, the *Shi'ur Komah* (Measurement of the Height), Sefer Haqqomah describes God thus: 'From the seat of His glory and up is a distance of 1,180,000,000 parasangs. From the place of the seat of His glory and down is a distance of 1,180,000,000 parasangs.' Another (Sefer Hashi'ur) returns a slightly different measurement: 'The distance from his knee to his thigh, may He be blessed, is 244,250,000 sheqalim. The name of his loins is *Asam Gig Vahu*, may He be blessed – the space between His thighs and His neck, from the seat of his glory up is a total of

80

1,180,000,000' (conversion table: 1 parasang = *c*. 5.5 km; 1 shequalim = *c*. 6 km).

This means that according to Sefer Haqqomah's measurement, God stands, from head to toe, only 1.298 billion km high – less than one hundredth of a light year and hardly a dot in the Milky Way!

— 64 —

Is God black? – Religious groups like the Black Jews of Harlem, Black Muslims of Detroit, Jamaican Rastafarians and the Peace Mission Movement of Father Divine have, for ages, been claiming that God is black. Given that he made man 'in his own image' (Gen. 1:27) and that modern geneticists have traced the first human beings back to Africa, it is as likely as not that Adam (and therefore God) were indeed black.

For scriptural evidence turn to the book of Daniel, the second section (probably not by the same author as the first) where God is described as seated upon a throne, wearing white garments 'with hair like lamb's wool'. John of Patmos in the book of Revelation had a similar apocalyptic vision of the deity a century or so later: 'His head and his hairs were white like wool,' he revealed (Rev. 1:14). To many, these passages confirm that the Ancient of Days looks like an old man with an Afro hair-do.

The issue of God's skin colour has been addressed by several prominent religious leaders. Wallace D. Fard who set up the Black Muslim Movement in the 1930s declared himself to be 'Allah, the Supreme Ruler of the Universe'. When a tenth-century wool-carder called Husayn ibn Mansur (known today as the poet al-Hallaj) did the same, declaring '*Ana 'l-Haqq*' (I am God), he was promptly hanged, drawn and quartered by furious Muslims. And what of Father Divine? Nobody knows his real name though he might have been George Baker, born in Monkey Run (the black quarter of Rockville, Maryland) in 1882. Baker's parents were slaves and his mother was the fattest woman in Maryland. After her death Baker emerged as a preacher,

81

first calling himself Messenger and later, the Reverend Major Jealous Divine. Under this name he attracted a small following which gathered to hear him preach at Sayville, chanting: 'Father Divine is God. He is the living tree of life, Father, Son and Holy Ghost. We may take the words of Father Divine – eat, drink and live for ever.' White residents of Sayville were not amused and in 1931 Major Jealous was arrested for causing traffic congestion and, on refusal to pay a five-dollar fine, sent to prison.

Justice Lewis J. Smith summed up: 'There may be those who believe this defendant is God. There are undoubtedly many who believe he is not, and those who believe he is not God are entitled to have their rights protected the same as those who believe he is God.' Two days after sentencing Judge Smith died of a heart attack. 'I hated to do it,' said Divine from his prison cell. This apparent miracle earned him thousands more devotees and after his release from prison Divine became so rich and famous that he was able to retire, consigning the duties of his church to Edna, his wife. She (whose maiden name was Ritchings) assumed the title 'Mother Divine'. He died in the 1960s and a few people still believe that he was God.

Meanwhile the Rastafarians of Jamaica continue to assert that God is/was Haile Selassie (1892–1975), erstwhile Emperor of Ethiopia. In 1955 Selassie gave 500 acres of land to Jamaican followers of the Rastafarian 'Back to Africa Movement'. But *ganja* (or marijuana) was enshrined as the religion's 'sacred herb' and only a few Jamaicans ever made it there. By 1970 fewer than twenty people were occupying the site. Haile Selassie's death in 1975 was not accepted by many Rastafarians who still believe him to be immortal – just hiding away somewhere.

— 65 —

God's gender. – God is supposed to be a male character, after all he is referred to as 'he' not 'she', he speaks in a voice like thunder, he helps

Israelites win battles and generally rampages around in an identifiably masculine kind of way. But God's masculinity is categorically rejected by the Roman Catholic Church which teaches its flock that 'In no way is God in man's image. He is neither man nor woman. God is pure spirit in which there is no place for difference between the sexes' (*Catechism of the Catholic Church*, 370). Others, however, have contended that pure spirit *can* be sexed. Sophia (Wisdom), for instance, is distinctly female. The Holy Spirit, too, was identified as a female by all ancient Semitic cults, in particular, the Spirit was noted as 'a woman' in the *Gospel of Philip* (17a), as the 'mother of Jesus' in Origen's account of the *Gospel of the Hebrews* and as a female progenitor with milk-filled breasts in the *Odes of Solomon* (*Odes Sol.* 19). Why does the church speak of God, the Father, and of God, the Son if there is no imputation of gender?

To those who subscribe to the notion of a Godhead comprising a Trinity, it might make sense to reflect that the Holy Ghost represents the female element, while the Father and the Son are obviously male. In the Jewish tradition, where the Trinity is denied, God is referred to as 'he' only because there is no neuter in Hebrew, but in the Cabbalistic doctrine of the *Sefirot* (by which God is represented as emanating ten powers) some strands of Judaism will concede a male emanation (divine wisdom, known as *Abba*, meaning father) and a female emanation (divine understanding, known as *Imma*, meaning mother).

In these respects God may be viewed as androgynous (having both male *and* female emanations), just as he seemed to be in Genesis and in the Mormon *Book of Moses*, where he creates an androgynous Adam: 'In the image of his own body, male and female, created he them, and blessed them and called their name Adam' (*Book of Moses* 6:9).

But how does God's androgynous form effect his genitalia? The evidence that God has sexual organs is so thin on the ground as to be non-existent. As a single-parent, Creator God he had need for neither male nor female organs of reproduction, for Adam, after all, was made from mud and Eve was constructed from Adam's rib. For this simple reason God would not have bothered to make sexual organs for himself, even if he had to make them for Adam and Eve.

— 66 —

Her feminine side. – While God is described in predominantly male terms in the Bible, supporters of the view that he is androgynous point to biblical passages to bolster their claim. Many of these are to be found in the book of Isaiah where God compares himself to a woman in labour: 'I have kept silent for a long time, I have kept still and restrained Myself. Now, like a travailing woman I will groan, I will both gasp and pant' (Isa. 42:14); to a breast-feeder (Isa. 49:15); and to a comforting mother (Isa. 66:13). In the Psalter, God is compared by David to a midwife (Ps. 22:9), and to a mistress (Ps. 123:2), while the book of Malachi speaks of God as Israel's wife (Mal. 2:14). A divine womb is mentioned as the place of Israel's gestation (Isa. 44:2) where the chosen people will continue to be nurtured, as God himself says: 'Hearken unto me, O house of Jacob, all the remnant of the house of Israel, who are carried by my bowels, are borne up by my womb. Even to your old age I am the same, and to your grey hairs I will carry you: I have made you, and I will bear: I will carry and will save' (Isa. 46:3–4). But these are all examples of symbolic imagery, no more than that. Whether the same can be said of passages in the *Odes of Solomon* where God, the Father, is portrayed with breasts bursting with milk, or in the numerous Semitic texts which describe the Holy Spirit as a feminine, mothering force is less certain.

In the thirteenth century God appeared before a mystic nun called Mechthild of Hackborn asking her to consider him as her mother:

Thou shalt call none other thy mother, and thine love for me shall be as unto thine mother. And, as children suck their mothers' breasts, even so shalt thou suck from My love inward consolation

and unutterable health, and My love shall also feed thee, and clothe thee, and provide for thee in all thy wants, like a mother who provideth for her only daughter. (*Select Revelations* 2:4)

Most ancient religions regarded the worship of both male and female gods and goddesses as an essential prerequisite to spiritual well-being. An androgynous monotheistic God was a radical departure for those who embraced the new religion at the beginning of the first millennium BCE. God, then, was a composite mixture of *aspects* of other gods and goddesses (like El, Ba'al and Asherah) that once had separate identities.

—— 67 ——

Keep your secrets. – Jesus' philosophy of the body enshrined the principle that any organ or limb that incited man to sinfulness ought to be amputated: 'for it is better for you to enter life maimed', he once said, 'than with two hands to go to Hell, to the unquenchable fire' (Mark 9:43), and further: 'If your right eye causes you to sin, pluck it out and throw it away; it is better that you lose one of your organs than that your whole body be cast into Hell' (Matt. 5:29). There were those who took Jesus' message to heart. Origen, for instance (*c.* 185–254), a Christian theologian and spiritual writer, castrated himself, as (according to Jesus) did many others: 'For there are some eunuchs, which were so born from [their] mother's womb and there be eunuchs, which have made themselves eunuchs for the kingdom of heaven's sake' (Matt. 19:12).

That Jesus believed testicles to be the cause of sin has never been thoroughly established, nor is it irrefutable that he was promoting castration as a virtue. If so Jesus would have been (not for the first time) guilty in the eyes of traditional Judaism, for contradicting the teachings of the Torah (the laws given by God to Moses on Mount Sinai). Although God may not have genitalia of his own, he makes it abundantly clear that castrated or genitally mutilated men will not be warmly welcomed at the Pearly Gates: 'He that is wounded in the balls,' ordains the Torah, 'or hath his privy member cut off, shall not enter into the congregation of the Lord' (Deut. 23:1)

In fact God is so confirmed in his dislike of castration that anyone who injures the male genitalia (even a wife, defending her husband's life) must be severely punished.

When men fight together one with another, and the wife of one draweth near for to deliver her husband out of the hand of him that smiteth him, and putteth forth her hand and taketh him by the secrets. Then thou shalt cut off her hand, and thine eye shall not pity her. (Deut. 25:11–12)

And Origen gravely miscalculated.

III

Furnace

68

Problem with Abraham. – The Bible is full of mysteries but perhaps the greatest of these is the question of Abraham. Of all the people, in all the countries at all times in the history of the human race, why did God choose precisely Abraham to be the father of his chosen people? The Bible offers no explanation whatsoever. In the Genesis account Abram (as he was first called) was an old Chaldean (not a Jew) from the Southern Mesopotamian city of Ur. He was dull, as many Mesopotamians were, a dishonest man, with no sense of humour, a cruel streak and a grimacing wife. Most of this is not revealed until after the incident of his divine calling.

For an explanation of his calling readers must turn to the ancient *Book of Jubilees.* Abram, the book reveals, hated people worshipping idols and tried to stop his father from indulging in this harmless folly on many occasions. One night, in a puritan rage, he crept from his bed and set light to his father's temple causing his own brother to burn to death in the process (*Jub.* 12:12–14). This was perhaps all it needed to excite God's interest.

'Leave your country, your family and your father's house,' God said to Abram, for a land I will show you. I will make you a great nation. I will bless you and make your name so famous that it will be used as a blessing. I will bless those who bless you and curse those who slight you. All the tribes of the earth shall bless themselves by you' (Gen. 12:1–3).

Abram had nothing to lose. Though he must have been bewildered by God's unexpected enthusiasm. That very day he collected his family – a barren wife, Sarai, and a nephew called Lot – and set off for Canaan. His what? His family? God had expressly commanded Abram to leave

89

his family behind and God, as everyone knows, does not tolerate disobedience.

From this point on God must have realised the error of his choosing. Could he not have found a better, brighter, more obedient person than Abram to father his chosen race? If God regretted his choice (as later he was to regret choosing Saul for king) he managed to conceal his feelings from Abram, for all was not lost. God had plenty of tricks up his sleeve. First, he struck Abram's reward (the land of Canaan) with a famine, forcing the zealot and his frumpy entourage to pack their bags immediately on arrival and head for Egypt instead. But there was worse in store for Abram.

God promised him and his seed all the land from the river of Egypt to the great River Euphrates, as well as a vast sweep of fertile territory known at that time as the lands of the Canaanites, Amorites, Hittites and Jebusites: 'To thee I will give it and to thy seed *for ever*,' he swore, without a hint of irony (Gen. 13:15). Abram was so excited he agreed on the spot to an act of fearful self-mutilation in order to please God, little realising, as he hacked at the flesh of his penis with a flint-stone, that three-and-a-half thousand years later God would still not have fulfilled his side of the bargain.

— 69 —

Fair deal. – God waited until Abraham was 99 years old before approaching him with the following proposal:

I, God, shall make you father of all nations; I shall magic it so that your barren wife Sarai, though ninety years old, shall bear you a son a year from now. Some of your descendants will be kings, the land where you presently live as an immigrant, Canaan, will be given to you and your descendants, to own in perpetuity. I shall be your God and the God of your descendants after you. That is my side of the bargain. Now, in return for all this, I

want you to change your name from Abram to Abraham and get
your wife to change hers from Sarai to Sarah. (Gen. 17: paraphrase)

On the face of it Abram had a pretty generous deal here: he and Sarai
get the land of Canaan, a whole lot of descendants (some of whom will
be kings) *and* a God all of their own in exchange for a harmless change
of name. Too good to be true? Of course it is – 'Ye ne'er get ought
for nought', as the old Lancashire saying goes. God required Abram's
signature to the deal; not just a scribble on a tablet or a footprint in
the sand, something far more indelible than that:

> You must circumcise the flesh of your foreskin, and that will be
> the sign of the covenant between myself and you. As soon as
> he is eight days old, every one of your males, generation after
> generation must be circumcised, including slaves born within
> the household or bought from a foreigner not of your descent.
> My covenant must be marked in your flesh as a covenant in
> perpetuity. The uncircumcised male whose foreskin has not been
> circumcised must be cut off from his people for he has broken
> my covenant. (Gen. 17:11–14)

Abraham removed his foreskin that very day, as well as the foreskins
of all his household.

—— 70 ——

Circumcision. – Egyptian boys are depicted enduring the operation
of circumcision on a 3,500-year-old mural painting at the temple of
Khonsu in Karnak. The Arabians did it and often still do, though the
Qur'an does not enforce the practice. Assyrians, Mandingos, Falashas,
Abyssinians, Tonga Islanders and Aztecs do it or did it; many Christian
Americans still do, and it was briefly considered the height of fashion
by the English upper classes. Israelites at the time of Joshua were so

enthusiastic that they sometimes had it done twice (Josh. 5:2)!

Given the weight of importance which God himself placed on the ritual of circumcision it matters that we understand what it entails. In simple medical terms male circumcision is the removal of the foreskin of the penis by cutting away the inner and outer layers of the foreskin and (nowadays) stitching the raw edges together. It can be done using local anaesthetic. In biblical times, however, there was no anaesthetic and the operation was accomplished with a sharp flint (Josh. 5:2), causing terrible pain for several days (Gen. 34:25).

By 1645, when the English diarist John Evelyn witnessed a circumcision in Rome, the instruments were less rustic but the horror and pain remained the same. The following description should provide the curious reader with all he needs to know:

With profound reverence and mumbling a few Words he waved the Child to and fro a while; then he delivered it to another Rabbie, who sate all this time upon a Table, he taking it in his hands put it betweene his thighs, whilest the other Jew unbound the blankets that were about it to come at the flesh: at this action all the company fell a singing of an hebrew hymn, and in as barbarous a tone, waving themselves to and fro, a ceremony they observe in all their devotions.

The Infant now strip'd from the belly downewards, the Jew tooke the yard of the child and Chaf'd it within his fingers till it became a little stiff, then with a silver Instrument (which was held to him in the basin) he tooke up as much of the Praeputium as he could possibly gather, and so with the Razor, did rather Saw, than cutt it off; at which the miserable babe cry'd extreamly, whiles the rest continu'd their odd tone, rather like howling than singing: then the Rabby lifting the belly of the child to his face, and taking the yard all blody into his mouth he suck'd it a pretty while, having before taken a little Vinegar, all which together with the blood he spit out into a glasse of red wine of the Colour of french wine: This done he stripp'd downe the remainder of the fore-skin as farr and neere to the belly as he could, so as it appeared to be all raw, then he strew'd the read powder on it to stanch the bleeding and covered it with the paper-hood, and upon all a Clowte, and so swath'd up the Child as before.

All this while they continue their Psalme: Then two of the Women, and two men, viz., he who held the Child, and the Rabbin who Circumcis'd it (the rest I suppose were the Witnesses) dranke some of the Wine mingl'd with the Vinegar, blood and spittle: so ended the slovenly ceremony, and the Rabbin cryes out to me in the Italian tongue perceiving me to be a stranger: '*Ecco Signior mio, Un Miracolo di dio*'; because the child had immediately left crying. (John Evelyn, *Diaries,* 15/1/1645)

—— 71 ——

Why the phallus? – Why did God ask Abraham to mark a sign of the covenant on the most private and sensitive part of his body? Could he not have pierced his ear or taken a small slice off the tip of his nose instead? If God did not like foreskins he should have created men without them in the first place. Angels were created by God ready-circumcised (*Jub.* 15:27). Why not mortal men as well?

Scholars and theologians have yet to agree why it was that God chose the penis as the best place to consecrate his covenant. Maybe the God of Israel was once a phallic deity *alla pagano* to whom the foreskin would have been offered as a cultish sacrifice.

Christian theologians, however, are more likely to point to original sin, the excision of the foreskin being a symbolic removal of human *flesh*, which, from the Fall of Adam, was thought to be contaminated by sin; the flesh of the penis – an organ of lust – especially so.

Jesus, though himself circumcised, denied to his disciples that circumcision was useful: 'If it were useful,' he once remarked 'their father would beget them from their mother already circumcised' (*Cop.*

Gos. Thom., Log. 53), while Philo of Alexandria, the Greek-speaking, Jewish philosopher and contemporary of Jesus, attempting to make circumcision palatable to the Greeks, gave six good reasons for doing it in his treatise *On Special Laws* (*De specialibus legibus*). Among them he pointed out how healthy it is to be circumcised, how beneficial for procreation, claiming also that the circumcised penis resembles the heart (which is nice) and that circumcision is a fitting symbol of the excision of pleasure.

The modern American sees it differently, as one scholar, Howard Eilberg-Schwartz, makes clear in his phallic study of God:

> In the priestly writings, circumcision is treated as a symbol of male fertility, of God's promise to make Abraham a father of multitudes. It is no accident that the symbol of the covenant is impressed on the male organ of generation rather than the ear or the nostril. By exposing the male organ, the rite of circumcision makes concrete the symbolic link between masculinity, genealogy and reproduction.

So there you have it!

— 72 —

Repercussions of the covenant. – God never worries about the conse- quences of his actions. He regrets his mistakes (Gen. 6:6 and else- where), but that is not the same thing. Many of God's actions have led, directly or indirectly, to the most terrible consequences, not least his insistence on circumcision as a sign of his covenant with Abraham. What started as one patriarch's willing consent to an act of genital self-mutilation led, in time, to grave problems which God may or may not have foreseen. A few examples of tragedies that might have been avoided if God had not demanded circumcision will suffice:

In the second century BCE when all things Greek were considered smart, many Jews took to wearing Greek clothes, talking the Greek tongue and enjoying the culture of naked relaxation at their local *gymnasia*. Since many Greeks found the sight of a circumcised male member distasteful, some Jews, from feelings of snobbery and social embarrassment, attempted to stick their foreskins back on by using a reverse surgical operation called *epispasm*. Things came to a head in the great persecution of 167–64 BCE when the Seleucid king, Antiochus IV (nicknamed 'the Madman'), attempted to enforce a programme of Hellenisation upon all the Jews both inside and outside of Jerusalem, enlisting, as his helper, a particularly vicious high priest called Jason.

Antiochus and Jason outlawed circumcision as well as abstinence from pork and other Jewish practices, ensuring the Orthodox Jews that resisted his measures were severely punished. 'Women who had had their children circumcised were put to death according to the edict and their babies were strung round their necks, members of their household and those who had performed the circumcision were executed with them' (1 Macc. 1:60–61). Eventually, the Jewish hero, Judas Maccabaeus, led a revolt against Antiochus's harsh regime. Once he had asserted his own authority Judas ordained his brother, Jonathan, as high priest and between them slaughtered as many uncircumcised Jewish males as they came across or, in the luckier cases, enforced circumcision upon them.

God's anger against those who are not circumcised knows no bounds. He tried to murder Moses on the journey from Midian to Egypt for being uncircumcised (Exod. 4:24–6), later informing him that 'anyone who is born whose flesh is not circumcised on the eighth day is not from the sons of the covenant but of the children of destruction to be smashed down and annihilated, to be uprooted from the face of the earth' (*Jub.* 15:26).

— 73 —

Phallic deity? – Ancient religions were chock-a-block with phallic deities. When gods had distinct roles to play, winning battles and

.

granting fertility were the most important of them all. Human fertility was usually the specific province of one god and sacrifices to that deity would range from a young bride's virginity (Augustine in *Of the City of God* records the use of a statue of Priapus, 'upon whose huge and beastly member the new bride was commanded to get up and sit'), to throwing the male foreskin into a sacrificial fire after circumcision. God's desire for Abraham and his descendants to circumcise themselves might well suggest that his origins were indeed phallic. Here is further evidence:

When God tried to kill Moses in the desert, Zipporah quickly circumcised their son and pushed the amputated foreskin against Moses' genitals in order to appease God (Exod. 4:25).

The fertility gods of Canaan, Assyria and Mesopotamia were worshipped with symbolic stone pillars. When Jacob awoke from a dream about God 'he took the stone he had used for a pillow, and set it up as a monument, pouring oil over the top of it,' later, offering his pillar to God as a house (Gen. 28:18). Jacob named the place Bethel, a word derived from *baetylia* which are heathenish rude stones. Joshua also erected rude stones in reverence to God (Josh. 24:26).

Moses railed against poles and pillars of all sorts, urging his people not to worship but to destroy them (Deut. 12:2–3; Lev. 26:1). Moses' job cannot have been made any easier by God himself who repeatedly appeared in front of the Israelites in the shape of a pillar. 'And the Lord went before them by day in a pillar of cloud, to lead them the way; and by night in a pillar of fire, to give them light; to go by day and night' (Exod. 13:21).

And it came to pass, as Moses entered into the tabernacle, the cloudy pillar descended, and stood at the door of the tabernacle, and the Lord talked with Moses. And all the people saw the cloudy pillar stand at the tabernacle door: and all the people rose up and worshipped, every man in his tent door. (Exod. 33:9–10)

That God is often described in the Bible as 'a rock' may not be an innocent analogy for divine strength or immutability after all, for the rock was, for thousands of years, the most potent symbol in phallic worship. Moses upbraided his people: 'You forget the Rock who begat you, unmindful now of the God who fathered you' (Deut. 32:18), while the Psalmist subtly suggested the same: 'Those that be planted in the house of the Lord shall be fertile. They shall bring forth fruit even in old age; they shall be fat and flourishing for the Lord is upright: he is my rock in whom no fault is to be found' (Ps. 92:13–15).

—— 74 ——

Need to be feared. – God was supposed to be fond of Abraham, he had set up a covenant that favoured his descendants and had magicked his barren nonogenarian wife to be fertile. To the Muslims Abraham (*Ibrahim*) is known as *Kalil Allah* (the friend of God). Yet God felt insecure in his friendship: 'Does Abraham really love me?' he may have wondered, 'Is he scared of me? Will he do anything in the world for my sake? Absolutely anything?'

God needed to know. The matter was festering and he wanted to end the uncertainty, once and for all. So, when Abraham was about 113 years old, God called out to him:

'Abraham, Abraham!'
'Here I am,' Abraham replied, and God said:
'Take now your son, your only son Isaac, who you love, and go to the land of Moriah and offer him there for a burnt offering on one of the mountains which I shall point out to you.' (Gen. 22:1–2)

God chose an inconvenient mountain that was three days' journey for Abraham and his son. When they arrived there, Abraham built an altar, loaded it with kindling and tied his son to the top. He had it in mind to stab Isaac to death, set light to his corpse and hopefully create a wafting, meaty 'smell pleasing to the Lord' (Lev. 1:9), but at the very

97

instant when the murder was about to happen God called out: 'Do not harm the boy, for now I know you fear God, you have not refused me your own beloved son.'

God was was so pleased that he blessed Abraham and repeated some of the unfulfilled promises that he had already made to him, several years before (from Gen. 22).

— 75 —

Happy end. – In the days when men were not supposed to sleep with other people's wives, the only hope was to kill the husband and then take his widow to your bed. When Abraham was visiting foreign provinces he asked his wife Sarah to pretend to be his sister so that if a foreign king should wish to sleep with her, he could have her, without having to kill *him* first. Sarah willingly consented to the plan.

When they went to Gerar, Abraham and Sarah introduced them-selves as brother and sister and she was duly sent for by the King, Abimelech. As she entered the King's chamber – laughing, perhaps, in anticipation at the pleasure she was going to receive (Gen. 18:12) – Abimelech must have been disappointed, not to say disgusted, for she was well over 90 years old. He decided to go to sleep on his own, but his sleep was spoilt, not by Sarah demanding sex, but by God in a furious rage: 'You are to die,' bellowed the Lord, 'because of the woman you have taken, for she is a married woman.'

Abimelech was astounded, for he had not gone near the hag and anyway, he had been informed (in good faith) that she was Abraham's *sister*, not his wife. 'Lord', he asked, 'Would you kill someone even if he was righteous? My conscience is clear.'

'Yes, I know that you have acted with a clear conscience since I myself prevented you from sinning against me. That was why I did not let you touch her. Now send the man's wife back; for he is a prophet and can intercede on your behalf for your life, but understand this: if you do not send her back this means death for you and all yours.'

As an extra punishment God made Abimelech, his wife and all their slave girls infertile. Abimelech was delighted to be rid of Sarah and so frightened that he showered Abraham with gifts including sheep, cattle, slaves and a thousand pieces of silver. In return Abraham generously interceded with God so that Abimelech's life was saved and the cruel infertility spell reversed (Gen. 20).

— 76 —

Wrestling match. – One night God saw a man on his own by a ford. Assuming the guise of a male human being, God started to wrestle with him and the two of them wrestled and wrestled all night long. But God wanted the fight to stop and so, to put an end to it, whacked the man's hip socket, dislocating it at the joint. The man continued to hold God in a vice-like grip.

'Let me go,' God pleaded, 'for day is soon breaking.'

But the man, who now recognised his opponent as God, remained adamant, 'I shall not let you go unless you bless me,' he said.

'What is your name?' asked God, still unable to release himself.

'Jacob,' replied the man.

'No longer are you to be called Jacob, but *Israel* since you have shown your strength against God and men and have been victorious.'

'Very well, but what is *your* name?'

'Why do you ask my name?' God rebuked. But he blessed Jacob and was duly released. Jacob stood up and named the place *Peniel* (meaning 'face of God') because 'here I have seen God face to face,' he said 'and have survived.' After that Jacob limped off to rejoin his two wives and eleven children who had crossed the ford before him.

And the moral of this strange tale? 'That is why to this day Israelites do not eat the thigh sinew which is at the hip socket' (Gen. 32:33).

99

— 77 —

Why the thigh sinew at the hip socket is not to be eaten. – God dislocated Jacob's hip socket so that strict Jews (in honouring the incident) are reluctant to consume the hindquarters of beef to this day. If the cut is eaten at all, the sciatic nerve must first be removed, entailing an intricate process of butchery known as 'porging'. Since skilled porgers are not easy to come by, thick flank is usually rejected as *terefah* (forbidden food) by the Orthodox.

Did God really intend his people to avoid unporged thick-flank for ever? Through Moses he left a great legacy of *other* dietary laws (Lev. 11; Deut. 14:3–21) and it would have been far easier if he had added 'thigh sinew at the hip socket' to those lists rather than endure the humiliations of a fordside wrestling rigmarole with Jacob. God *may* have intended to stop people eating 'thigh sinew at the hip socket' it is true, but is it not equally possible that God may have intended the reverse – that he dislocated Jacob's hip in order to *draw attention* to this particular cut and persuade his people to eat it? Back-shank is not particularly good, porged or unporged, but Orthodox Jews prefer not to look at it this way, adhering instead to the well-worn rabbinic dictum that 'a man should not say: "I dislike intensely the meat of the pig." He should rather say: "I would like to eat it but my father in heaven has declared it to be forbidden."'

— 78 —

Usual suspects. – Jacob's wrestling match (Gen. 32) forces embarrassing questions about God into the open. Why wrestle with Jacob in the first place? Why can't God win the fight? Why is he *forced* to bless Jacob? Why won't he give his name? Why does he appear to be afraid of the dawn light? If it *is* God who wrestles with Jacob,

do his whimsy, his impotence and his eccentricity really know no bounds?

One common suggestion is that God is not God at all in this story but some sort of angel, possibly Uriel, or Michael acting off his own bat. This, however, is contradicted by Jacob's testimony: 'I have seen *God* face to face and survived,' he said. A Christian compromise is reached by Matthew Henry (1662–1714) in his famous Bible Commentary: 'The Angel who wrestled with Jacob', he wrote, 'was the second Person in the sacred Trinity, who was afterwards God manifest in the flesh, and who, dwelling in human nature, is called Immanuel.' (*Exposition of the Old and New Testament*, Matthew Henry) In other words it was Jesus who dislocated Jacob's hip! Whatever next?

— 79 —

Israel in Egypt. – Some theologians believe that Israel (the name Jacob was ordered to adopt at Jabbok) means 'He will fight with God', or even, 'Struggle with God', in a strange, perhaps forgotten, Hebrew dialect. This allows the exegete to suggest that the whole story of Jacob's wrestle is not about thick flank at all, but an allegory of the difficult path which any believer must follow in order to enter the kingdom of heaven.

Others are not so sure. The etymology of Israel can just as easily be traced to a compound name rooted in the divine pantheon of ancient Egypt: Isis (Egyptian queen of the gods represented by the moon), Ra (Egyptian king of the gods, represented by the sun) and El or Ali (the council of the lesser gods, represented by the stars). Thus ISRAEL originally meant 'Land of the Heavens', the twelve tribes of Israel being the twelve constellations that environ the ecliptic through which the sun makes its annual circuit. It should be noted that the earliest mention of Israel is found, not in the Hebrew Bible, but in Egypt, on a commemorative stele inscribed to King Meneptah (*c.* 1200 BCE).

Naked ecstasy in the huts at Ramah. – Saul was incensed against David. His fury fired, for the most part, by a burning homosexual jealousy, which, on this occasion, was exacerbated by David's incessant twanging on the harp. So God put an evil spirit onto Saul who sprang up and pinned the wretched harpist against the wall with his spear. David was so petrified that in the evening he escaped from Saul's palace leaving a dummy in his bed and went to live with Samuel at Ramah.

When Saul got word of where David was hidden he sent agents to arrest him, but 'God came on Saul's agents' who, instead of apprehending David, stripped off their clothes and joined him and Samuel in naked ecstasy. Saul, distraught, sent more agents, but the same thing happened. He sent a third lot, and they too fell for the lure of David's ecstatic nudity. Eventually Saul decided to come to Ramah himself.

'Where are Samuel and David?' he asked, and someone answered, 'Why, they are in the huts at Ramah.' So Saul went on from there to the huts at Ramah and the spirit of God came on him too, and he went on his way in an ecstasy until he came to the huts at Ramah. He too stripped off his clothes and he too fell into an ecstasy in the presence of Samuel, and falling down, lay there naked all that day and night. Hence the saying: 'Is Saul one of the prophets too?' (1 Sam. 19:18–24)

Nude. – When Adam and Eve ate the forbidden fruit they became aware, for the first time, of their own nakedness. Before that, they had not noticed a thing; neither were they roused by each others' bodies, nor ashamed of their own. How was it that God discovered they had taken that fruit? Not by counting the apples on the tree, nor by talking to the serpent, nor by smelling Adam and Eve's appley breaths. No – he discovered their sin when Adam admitted hiding himself from God 'because he was naked'.

'Who told you that you were naked?' God asked Adam, 'You must have eaten the forbidden fruit to know that.' He was furious with both of them. 'Behold, the man is become as one of us,' he bellowed to the rest of the *elohim*, 'He has come to know good and evil' (Gen. 3:22). Gods have always understood about nakedness but now (Oh horror!) humans understand it too.

The sequence here is bizarre, for God (who always understood nakedness) decided to make animal skin suits for Adam and Eve (Gen. 3:21) *after* they had eaten the fruit and had just come to understand the full embarrassment of nakedness for themselves. As it happens they had already covered their privy regions in fig-leaf aprons *before* God started sewing them extra clothes. What was God up to? Was he just being helpful to Adam and Eve? Or did he himself dislike the sight of naked human flesh?

When Moses was ordered to build an altar in his honour, God stipulated: 'You must not go up to my altar by steps, in case you expose your nakedness on them' (Exod. 20:26). This refers to the fact that Israelites, following ancient Egyptian practice, wore loincloths (without underpants) when offering sacrifices at the Temple. The importance of not offending God with the sight of human nakedness has been enshrined in religious practice ever since. Muslims, Jews and Christians must be fully clothed when they pray to God, while some Christian monastic orders refused to allow monks or nuns to strip naked under any circumstances, even to wash themselves.

In the Jewish Mishna and Tosefta (second-century documents of Rabbinic law) it is commanded that a man must have his genitals covered when he is expressing his love of God by reciting the *Shema* (i.e., Deut. 6:4–9). This prayer is strictly to be recited *before* dawn. So what happens if the faithful Jew is in his bath just as the sun comes up above the horizon? The law anticipates this problem, stating that bathers caught in such circumstances must cover their penises with towels or stand in the tub with water up to their waists so that their genitals cannot be seen (*Mishnah Berakhot*, 3:5).

A recurring concern for Christians is that once they have died they might resurrect *naked* up to heaven. Philip talks of those who 'are afraid lest they rise naked' (*Gos. Phil.*, Log. 23a), and St Paul writes to the Corinthians 'we would like to be found wearing clothes and not without them' (2 Cor. 5:3). In any event Paul believed that he would eventually ascend into heaven wearing a spiritual mantle that would conceal his naked form from prying eyes. It is curious that David, Samuel and other prophets tried to attract God's attention by dancing before him with all their might in a state of naked ecstasy (1 Sam. 19:18–24), for there is no evidence that God was remotely pleased by this. David was reprimanded by his wife for 'uncovering himself to the eyes of all his servants,' but David answered, 'I was dancing for God, not for them. I shall dance for God and demean myself even more. I may be base in your eyes, but by the servants you speak of, I shall be held in honour. And to the day of her death David's wife had no children!' (2 Sam. 6:21–3).

— 82 —

Hard to justify. – Through his servant Moses, God issued the following proclamation concerning those who may not be permitted to serve in his Temple:

> For no man that is botched may serve me, neither a blind man, nor a lame, nor he that has a flat nose, or anything superfluous. Nor a man that is broken footed or broken handed, or crookbacked, or a dwarf, or someone with a blemish in his eye, or with scurvy, or who is scabbed, or has damaged testicles. No man that has a blemish shall come nigh to offer sacrifices to the Lord by fire:

Anyone who is botched shall not come near so as to offer the
bread of his God. (Lev. 21:18–21)

— 83 —

Irritating Moses. – In the end God decided to kill Moses. The reason
he gave was that the prophet had broken faith with him, though in
the passage relating to that incident (Num. 20:1–12) some editorial
tinkering seems to have taken place so that the exact detail of Moses'
sin has disappeared from the text. 'Because you did not believe that I
could proclaim my holiness in the eyes of the sons of Israel, you shall
not lead the people into the land I am giving them.'

What had Moses done wrong? Some suspect that he had refused
to believe water would miraculously gush from a dry rock (this is the
immediately preceding scene), but given the quantity of miracles that
God had already shown to Moses, this seems unlikely.

Might it be that God had simply lost his patience with Moses? As
a rule God is always treated by mortals with the utmost respect. There
are few isolated exceptions. In the Pseudepigrapha, for instance, God
is summoned by name and told to perform miracles 'right away', and
Job once commanded God to: 'Listen, I have more to say, now it is
my turn to ask the questions and yours to answer' (Job. 42:4), but such
impudence is rare in the Bible. Moses, however, consistently treated
God as he would a naughty boy, flattering, advising, rebuking and
instructing him what to do. He reprimanded God for trying to avoid
the journey to Canaan without giving a proper reason (Exod. 33:12)
and told him to 'stop being angry and relent' when God threatened
to torch the Israelites for worshipping a golden calf (Exod. 32:12).
When God expressed his disappointment at Israelite stubbornness
Moses ticked him off again:

Remember your servants Abraham, Isaac and Jacob, take no
notice of this people's stubbornness, their wickedness and sin,

105

so that it may not be said in the land from which you brought us, 'God was not able to bring them to the land he promised them. It was because he hated them that he brought them out to die in the wilderness.' (Deut. 9:27–9)

What? Moses is telling God to tolerate the 'stubbornness, wickedness and sin' among the Israelites in order stop the Egyptians from gossipping about him? Was this the final straw for the prophet that once 'had won God's favour'? A trumped up charge was needed: 'Die on the mountain,' God said to Moses, 'because you broke faith with me at Meribah-Kadesh, in the wilderness of Zin, because you did not display my holiness among the sons of Israel, you may see this land only from afar; you cannot enter it, this land that I am giving to the sons of Israel' (Deut. 32:50–52).

Ha! ha!

— 84 —

Where did Moses get God from? – An exilic leader who goes by the Egyptian name of Moses is found in many histories that are not biblical. He is mentioned, for instance, by Manetho, the Egyptian historian of the first half of the third century BCE, by Hecateus of Abdera around 320 BCE, by Lysimachos in the second century BCE, Chaeremon, another Egyptian historian, of the first century BCE and by the Latin historians, Pompeius Trogus and Tacitus. All of their accounts differ in detail, but what remains clear is that there were two sides to the Moses story: the biblical (the story told from the point of view of those people who escaped with him from Egypt) and the Egyptian (or the account of those he escaped from).

According to Egyptian versions Moses was an Egyptian leader (possibly a priest) who took command of a large group of disaffected people within Egypt at a crucial moment in the nation's troubled history. In about 1375 BCE an eccentric Egyptian king, Amenophis

IV, audaciously declared that only one God was to be worshipped throughout Egypt and his name was Aton, the sun god. The king became known as 'He who serves the Aton', or Akhenaton. His monotheistic revolution was violent; temples and icons dedicated to the traditional gods of Egypt were destroyed and the hideous king (depicted with drooping jaw, scrawny neck, pot-belly and thunder thighs), and his beautiful queen, Nefertiti, built a virgin city at Amarna in Upper Egypt, where they tucked themselves away worshipping Aton to the detriment of the country at large.

Later generations of Egyptians were so ashamed at Akhenaton and his monotheistic religion that everything possible was done to wipe him out of their history books. When Akhenaton died (*c.* 1360 BCE) his son-in-law Tutankhaton was forced to abandon the worship of Aton, change his name to Tutankhamen and move the Pharonic priesthood back to Thebes where it had previously been. It has been suggested that a plague in Egypt may have resulted in the purgatory cleansing of Amarna, as if Akhenaton's new monotheism had been the cause of Egypt's misfortune. This may have been the reason why Amarna was abandoned.

Around this time Moses (possibly a priest with Akhenaton) became the leader of a large, isolated group of people. Who these people were and why they were dispossessed has been the subject of much disagreement among scholars who continue to offer a bewildering array of alternative answers. Some claim that they were *hapiru* (homeless builders – note the similarity to Hebrew); others that they were remnants of the *hyskos* (originally invaders from Palestine but who, after several centuries, had become a social underclass in Egypt); or were they possibly lepers (as described by Manetho – more likely plague victims) or monotheistic outcasts from Amarna? We are left guessing who they were and why they set off *en masse* for Palestine under Moses' command. Were they indeed descendants of the *hyskos*? Or was it because Palestine was one of the last remaining colonies of the crumbling Egyptian empire that they headed there?

There remains the possibility that God originally came out of

Egypt not as *Yahweh* but as *Aton* in the middle of the fourteenth century BCE and was none other than the monotheistic sun god worshipped by Akhenaton and Nefertiti at Amarna. Psalm 104 looks startlingly like a Hebrew translation of *Akhenaton's Prayer*, discovered by archaeologists at Armana in the nineteenth century, while etymologists argue that the similarity of the Egyptian name *Aton* to the Hebraic term for God, *Adonay*, is no coincidence.

— 85 —

Sun god. – Remnants of a sun worshipping culture are found scattered all over the Bible. Time and again God is described just as the sun itself might be described: bright, dazzling, hot and radiant. In Psalm 104 – drawn from Akhenaton's Atonist prayer – God is praised for 'wearing light as a robe' while Joshua, at Gibeon, addressed him as though he were the sun itself: 'Then Joshua spoke to the LORD in the day when the LORD delivered up the Amorites before the sons of Israel, and he said in the sight of Israel, "O Sun, stand still at Gibeon"' (Josh. 10:12). In the Psalms God is frequently identified with the sun: 'From the rising of the sun to its setting, the name of the Lord is to be praised' (Ps. 113:3); 'For the Lord God is our sun' (Ps. 84:11). God told Isaiah, 'I shall look down from my dwelling, like the burning heat of daytime' (Isa. 18:4), and shortly before his death Moses, in a blessing of the Israelites, calls out in prayer: 'God rose up from Sinai, dawning on them from Seir; blazing out from Mount Paran' (Deut. 33:2).

— 86 —

Nasty Aaron. – Of all the characters in the Bible, by far the most seedy is Moses' half-brother Aaron. He is presented as the close companion, whose eloquence saved the stammering prophet from making a public fool of himself and crucially persuaded the people to follow his brother out of Egypt. But there was more to Aaron than that. He was quick to take advantage. Setting himself up as high priest, he gave his sister, Miriam, job of top-prophet, elected his sons to the ruling priesthood and engaged upon a meticulous campaign to ensure that he and his heirs would for ever have the right to collect taxes from the people in the name of God. True, it was Moses and not Aaron who spoke to God (most of the time) and it was Moses who issued all of God's proclamations, but evidence suggests that the 'heavy-tongued' prophet, so reliant on his brother for all things, was Aaron's puppet.

God told Moses to 'muster the tribe of Levi and put it at the disposal of Aaron' (Num. 3:6). Then God arranged a special tax inciting Moses to take 1365 shekels from the Israelites and to hand it all to Aaron (Num. 3:49). But Aaron was still not happy; he needed attractive clothes and would not object to a bit more money. So God spoke to Moses again and said, 'Tell the Israelites to set aside a contribution for me. This is what I will accept from them: gold, silver and bronze; materials dyed violet purple, red-purple and crimson, fine linen, goats' hair, rams' skins dyed red, fine leather, acacia wood, oil for the light, spices for anointing oil and fragrant incense' (Exod. 25:1–6).

Good! Aaron had his material, but now he needed a tailor. God miraculously intervened again:

> You will instruct all of the skilled men who I have endowed with skill to make Aaron's clothes. They will make an embroidered tunic and waist-bands, a robe of violet-purple. In the centre it will have a hole for Aaron's head with a lavish woven hem, on its lower hem an embroidered pattern with pomegranates all the way round and golden bells adorning it. Also a golden seal which he can wear on his turban to lend him dignity and magnificence. You will dress your brother Aaron and his sons in these. (Exod. 28:31–35 paraphrase)

Once Aaron had set himself up in all his finery, he realised he was in need of a regular income in order to keep his show on the road. Once again God went to Moses on Aaron's behalf: 'When you count the Israelites by census, each one must pay a ransom for his life to avoid any incidence of plague among them, each one will pay half a shekel.' This 'ransom money' was payable every month.

What about food? God ordered two yearling lambs, with flour and olive oil and half a gallon of wine to be presented every day to Aaron and his sons, in perpetuity. Most important of all, Aaron and his friends must be given the best cuts, no scrag end or brisket for them: 'You will set aside the right thigh; the right thigh and the forequarters will revert to Aaron and his descendants' (Lev. 7:28).

When Aaron encouraged rebel Israelites to make a golden calf and to leap about naked in adoration of it, God put 3,000 Israelites to the sword, but Aaron was not among them. When he and his sister, Miriam, criticised Moses, God covered Miriam in filthy white skin-sores, but Aaron, once again, got off scot-free (Num. 12).

— 87 —

Preparations for speech day. – God wanted to tell his people, the Israelites, ten important things. They were for the most part legal prohibitions, which in time would be hailed as the mighty *Decalogue* (Ten Words), otherwise known as the Ten Commandments. He intended to deliver them in a speech from the top of Mount Sinai; but this needed careful planning, so he went to Moses and said: 'Look, I shall come to you in a dense cloud so that the people will hear me speaking to you and believe you ever after.'

Nothing is that simple. There were details to organise and movements to rehearse. God was not prepared to address himself to a dirty audience so he had to make sure that Moses would see to it that his people cleaned themselves up – two days to wash and get ready in which time they were also to abstain from any sexual intercourse. And then there were all the security issues to worry about – God did not want to be seen and Moses had to make sure that the whole mountain was properly cordoned off well in advance of the event. Anyone caught touching even the edge of the mountain would be 'stoned or shot by arrow'. The sign, God said, that he was ready to deliver his speech would be a loud trumpet.

Two days passed in which the people scrubbed and polished themselves in chaste preparation for the divine address. Finally God descended on the mountain. The trumpet blast grew louder and louder, the mountain shook and there was smoke, thunder and flashes all around. The people were terrified. But before making his ten points, God too must have been anxious, for he suddenly called for Moses. The prophet came panting to the top of the mountain to see what was wanted:

'Go back down again,' God ordered 'warn the people that they must not break through to peer at me, for if they do they will die.'

'But they cannot possibly come up here said Moses, for you yourself told me to cordon off the mountain.'

'Away with you,' snapped God 'Go back down the mountain and come up again with your brother. And remember – do not let anyone else come up and look at me.'

The people must have been wondering what the hell was going on, but in the end their patience was rewarded and God delivered his speech from the heart of the fire on the top of the mountain (Exod. 19).

—— 88 ——

Going to press. – God decided that the speech he had delivered to the Israelites from the top of Mount Sinai was good enough to be published, but he needed Moses' help and invited the prophet to stay with him on the mountain for forty days and forty nights while the 'Ten Words' were etched (by God's finger) on to both sides of two tablets of stone. But when the job was completed God told Moses that he was in a blazing rage and wished to exterminate the Israelites, for he happened to know that while he and Moses were working, the Israelites were larking around at the foot of the mountain with a metal calf.

Moses thought God was overeacting: 'Give up your burning wrath', he protested, 'and relent,' but God fumed as Moses carried the sacred tablets down the mountain to show his people. As Moses reached the foot he spotted the metal calf and he too lost his temper, smashing the sacred tablets on the ground and threatening everyone with death. Returning to the summit, Moses found God in sunnier mood, loudly exalting his own special virtues: 'The Lord, the Lord, God of tenderness and graciousness, long-suffering and abundant in goodness and truth. Keeping mercy for thousands; forgiving fault, crime and sin, but by no means clearing the guilty, punishing the parents fault in the children and in the grandchildren to the third and fourth generation' (Exod. 34:6–7). And so Moses and God stayed happily together for another forty days and forty nights, eating and drinking nothing, rewriting the tablets exactly as they were before Moses had smashed them (Exod. 20).

— 89 —

God's first word. – The first Commandment and possibly the most important of them all is this: 'I am the Lord your God and I brought you out of the land of Egypt, out of the house of bondage. You shall have no other gods before me.' God was in a tense state as he prepared to declaim the Decalogue from Mount Sinai. He had been fretting about security. Worrying lest Israelites should break the cordon and look at him. His first Commandment reflects this unease.

God could not trust the Israelites so he prohibited them from worshipping other gods. Since other gods did not exist, it is hard to understand what damage would have been done either to God or to the idolaters, if non-existences were worshipped. God gave no reason

112

for proscribing idolatry but consistently upbraided it, encouraging his people to punish idolaters with unflagging zeal:

> If thy brother, the son of thy mother, or thy son, or thy daughter, or the wife of thy bosom, or thy friend which is thine own soul, entice thee secretly saying 'Let us go and serve other gods,' thou shalt not consent unto him, nor hearken unto him; neither shall thine eye pity him. But thou shalt surely kill him; thine hand shall be first upon him to put him to death, and afterwards the hand of all people. And thou shalt stone him with stones that he die. (Deut. 13:6–10)

Modern sensitivity recoils from such harsh punishment of harmless folly, but 'the Lord, whose name is Jealous, is a jealous God' (Exod. 34:14), and this sort of thing should be expected.

—— 90 ——

His second word. – In his second Commandment God prohibited the making of any image. What he particularly disliked were 'graven images' of other gods that might lead to idolatry, but he was equally afraid that people would want to make images of *him*. This Commandment, like the first, has an air of panic about it; the rule is exaggeratedly sweeping in its prohibition of any 'likeness of any thing that is in heaven above, or that is in the earth beneath, or that is in the water under the earth'. It means no photographs, maps, models, illustrations, paintings, films, sketches, statues, doodles – anything at all that *depicts*. The second Commandment has proved quite impossible to honour. Even God himself could not adhere to it, ordering Moses to make two cherubim with outstretched wings out of pure beaten gold and stick them onto each end of his 'mercy seat' (Exod. 25:18). Later Moses, off his own bat, 'made a serpent of brass, and put it on a pole so that if a real, poisonous snake struck, the victim, just by looking at Moses' model, would be miraculously cured' (Num. 21:9).

113

— 91 —

His third word. – 'Thou shalt not take the Lord's name in vain.' God was at first reluctant to tell anyone his name. When Moses asked him, he dismissed the question: 'I am who I am,' (Exod. 3:14), but later let it be known that his name was *Yahweh*. At that time it was believed that the holy name could bring magical powers to any person who uttered it, which may have been why God wanted its use controlled. However, if the name did not of itself possess any special power, it is not at all obvious why the infinite, omnipotent God should care less if any mortal chose to pronounce it in a deep, reverent tone, or lightly, with a touch of irony.

— 92 —

Mixed reasons. – There are two versions of God's fourth Commandment, one can be found in the Decalogue of Exodus (Exod. 20:2–17) and the other in Deuteronomy (Deut. 5:6–21). The Exodus version – thought to be the older and more dignified of the two – reads thus:

> Remember the sabbath day, to keep it holy. Six days shalt thou labour and do all thy work: But the seventh day is the sabbath of the Lord thy God: in it thou shalt not do any work, thou, nor thy son, nor thy daughter, thy manservant, nor thy maidservant, nor thy cattle, nor thy stranger that is within thy gates: For in six days the Lord made heaven and earth, the sea and all that in them is, and rested the seventh day: wherefore, the Lord blessed the sabbath day and hallowed it.

The Deuteronomic version gives a different reason for resting on the sabbath: 'And remember that thou was a servant in the land of

Egypt, and that the Lord thy God brought thee out thence, through a mighty hand and by a stretched out arm; *therefore* the Lord thy God commanded thee to keep the sabbath day.'

Neither explanation makes much sense and the mere fact that God gave two different reasons for observing the sabbath rule suggests that either he, or the subsequent editors of these passages, have forgotten why the rule was originally conceived. Whatever the reasons for the sabbath Commandment God shows no mercy to those who break it:

> While the Israelites were in the desert, a man was caught gathering sticks on the sabbath day. And God said to Moses, 'This man must be put to death. The whole community must drag him outside the camp and stone him with stones,' and so, as God had ordered, the whole community took the man out of the camp and stoned him until he was dead. (Num: 15:32–6)

—— 93 ——

How to live a longer life. – To those who are obedient to the fifth Commandment ('honour thy father and thy mother') God promises 'that thy days may be prolonged and that it may go well with thee in the land which the Lord thy God giveth'. God, at the time he issued this Commandment, was probably concerned at the casting out of old parents who were no longer economically useful. While it has always been assumed that old parents who are looked after 'will have their days prolonged', God promises that the carers too will have longer lives, but this promise has not been demonstrably kept.

Perhaps what he really meant was that by honouring your parents *they* will not shorten *your* life by killing you, for God's law also prescribes the death penalty to disobedient children:

> If a man have a stubborn and rebellious son, which will not obey the voice of his father, or the voice of his mother and will not

115

listen to them. Then shall his father and his mother lay hold on him, and bring him out to the elders of the city. 'This son is stubborn and rebellious, he will not obey our voice!' And all men of his city shall stone him with stones until he dies. So shalt thou put evil away from among you; and all Israel shall hear and fear. (Deut. 21:18–21)

Jesus taught, in the face of the fifth Commandment, to 'call no man your father' (Matt. 23:9) and further urged that he who 'hateth not his father and his mother cannot be my disciple' (Luke 14:26). In normal circumstances, Jesus would have been dragged out to the city elders and stoned, but since his father's identity was confusing, he got away with it.

— 94 —

Thou shalt not kill. – God's sixth Commandment has been widely interpreted to mean 'Thou shalt not kill any other human being'. We can assume that animals are not included in the prohibition, for God himself encouraged animal sacrifices and meat-eating long after he issued the decree at Sinai. But if 'Thou shalt not kill' is a rule that is not supposed to apply to animals, how can we be so sure that it *is* meant to apply to human beings? Seconds after reaching the foot of the mountain with the tablet inscribed with these words by God's fair finger, Moses instructed his people: 'God says this, "Every man must buckle on his sword and run up and down the camp, from gate to gate, slaughtering his brother, his friend and his neighbour." The Levites did as Moses asked and about three thousand men were killed that day' (Exod. 32:27–8). Later, when they fought the Midianites, Moses commanded his people to 'kill every male among the little ones, and kill every woman who is not a virgin' (Num. 31:17). God approved these measures, himself boasting, 'I shall destroy both the youth and the virgin maid, the suckling infant and the man of grey hairs'

(Deut. 32:25). When he ordered Saul to exterminate the Amalekites 'and utterly destroy all that they have', God was horrified that a single Amalekite life had been spared, and repented that he had chosen Saul to be king of Israel (1 Sam. 15:35).

Jesus, who revered the Decalogue and preached, 'if you would enter life, keep the commandments' (Matt. 19:17), interpreted the sixth Commandment as 'Thou shalt not murder' (Matt. 19:18) which left a loophole for him to declare: 'Think not that I am come to send peace on earth: I came not to send peace, but a sword' (Matt. 10:34). Jesus' buccaneering spirit has led to many of history's religious blood baths, like the 'justified' slaughter of 40,000 Muslims and Jews at Jerusalem in 1097.

Let the bold Christian knight, Comte Raymond d'Aguilers explain:

We saw wonderful things, Some of our men cut off the heads of our enemies, others shot them with arrows so that they fell from the towers; others tortured them longer by casting them into the flames. Piles of heads, hands and feet were to be seen in the streets of the city. What more shall I tell? Not one of them was allowed to live. We did not spare the women or children. Our horses waded in blood up to their knees, nay up to the bridle. It was a just and wonderful judgement of God. (*All in the Mind*, Ludovic Kennedy)

If it was indeed God's wonderful judgement then how does he expect his sixth Commandment to be interpreted? If the killing of animals is permissible and so is the killing of human beings then what is there left? Thou shalt not kill – what?

—— 95 ——

Limited appeal. – God's seventh Commandment is directed not to everyone, but to that diminishing group of adults which is married.

'Thou shalt not commit adultery' proclaims that since marriage is a divine blessing in which a couple promises to be faithful to one and other, adultery (the breaking of that promise) is an insult to God. The old-fashioned punishment for adultery was death to both parties (Lev. 20:10; Deut. 22:22), but in later biblical times death was replaced by 'blows, contempt and dishonour never to be blotted out' (Prov. 6:32–3). Jesus broadened the definition of 'adultery' to include looking at a woman lustfully (Matt. 5:27–8), marrying a divorced woman and even *being* a divorced woman (Matt. 5:32). If Jesus wished punishments to be extended to all these groups he was a harsh man, for that bandwidth makes adultery difficult to avoid. But as St Paul always warned: 'It is not good for a man to touch a woman' (1 Cor. 7:1).

— 96 —

Thou shalt not steal. – God told Muhammad that 'if a man or woman steal, cut off their hands in retribution for that which they have committed' (Qur'an 5:42). This was later fine-tuned by Muslim exegetes so that the punishment was only to be carried out if the thief had taken more than four dinars in value. At the first offence he would have his right hand hacked off at the wrist, at the second, his left foot at the ankle, then his left hand would have to go and finally his right foot. After this it was at the judge's discretion how to punish the stump. In the Hebrew Bible amputation of limbs is not recommended.

At the battle of Jericho, Joshua decreed that all loot should be 'consecrated to God' (for which read: 'stashed in the coffers of the ruling priesthood'). When a man called Achan confessed to holding 200 shekels and a gold ingot aside he was stoned and burned to death (Josh. 7:25), but Achan's punishment was stiff not because he had stolen but because he had stolen *from God.* Elsewhere the punishment for theft is milder. A thief who steals to avoid starvation is made only to 'pay sevenfold and hand over all his family resources' (Prov. 6:31).

118

If the punishment for thieving is too mild on earth, God has restored the balance by devising a particularly savage bowge for thieves when they get to hell. Dante, who visited the place, recorded in the department of thieves that

a most loathsome welter filled the sink of it, a mass of serpents so diverse and daunting. My blood still turns to water when I think of it. Amid this cruel and repulsive crop of monsters, naked men ran terrified. Their hands were held behind their backs and tied with snakes, whose head and tail transfixed the loin, writhing in knots convolved on the hither side. (*L'Inferno*, 24:91–6)

When Israel escaped from Egypt, God cast a spell on the Egyptians so that they 'willingly' handed over gold and silver jewellery as well as fine clothes to the departing Israelites (Exod. 12:35–6). Was God himself thereby guilty of breaking the eighth Commandment? What does it matter? The Egyptians would never press charges.

—— 97 ——

False witness. – The Catholic Church and many rabbinic sources, have long viewed the ninth Commandment as a prohibition against *all* lying. But God was more specific than that. Had he intended to proscribe lying *per se*, he would surely have declaimed from the fire on Mount Sinai, 'Thou shalt not lie,' but he chose not to say that. He said something else instead: 'Thou shalt not bear false witness against thy neighbour.'

The Catechism of the Catholic Church uses this Commandment to rail against any form of misrepresentation including boastfulness and satiric irony (*Catechism*, 2481), but this is to miss the point of God's specific message. God was referring to one type of lying only, the bearing of false witness. According to the Torah, whatever the offence, the evidence of two or more witnesses is required to sustain the charge:

119

'a single witness will not suffice to convict anyone of a crime or offence of any kind' (Deut. 17:6). The punishment for bearing false witness is the same as the victim of the perjury *would have* received, if it had succeeded in convicting him (Deut. 19:16–21).

— 98 —

Mystery of mysteries. – Why God decided to limit himself to only ten commandments is a mystery, and why, having done so, he chose to proscribe this mild little thing out of all the most abominable crimes that could have been stopped is, of itself, the mystery of mysteries. 'Thou shalt not covet thy neighbour's house, nor his maidservant, nor his ox, nor his ass, nor anything that is thy neighbour's.'

Why not? What is wrong with desiring other people's things? To desire only one's own possessions (the things we already have) would admittedly be odd. To desire other people's things (things we do not own) is, surely, the most natural form of desire. If God is not intending us to abandon all desire, what then is he wanting?

Far be it for a humble scribe to criticise the phrasing of the Almighty, but could it be that God did not word this Commandment properly? What he might have been trying to say is that some of the *consequences* of covetousness (e.g. theft, adultery, causing a neighbour embarrassment by slavering over his things, spoiling friendships through jealousy etc.) are undesirable. Discreet coveting of a neighbour's ass is harmless of itself, and may even lead, in some cases, to an industrious life spent in the honest pursuit of bigger and better asses. In this respect covetousness might be viewed as a virtue.

— 99 —

Ten more commandments. – Here are some of the *other* laws which God gave to Moses:

120

1. 'If, when out walking, you come across a bird's nest in a tree or on the ground, with chicks or eggs and the mother sitting on the chicks or the eggs, you must not take the mother who is brooding the chicks. Let the mother go; the young you may take for yourself. So shall you prosper and have a long life' (Deut 22:6–7).
2. 'If a man dies childless, his brother shall marry his widow' (Deut 25:5), or, 'To marry a brother's widow is an unclean thing' (Lev. 20:21).
3. 'You are to make tassels for the four corners of the cloak in which you wrap yourself' (Deut. 22:12).
4. 'If a woman conceives and gives birth to a boy, she is to be unclean for seven days, just as she is unclean for her monthly periods. If she gives birth to a girl, she is to be unclean for two weeks, as during her monthly periods, and she must wait another sixty-six days for her blood to be purified' (Lev. 12:2–5).
5. 'When a boil appears on a man's skin, which, after healing leaves in its place a whitish swelling or a shiny spot of redish white, the man must show himself to a priest' (Lev. 13:18–19).
6. 'A woman must not offer herself to an animal to have intercourse with it. This would be a foul thing' (Lev. 18:23).
7. 'You must not shave your foreheads for one that is dead' (Deut. 14:1).
8. 'A man whose testicles have been crushed or whose male member has been cut off is not to be admitted to the Assembly of God' (Deut. 23:2).
9. 'If a servant says "I love my master and my wife and children, I do not wish to be freed" his master may bring him out to the door-post, bore a hole in his ear with an awl; and the servant shall serve him forever' (Exod. 21:5–6).
10. When 'the spirit of jealousy' comes upon a man, he must take his wife to see a priest. The priest will give her to drink some bitter water with dust from the floor mixed into it and the woman must gulp it down reciting the words 'Amen, Amen'. If her belly distends, her thigh rots and her organs shrivel, she must have been guilty

all along. If not, she is free to go forth and have children (Num. 5:19–28).

— 100 —

Persuasive. –

'If you do not listen to me and do not put all these command-ments into practice, if you reject my laws and insult my customs, and you break my covenant by not putting all my commandments into practice, this is how you shall be treated: I shall subject you to terror, consumption and a burning fever that will consume your eyes making you blind and short of breath.

'You shall sew your seed in vain, for your enemies shall eat it. And I shall set myself against you and you shall be slaughtered by your enemies. You shall be ruled by the people who hate, and you shall run in terror when no one is pursuing you. And, if, in spite of this you still will not listen to me, I shall punish you seven times over, breaking your proud strength. I shall heap seven times more plagues on you and send wild animals to rip you and your children apart, destroy all your livestock and leave your lands deserted. I shall bring the sword on you and when you huddle together I shall send a plague in among you.

'You will fall into your enemies' hands. I will snatch the bread from you which you need to survive. And if, in spite of this you still will not listen to me, I shall make you eat the flesh of your own sons, I shall make you eat the flesh of your own daughters, I shall destroy your sacred places and smash your altars. I shall pile your corpses on the carcasses of your idols and my soul shall hate you.

'I shall flatten your cities and bash up your sanctuaries. I will refuse to inhale the sacrificial smells which you make to please me. I shall send the sword against you, reduce your lands to desert and your towns to ruins. You shall be scattered among your enemies and those that survive will live in such terror as to scream at the falling of a leaf. You shall run away, as though running from the sword though there is no one in pursuit. In your fleeing you will stumble and fall over one another.

'You will be powerless to stand up to your enemies, you will perish and the land of your enemies will swallow you up. Those who survive will pine away in guilt in the countries of their enemies and their descendants, bearing the guilt of their ancestors too, will pine away like them.

'Yet in spite of all this I shall not so utterly reject or detest you as to destroy you completely and break my covenant with you; for I am the Lord your God.' (Lev. 26:14–45)

—— 101 ——

Take that! – God must have been listening when Moses was approached by three men called Korah, Dathan and Abiram. They had summoned up the courage to complain to Moses that he and Aaron were giving themselves airs and graces, running the priesthood as though it were an elite family firm. The three men were supported by 250 respected community leaders who equally agreed that Moses and Aaron were being unfair. Moses did not deny the charges, but 'flew into a rage'. At which point God stepped in. 'Stand back,' he bellowed, 'I am going to destroy them here and now.' Thus saying, he split the ground into a wide crack under the feet of the three unfortunates, so that they, their wives and all their families were swallowed into the earth. The community leaders who had supported them ran in terror, but God sent a blast of fire to burn all 250 of them to cinders. When the Israelite people mourned their dead, God, in his fury, sent a retributive plague which caused 14,700 of them to perish (Num. 16–17).

Egyptian cat and mouse. – There is a Deuteronomic law which states 'you must not regard the Egyptian as detestable' (Deut. 23:8), yet God himself has not forgiven them for 'making the children of Israel serve with rigour'. He is disgusted by their bodies, deriding them to Ezekiel as 'profligates with cocks the size of donkeys' which ejaculate as violently as stallions' (Ezek. 23:20); at one point he mingled a perverse spirit among them that caused the whole of Egypt to 'err as a drunken man staggering in his own vomit' (Isa. 19:14).

When Moses first went to the Egyptian Pharaoh to ask him if the Israelites might leave the land of Egypt, God 'hardened Pharoah's heart' so that Pharoah could not release the Israelites even if he wanted to. To punish Pharaoh for his stubbornness, God turned his rivers to blood, so the fish in them died and stank. Then he sent a plague of frogs. They also died and stank. The frogs were followed by mosquitoes, followed by horseflies, followed by the sudden death of all the Egyptians' livestock.

What next? Boils and sores for their faces. By this stage Pharaoh had had enough, he was desperate to rid himself of the Israelites, but God wished to play on, so he 'hardened the heart of Pharaoh' once again, telling him: 'You would have been swept from the earth, but I have let you survive for this reason: to display my power to you and to have my name talked of throughout the world' (Exod. 9:16).

That said, he sent a mighty hail-storm to wreck Pharoah's crops and drown anybody caught in the deluge; then locusts, millions of them, but once again Pharaoh was unable to release the Israelites from their bondage for his heart had been hardened by God. God's next trick was to switch out the lights over Egypt for three whole days. In the darkness Pharaoh spluttered to Moses, 'Go, and take your wives and children with you.'

But God was enjoying the game too much for it to end right

there. A technicality arose and God made Pharaoh recant. His next ploy, intended as the denouement, was to kill every first-born thing of Egypt (people as well as animals) and only when there was 'great wailing all over Egypt', would he allow the Pharaoh to let the Israelites go. Pharaoh must have been pleased to see the back of them and return, at last, to normal life in Egypt.

But no! God had not quite finished: 'I shall make Pharaoh stubborn,' he said, 'and he will set out in pursuit of them; and I shall win glory for myself at the expense of Pharaoh and his whole army, and then the Egyptians will know that I am God.' And so God impelled the Egyptians to chase the Israelites to the Sea of Reeds, where their chariots' wheels clogged up with mud and every last one of them was drowned (Exod. 14:28).

— 103 —

Not women. – The Hebrew Bible and the Qur'an are both written for, and addressed to, men – not women. This is possibly out of God's respect for prevailing human custom at the times of their revelation. 'Your women are your furrows,' says the holy messenger of Muhammad, 'so come to your furrows as you wish' (Qur'an 2:223).

On the whole, God treats women with respect not just as mothers and wives but as serving prophets (Exod. 15:20) and Judges (Judg. 4–5) too. Cruel treatment of women by men is severely punished in the scriptures and yet God is not unbiased. While it would be unfair to describe him as a misogynist there is no doubt that for God, while the sexes may be equal, one is decidedly more equal than the other. In the Qur'an, for example, he advises Muhammad that, 'women ought to behave in like manner to their husbands as their husbands should behave towards them, according to what is just: but the men ought to have a superiority over them' (Qur'an 2:227).

So what is wrong with women? Thomas Aquinas explained the problem with a helpful lesson in biology: 'The particular nature of the active male seed', he wrote, 'intends to produce a perfect likeness of itself, and when females are conceived this is due to weak seed, or unsuitable material, or external influences like the dampness of the south wind' (*Summa Theologiae*, 13:92:1). But when it comes to who might and who might not enter the kingdom of heaven, women are just as unlikely as men to be admitted:

Men and women who have surrendered, believing men and believing women, obedient men and obedient women, truthful men and truthful women, enduring men and enduring women, humble men and humble women, men and women who give in charity, men who fast and women who fast, men and women who guard their private parts, men and women who remember God often – for these God has prepared forgiveness and a mighty wage. (Qur'an 33:35)

Such unequivocal messages never got through to the disciples in Jesus' coterie. Simon Peter in particular wanted Jesus to throw the women out from among them, while Jesus, for his part, came up with a typically ingenious solution:

And Simon Peter said unto them: Let Mariham go out from among us, for women are not worthy of the life. Jesus said: Look, I will lead her that I may make her male, in order that she too may become a living spirit resembling you males. For every woman who makes herself male will enter the kingdom of heaven. (*Cop. Gos. Thom.* 114)

If Jesus had known God's position regarding the equal rights of women in gaining access to heaven, he need not have bothered to disguise them as men. His plan, if actuated, would in any case, have incurred the wrath of God, for it is written: 'A woman must not wear men's clothes nor a man put on a woman's dress. Anyone who does this is detestable to the Lord your God' (Deut. 22:5).

— 104 —

Vile bodies. – The origins of the Christian mistrust of sex lie hidden deep in the Hebrew Bible. From the very start squeamishness about naked human bodies emerges from the shame that Adam and Eve were made to feel after their disgrace at Eden. But what starts as a feeling of embarrassment, a coy need to cover up, leads eventually to an out-and-out hatred of human bodies and their sexual or lavatorial functions. Was this an inevitable consequence of the Fall, or did God himself have problems in this area?

God focused his own loathing on genital discharges, particularly sperm and the blood of female menstruation: 'And if a man shall lie with a woman in her sickness, and shall uncover her nakedness, he hath discovered her fountain, and she hath uncovered the fountain of her blood: and both of them shall be cut off from among their people' (Lev. 20:18).

In the Qur'an God is even stricter insisting that a woman in *perda* should not be approached by a man. God told Muhammad:

They will ask also concerning the courses of women: Answer, They are a pollution: therefore separate yourselves from women in their courses, and go not near them until they be cleansed, go in unto them as God has commanded you, for God loveth those who repent, and loveth those who are clean. (Qur'an 2:222)

From small beginnings a widespread disgust with bodies (particularly women's bodies) reached its climax in the letters of the Fathers of the Christian church, notably saints Paul, Augustine, Jerome and Odo of Cluny, the latter observing that all women were 'but blood, mucous and bile. If we refuse to touch dung and phlegm, even with a fingertip, how can we desire to embrace a sack of shit?' (*S. Odonis abbatis Cluniacensis Collationes*, lib. ii, cap. IX, in Mignes Edition).

Odo may have been writing from experience yet his rhetoric is remarkably similar to ancient Hindu scripture. The Vedic Upanishads, written 1500 years before Odo of Cluny was born, make a similar point, not as an invective against women, but against bodies in general: 'In this ill-smelling, unsubstantial body, which is a conglomerate of bone, skin, muscle, marrow, flesh, semen, blood, mucus, tears, rheum, faeces, urine, wind, bile, and phlegm, what is the good of enjoyment of desires?' (*Maitri Upanishad*, 1:3).

When Paul asked the Church at Philippi, 'Who shall change our vile bodies that they may be fashioned like unto his glorious body?' (Phil. 3:21), he may too have been thinking of the horrors of defecation, menstruation and semenal discharge. God later informed Muhammad that no man must pray to him 'when polluted by the emission of seed' (Qur'an 4:46).

Like Muhammad, Moses too was fully aware of God's sensitivities in these areas and gives the Israelites a tutorial on hygiene:

When you are in camp, at war with your enemies, you must avoid anything bad. If any one of you is unclean by reason of a nocturnal emission, he must leave and not come back into the camp, but towards evening wash himself and return to camp at sunset. You must have a lavatory area outside the camp, and go out to this; you must have a trowel in your equipment and, when you squat outside, you must scrape a hole with it, then turn around and cover up your excrement. For the Lord your God goes about inside your camp to guard you and put your enemies at your mercy. Your camp must therefore be a holy place; God must not see anything indecent there, or he will desert you. (Deut. 23:10–15)

The Jewish solution is a *mikveh* or ritual bath, the significance of which has died a little with time. At first a ritual bath was ordered for anyone who had come into contact with anything unclean (e.g. a dead mouse), but later was used only to wash away post-coital, post-natal and menstrual impurities. Orthodox Jews do not allow a normal bath to be used, it must be a specially constructed basin which collects only *pure* liquid, such as rain water. The Talmud states that all men who have ejaculated (by whatever means) must immerse themselves in a *mikveh* before studying the Torah, and strict Jews are also of the opinion that a wife must count seven 'clean days' after her menstrual period has ended, followed by a total *mikveh* immersion before she may entertain herself and her husband in any further acts of sexual intercourse. These things are done in order to please God.

—— 105 ——

Major offence. – Tamar had a husband called Er who offended God, so the good Lord killed him. Now, holy law states that a dead man's brother *must* marry his widow (Deut. 25:5), and thus the dutiful, pious Onan took Tamar, his-sister-in-law, to be his bride; but every night, instead of fathering her children, Onan shot his sperm upon the floor. God was so offended that he killed him too (Gen. 38:7–11).

—— 106 ——

More to it. – It has often been remarked how peculiar it was of God to tell his trusted prophet Hosea to marry a prostitute. 'Go marry a whore,' he instructed, 'and go and have children by a whore' (Hos. 1:2), for God's written laws strictly forbid any such thing, particularly among the priesthood: 'They shall not take a wife that is a whore,' he states, nor shall they allow whoredom within the family, for 'the daughter of any priest if she profane herself by playing the whore, she profaneth her father and she shall be burnt with fire' (Lev. 21:9). Thomas Aquinas thought that prostitution ought to be tolerated on the calculated basis that if you 'take away the sewer, you fill the palace with shit; take prostitutes away from the world and you fill it with sodomy' (*De regimine principum*, 1:14). Centuries later, the British

Prime Minister, William Gladstone, who professed a virulent dislike of prostitution, took to spending his evenings away from his wife in the dark alleys of London's whoring district, trying to persuade young women of the error of their ways. Some historians believe there was more to it than that – perhaps he was jealous of Hosea.

— 107 —

Between the sheets. – The history of Christianity reveals a dogged dislike of sex. According to the church Fathers, Paul, Ambrose, Jerome and in particular Augustine, both the sexual act itself and concupiscence (the desire by which it is provoked) are wicked sins. Sin is defined as any act committed against the will of God; so the great challenge for the Fathers was to find proof that the divine will forbade sex and concupiscence.

God did indeed lay down a number of sexual laws in the Pentateuch; in particular he proscribed incest of most kinds (though he does not explicitly outlaw intercourse between a brother and his full sister), bestiality, rape etc., but these laws do not of themselves amount to sufficient evidence in support of Augustine's radical Christian chastity. Obviously a bit of sex needs to go on, or nobody will be born and then there will be no one left to go to heaven and praise God and do all those good things which the Fathers believe to be paramount, yet to Augustine, Jerome and Paul, even sex within marriage must be regarded as a necessary evil. Christian arguments against sex have tended to focus on the opinion that it is dirty and distracting, enticing righteous people away from their obligations to God.

Augustine was particularly concerned about one sentence from the Latin Vulgate: '*ecce enim in iniquitatibus conceptus sum et in peccatis concepit me mater mea*' (For behold I was conceived in inquities; and in sins did my mother conceive me). It is taken from Psalm 50. This passing remark led Augustine to believe that the sin of sexual desire is handed down through the generations and must therefore have originated in the disgrace of Adam and Eve. But wait a minute! There is a problem here. If the sin of concupiscence is inherited from Adam as part of that package called 'original sin', how come it is not washed away by the sacrament of baptism? Baptism is, after all, supposed to be the cleansing and purification of all original and personal sin. An explanation was given by the noble bishops at the Council of Trent in 1546:

> Yet certain temporal consequences of sin remain in the baptised, such as suffering, illness, death and such frailties inherent in life as weaknesses of character and an inclination to sin that tradition calls concupiscence, or, metaphorically, 'the tinder of sin' (*fomes peccati*); since concupiscence is left for us to wrestle with, it cannot harm those who do not consent but manfully resist it by the grace of Jesus Christ. (*Catechism of the Catholic Church*, 1263)

But where does that leave Jesus Christ himself? He was, after all, born of a woman who was (was she not?) descended from Adam; if Jesus' baptism failed to wash away his concupiscence, then he too must have been as guilty as the rest of us. Augustine tried his hardest to explain why not:

> Therefore he [Jesus] alone having become also a human being while remaining God, never had any sin and did not assume sinful flesh, although his humanity was taken from his mother's sinful flesh. For, assuredly, the flesh that he assumed from her he either cleansed before assuming or cleansed in assuming. And so God created and chose the Virgin Mother, who conceived not by the law of sinful flesh but who, because of her devout faith deserved to have the embryo made within her. (*De Peccatorum Meritis et Remissione*, 2:24:38)

Obviously then it is crucial if concupiscence is to remain a sin in Christian dogma that Jesus himself be free of it. Much scholarship has been exhausted on the issue of Jesus and sex, leaving many with the conclusion that some of the New Testament redactors (possibly James, the brother of Jesus, and Paul) may have consciously suppressed evidence of Jesus' libertinism. There are hints of it in the Gospel of John where it is revealed that the Son of Man stripped off his clothes, girded himself with a towel, washed the disciples feet and removed the towel to dry them (John 13:4–5). Later, when Jesus was presumably stark naked, Simon Peter wished to ask him a question, but a disciple (several times alluded to as 'the disciple whom Jesus loved') was lying on Jesus' chest: 'Now there was lying on Jesus' bosom the disciple whom Jesus loved. Simon Peter therefore beckoned to him, that he should ask who it should be of whom Jesus spake. He then lying on Jesus breast said unto him. Lord who is it?' (John 13:23–5).

In 1958 a quotation from a fragment of what is believed to be a passage of the original Aramaic version of the Gospel of Mark was discovered in the library of a Greek Orthodox Monastery at Mar Saba, south east of Jerusalem. The short gobet, which is thought to have been originally located between Mark 10 verses 34 and 35 in the canonical gospel, reveals how Jesus raised a man from the dead at a tomb outside Bethany:

And immediately he went in where the young man was, stretched out his hand and raised him up, grasping him by the hand. But the young man looked upon him and loved him and began to entreat him that he might remain with him. And when they had gone out from the tomb, they went into the young man's house for he was rich. And after six days Jesus commissioned him and in the evening the young man came to him clothed only in a linen cloth upon his naked body. And he remained with him that night; for Jesus was teaching him the mysteries of the Kingdom of God.

In a second smaller fragment from the same source it is written, 'He came to Jericho and there were there the sisters of the young man Jesus

loved, and his mother and Salome; and Jesus did not receive them' (*Sec. Gos. Mark*, frags. 1 and 2).

Augustine may have chosen to ignore such evidence, continuing to preach the evils of lust instead: 'Indeed we hate the desire by which our Flesh desires contrary to our Spirit, and what is this desire except an evil love? Moreover we love the desire by which our Spirit desires contrary to the Flesh and what is this desire except a good love?' (*Enarrationes in Psalmos*, 118.8.4). Despite all of this, there is no evidence to support Augustine's belief that God has ever regarded sex within marriage (or concupiscence) as sinful. The Catholic Church points to the sin of Onan (Gen. 38:9) as a good reason to prohibit contraception to this day, but in so doing is made a laughing stock by our sexually mature modern world.

— 108 —

Divine amnesia. – How is it possible to question the merits of God's memory? Surely he never forgets a thing? Yet clues scattered in the Bible suggest the divine memory is not all that it should be. In the book of Genesis, for instance, God has trouble remembering Jacob's name (Gen. 32:30) even though he had met him on several occasions and sworn to 'keep him safe' and 'never desert him'. When Jacob reminded God of his name he was ordered to change it to Israel. A short while later when Israel (as he then called himself) was at Bethel, God (forgetting their earlier conversation) said: 'Your name is Jacob, but from now on you will be called not Jacob but Israel' (Gen. 35:10).

'Very well, then. I shall no longer call my self Jacob but Israel. You have told me twice now.'

Two pages on: 'God spoke to Israel at night: "Jacob, Jacob," he said, "I am El, God of your father"' (Gen. 46:3).

These are problems which cannot be ironed out by any amount of exegetical spin. From time to time God helps himself with the use of an *aide-memoire*. After the flood, for instance, he sent a rainbow so that he might in future be reminded of his promise to Noah, never to deluge the world again (Gen. 9:12–17). Without a rainbow he might well forget.

Abraham was reminded of his covenant every time he looked at his circumcised penis, but God has still not fulfilled all of his promises to Abraham (Gen. 13:15; 15:18). He needs prompting. After the Israelites had languished in captivity for 400 years God was reminded of his promise to them only when he heard their groans rising up from Egypt (Exod. 6:5). Aware of the problem, God asked Moses to blow a loud trumpet to remind him occasionally to think of Israel (Num. 10:9).

In order not to forget the most important things (who should be raised to heaven and who should be cast into eternal darkness) God writes notes in his 'book of remembrance', sometimes known as the Book of Life (Mal. 3:16–18). If you are not in it you are in big trouble, for 'whosoever was not found written in the Book of Life was cast into the lake of fire' (Rev. 20:15). On the Day of Judgement the chosen few will be sent to heaven so long as their names are written in the register, but even the most saintly among us cannot afford to be too cocky, for while God may have had every intention of entering their names into his book – he may equally well have forgotten.

— 109 —

Vignette. – In a moment of generosity a man called Ananias agreed to sell his property and give the proceeds to the Christian church. He took the money and handed it to Jesus' disciple Simon Peter, but somehow Simon Peter discovered that Ananias had received more for his property than he was handing over, and was furious with him. Taking the money Simon Peter railed: 'Ananias, how can Satan have possessed you that you should lie to the Holy Spirit and keep back part of the price of the land?' God, who must have been listening, took Peter's side in the argument and struck Ananias to the floor. When Ananias's wife,

Sapphira, turned up, expecting a grateful attitude from the apostles, she was told by Peter: 'Listen! At the door are the footsteps of the undertakers that have buried your husband; they will carry you out too,' and God struck her down as well (Acts 5:1–11).

MORAL: Do not marry a man who gives money to the church.

— 110 —

Acquired taste. – The Eucharist, a Christian sacrament, is celebrated by millions of people every Sunday who believe themselves to be eating the body and imbibing the blood of Christ – the food, as it were, of immortality. Their cue is taken from Jesus himself, who at the last supper ordered his disciples to: 'take, eat: this is my body' (Mark 14:22), and had voiced a similar idea at the synagogue in Capernaum:

> I am the living bread. Unless you eat the flesh of the Son of Man, and drink his blood, you have no life in you. Whoever eats my flesh and drinks my blood will have eternal life and I will raise him up at the last day. For my flesh is meat indeed, and my blood is drink indeed. He who eats my flesh and drinks my blood, lives in me and I in him. (John 6:53–6)

The ancient, pagan notion that eating God's flesh will somehow bring his worshippers closer to him is kept alive by Christian denominations which hold to the doctrine of divine *transubstantiation*, whereby bread and wine are literally converted, so that 'the body and blood, together with the soul and divinity of our Lord Jesus Christ and, therefore, the whole Christ is truly, really and substantially contained therein' ('Council of Trent', *Christian Faith*, 1551).

Oneness with God can be achieved not just by eating him, but, as the twelfth-century Cistercian Abbot, Bernard of Clairvaux, observed, by eating him while he is also eating you:

135

I am ashes, because I am a sinner, and therefore am I eaten by Him. I am masticated when I am reproved; I am swallowed when I am instructed; I am undergoing decomposition in the stomach when I begin to change my life; I am digested when I am transformed into his image; I am assimilated when I am conformed to his will. For were I to feed on Him whilst He did not feed on me, He would appear to be in me, yet I should not truly be in Him. (*Sermons*, LXXI)

St Catherine of Siena thought she could improve her chances of being chosen by licking pus from the wounds of hospital patients, while the mystic Angela of Foligno (1248–1309) was inspired to drink a tub of putrid discharge which had dripped from the rotting skin of a leper. As she took it a morsel of flesh stuck in her throat. Angela was determined to force it down even though she was choking to death. In the end, instinct prevailed over piety, and she spat it out.

— 111 —

Blood stain. – God believes that blood is life, or somehow contains the spirit of life within it. He told Noah, as he and his family clambered from the ark, that 'Everything that moves will be yours to eat, I give you everything with this one exception you must not eat flesh with life, that is to say blood in it' (Gen. 9:3–4). And to Moses he reiterated: 'If any member of the House of Israel or any resident alien consumes blood of any kind, I shall set my face against that individual and shall outlaw him from his people. For the life of the creature is in the blood' (Lev. 17:10–11).

Although the blood of an animal was sacrificed to God on his altar, the Israelites were also aware that by smearing blood on their door posts at the Passover they could prevent God from entering their houses and slaughtering their firstborn. Blood had been superstitiously smeared on door posts for centuries to ward off evil spirits.

Jesus took a more cavalier attitude to blood, exhorting his disciples to drink his own (John 6:53) and to stick their fingers into his wounds after the crucifixion (John 20:27). One of Jesus' most committed devotees, Julian of Norwich, extolled the wound in his side as 'a fair and delectable place', but John Mirk, a Shropshire prior of the late fifteenth century, urging his congregation to Lenten confession, told a different story. Jesus, he claimed, had appeared 'with blody woundys stondying before a seke manys bed', urging him to confess of his sins. But the sick man did not wish to do so and remained silent, so 'Cryst toke out of hys wounde yn hys syde his hond full of blod and sayde "Thu fendys chyld, thys schall be redy token bytwyx me and the yn the day of dome," and therwyth cast the blod ynto hys face, and therwyth anon thys seke man cryed and sayd: "Alas! Alas! I am dampnest for ever!" And so deyd' ('Liber Festialis', XIV *Mirk's Festivals*).

IV

Strange Oaths

For the love of God. – 'Love' is the vaguest of terms which can be used to encompass any number of complex, indefinable feelings that living beings have towards other living beings, places or things. In the Bible God orders us to love him 'with all our heart, with all our soul and with all our might' (Deut. 6:5), but what does 'love' mean? Perhaps we believe that we know what is meant by 'I love my brother' 'I love my cat' or 'I love chocolate' – a different thing in each case – but what does it mean to love a transcendent untouchable, unknowable, invisible spirit?

The Catholic Church asserts that 'one cannot adore God without loving all men, his creatures' (*Catechism of the Catholic Church*, 2069), which puts the loving of God beyond the ken of most people. The mysterious author of the Johanine letters baldly states that 'God is love' (1 John 4:8), but without further commentary, this is not a helpful definition either of God or of love. Psalm 63 does better in attempting to describe man's love of God in more human, even sexual terms:

> God, You are my God; I search for You and my soul thirsts for You, as a parched and thirsty land that has no water. I shall behold you in the sanctuary, and see Your might and Glory. Truly your faithfulness is better than life; my lips declare your praise . . . I sing with joyful lips, when I call you to mind upon my bed, when I think of you in the watches of the night. (Ps. 63:1–6)

Others see loving God as part of a merging process. The tenth-century Muslim Husayn ibn Mansur (al-Hallaj) believed that he had succeeded through the power of his love in transforming himself into God:

'I have become the one I love' he declared, 'and he whom I love has become myself! We are two spirits mingled in one body! Thus to see me is to see him, and to see him is to see us both.' Al-Hallaj was executed in Baghdad for this blasphemy, but his example did not deter others. Four centuries later the Rhineland mystic Johannes Tauler yearned for an opportunity to merge with God by melting himself in a burning furnace of divine love:

O God, thou art love that ever burnest, set me also on fire, burn into my whole being, that in myself I may wholly fall away, and be wholly transformed by thy love; melt my whole body, that I may wholly lose myself in thee. Consume me wholly, O my God, in the fire of thy burning love, that utterly forgetful of my own self and of all that is in the world, I may, with the arms of love embrace thee, the highest and most excellent Good. (*Meditations on the Life and Passion*)

None of Tauler's steamy passion is accepted in the Qur'an for Muslims believe that God quite 'likes' or 'approves' of certain mortals, but does not 'love' any of them.

— 113 —

How God got Teresa to love him. –

It was our Lord's will that in this vision I should see the angel in this way. He was not large but small of stature, and most beautiful – his face burning, as if he were one of the highest angels, who seem to be all of fire. I saw in his hand a long rod of gold, and at its tip there seemed to be a little fire. He appeared to me to be thrusting it at times into my heart, and to pierce my very entrails; when he drew it out he seemed to draw them out also, and to leave me all on fire with a great love of God. The pain was so great that it made me moan; and yet so surpassing was the sweetness of this excessive pain that I could not wish to be rid of it. The soul is satisfied now with nothing less than God. The pain is not bodily, but spiritual; though the body has its share in it, even a large one. It is a caressing of love so sweet which now takes place between the soul and God, that I pray to God in his goodness that he may also experience it who thinks that I am lying. (Teresa of Avila, *Life*)

— 114 —

How to unite your soul with God (a lesson in four parts). – Ultimate union with God consists of a blissful merging of souls; a process that has been described by several mystics as one the greatest delights that life can afford. How to achieve it:

1. DETACHMENT. First you must cleanse yourself of all earthly things: 'Union with God can only be obtained according to the degree in which the soul is detached from all things created which are the source of continual corruption and impurity,' says Jean-Pierre de Causade (1675–1751). 'This detachment, which when it has attained perfection is called *mystical death*, is the complete release from two objects; the exterior, that is to say all things around us and the interior, that is to say our own ideas, satisfactions and interests – in a word – ourselves' (*Spiritual Counsels*, 7:14).

When detachment is complete move along to stage two.

2. THE FLIRT. John of Ruysbroeck (1293–1381) describes this bit well:

By God's working and by the power of love, our spirit presses and inclines itself into God: and thereby, God is touched. These two spirits, that is, our own spirit and the Spirit of God, sparkle and shine one into the other, and each shows to the other its face. This makes each of the spirits yearn for the other in love. Each demands of the other all that it is; and each offers to the other all that it is and invites it to all that it is. (*Adornment of the Spiritual Marriage*, 54)

Once the flirt has been achieved it is time to kiss:

3. THE KISS. 'There is then a bodily kiss, a spiritual kiss, and an intellectual kiss. The bodily kiss is made by the impression of the lips; the spiritual kiss by the union of the spirits; the intellectual kiss through the spirit of God, by the infusion of grace' (Aelred de Rievaulx, *Spiritual Friendship*, 2:24).

So what can there possibly be beyond kissing? Luis de Leon (1528–91) has the answer.

4. PENETRATION.

When we have the most complete possession of bodily pleasure, the bond is weak and loose compared with this union. For the senses (and what is connected with them) only touch those things which are external: we only see the colour, hear the sound, taste the sweet or bitter, feel the hard or soft. But when God embraces the soul, he wholly penetrates it throughout, passing through its secret division and uniting himself with its most intimate being; there becoming, as it were, its soul, he embraces it most intimately. (*De los nombres de Cristo*)

The lesson is ended, go forth in peace.

— 115 —

Gadding about. – In the Hebrew Bible God is neither omnipresent, nor can he get himself from A to B by magic; he needs to travel just like everyone else. At first, his preferred method is walking. Adam heard his footsteps clomping in the Garden of Eden (Gen. 3:8) and hid; God told David to interpret the mighty sound of his feet as a signal to launch an attack on the Philistines (2 Sam 5:24) and during the Exodus he marched at the front of his people causing the whole earth to wobble (Ps. 68:7). Deborah and Barak describe how God once 'trod the land of Edom and the earth shook and the heavens quaked; the clouds dissolved into water and the mountains melted before him' (Judg. 5:4–5).

Later God developed a new technique for travelling within a column of mist like a tornado, which, according to Jeremiah, could go extremely fast (Jer. 4:13). The tornado is used in emergencies and on specific missions only; as a more dignified mode of transport God allows himself to be carried on poles by his people as he sits on a mercy seat between two carved cherubs high above the Ark of the Covenant. Daniel noticed that in heaven, his chair has wheels on it (Dan. 7:9) suggesting that the angels sometimes push or drag him around in his throne.

When crossing the heavens at speed God rides a fiery chariot driven by cherubim whose wings provide the necessary lift to prevent it from falling. Sometimes God rejects the chariot, mounting directly on the cherub's back instead (Ps. 18:10). In Psalm 104 David (or Akhenaton) revealed that God used 'the clouds as his chariot, advancing on the wings of the wind; using the winds as messengers and fiery flames as servants', but he does not have to rely on cloudy weather to get about. On clear days God raids the celestial equipage where a number of fantastic horses are stabled. These horses are made of fire (2 Kings 2:11) and, according to Jeremiah, can move 'swifter than eagles' (Jer. 4:13). The crazy prophet Habakkuk swears that God rides them himself from time to time, galloping in a furious rage 'across the sea and through the surging abyss' (Hab. 3:8; 3:15).

— 116 —

Seven things God abhors. –

There are six things that God hates: yea, seven things that are an abomination to him: a haughty look, a lying tongue, hands that shed innocent blood, a heart that weaves a wicked plot and feet that are swift in running to mischief, a false witness that lies with every breath and one who sows discord among brethren. (Prov. 6:16–19)

— 117 —

One thing he does not abhor. – 'God of God, light of light, lo, he abhors not the virgin's womb' ('O come all ye faithful!').

— 118 —

Seven things he loves. – A cheerful giver (2 Cor. 9:7); the gates of Zion (Ps. 87:2); none but him that dwelleth in wisdom (Wisd. of Sol. 7:28); Hephzibah of Beula (Isa. 62:4); judgement (Ps. 37:28); righteousness (Ps. 11:7); the smell of a burnt ram (Exod. 29:18).

146

— 119 —

The scent that God will not share. – God ordered Moses to make his favourite perfume:

'Take spices,' he said, 'storax, oncha, galbanum, sweet spices and pure frankincense in equal parts and pound them into an incense, just as a good perfumer might make it, salted, pure and holy. Once you have ground it up well put it in front of the Testimony in the Tent of Meeting where I shall meet you. You will regard it as especially holy. You are forbidden from making any incense from the same recipe for your own use. You will regard it as sacrosanct, and reserve it all for me. Anyone who takes up the same substance to use as perfume will be outlawed from his people. (Exod. 30:34–7)

— 120 —

Fuss pot. – God is not a great eater. Most religions believe that as pure spirit, God cannot eat, even if he wants to, though Christians agree that Jesus (God incarnate) who 'dippeth his hand into the dish' enjoying fish, unleavened bread, beakers of red wine at the last supper, ate continuously throughout his life. The Qur'an parades Jesus' eating as proof that he cannot have been divine. In the Bible, however, divine beings *do* eat food. Angels, for instance, eat manna (Wisd. of Sol. 16:20), and 'the Mighty One' eats bread (Ps. 78:25).

It is not stated if God intended to eat the apples of the Tree of Knowledge that were stolen by Adam and Eve but he certainly ate a large meal in the shade of a terebinth outside Abram's house. God, and two mysterious companions, had griddle cakes, butter, milk and veal prepared by Abram's wife Sarai (Gen. 18:8). It may not have been to God's liking, for later he insisted on dietary laws which to this day have restrained Orthodox Jews from eating meat and dairy products at the same time. Although he tantalised the Israelites with the promise of a land flowing with milk and honey; he ordered them not to sacrifice either to him (Lev. 2:11), disliking in particular, the smell of burned honey rising from his altar.

So what *will* God accept? From unblemished male cows and sheep he will take the fat covering the entrails, both kidneys and the fat on them, as well as the loins; he will have young pigeons and turtle-doves and unleavened bread only if coated with plenty of oil and salt (Exod. 29).

But God is ultimately more concerned with restricting the diet of human beings than with his own nourishment or lack of it. Of the four-legged animals, mortals are only to eat those which have *both* cloven hooves *and* chew the cud. This, for the orthodox, means *no* to pork, camels, whales and *yes* to cows, sheep, goats, deer, gazelle, roe-buck, wild goats, ibex, antelopes, mountain sheep etc. The animals which God calls 'detestable' are lizards, chameleons, moles and rats, on the one hand (Lev. 11:29–30); and bats, buzzards, pelicans, seagulls and ravens on the other (Deut. 14:11–19). No loss there! These animals probably taste disgusting anyway, but two dishes, which are known to be delicious, have mysteriously found their way onto God's list of 'detestables' – ostrich steak and kid-goat seethed in milk – dichotomies for the pious gourmet.

— 121 —

Fat. – In some deprived countries fatness, even obesity, is a sign of prosperity, good health and sexual prowess. God does not share this view and is enraged by anything overweight. Fatness, as revealed by Moses in a poetic incantation shortly before his death, is viewed as an indulgence which will lead inevitably to pride and hence to the rejection of God. 'Israel has now grown fat and is lashing out,' he complained, 'gross and bloated, he has disowned the God who made him' (Deut. 32:15). When God took the Israelites out of Egypt he worried that they would get too fat, conceited and spoiled: 'I pastured them and they were satisfied,' he observed, 'once satisfied their hearts grew proud, and therefore they forgot me' (Hos. 13:5–6).

To keep the Israelites slim, God demands that all the fat from animals be given to him. 'The fat belongs to Me!' he declared. 'This is a perpetual law for all your descendants wherever you may live' (Lev. 3:17).

Gluttons are punished in the afterlife, left to rot in a dank, putrid pit where 'hail stones, turbid water and snow, pour incessantly upon them' (Dante, *L'Inferno*, 6:10). In life, those who complain of hunger are stuffed to death with quail meat (Num. 11:31–3), those who ask for bread are sent fiery serpents to kill them all (Num. 21:6), and those who eat and drink without first obtaining God's consent are mauled to death by lions (1 Kings 13:1–27).

By these measures God's Chosen People soon learned that obesity would not be tolerated. Fatness was a curse from God: 'You will grow weary and will not rest,' God had threatened Adam, after the Fall. 'You will be afflicted with bitterness and not taste sweetness; be oppressed by heat and burdened by cold; you will toil much and not gain wealth; you will grow disgustingly fat and fail to reach your goal' (*LAE* 24:3).

According to Muslim tradition Adam, who retired to Sri Lanka after his expulsion from Eden, was so enormous that one of his footprints (found on the Sri Lankan mountain once known as 'Pico de Adam') was said to measure 70 cubits long. Eve was equally gross. The same legend describes her resting her head on one hill near Mecca while her knees were draped over two mountains in the plain about a mile and half asunder!

— 122 —

In search of a square meal. – The Israelites were moaning among themselves and the sound of it 'was offensive to God's ears'. His anger boiled over and he let loose a terrible fire among them which frazzled half the camp. Moses pleaded with God to desist and the fire eventually died down. But God heard the Israelites whingeing again. What is it this time?

They were famished, after years of wandering through the desert, some of them were withering away and blubbing like babies. 'Who will give us meat?' they wailed. 'Think of the fish we used to get for free in Egypt, the cucumbers, melons, leeks, onions and garlic!' How dare they? They had no right to complain for God had provided them with manna for breakfast, lunch and supper, for the past thirty years, and what was wrong with manna? 'Its appearance was like gum-resin' (Num. 11:7) and it 'tasted like cake made with oil. When dew fell on the camp at night time it went mouldy.' Who could complain at that?

God was beside himself with rage and Moses too was outraged.

'Since you have wept in God's hearing,' he rebuked, 'saying "Who will give us meat to eat? How happy we were in Egypt!" Very well, God will give you meat to eat. Lots of it. You will eat it not for one day, or two or five, or ten, or twenty, but for a whole month, till it comes out of your nostrils and you vomit from it.'

With over 600,000 of them God may have been nervous that he would not be able to fulfil so rash a promise: 'If all the flocks and herds were slaughtered, would that be enough for them?' He asked of Moses, 'If all the fish in the sea were collected, would that be enough for them?'

Something had to be done. God hatched a plan. By sending a wind from the sea he blew hundreds of thousands of quail inland towards the Israelite camp. There were so many that the land around the camp was two cubits thick with them. The people were delighted at seeing an end to their starvation and spent two days cheerfully collecting them up, but 'the meat was still between their teeth, not even chewed, when God's anger flared against the people. God struck them with a terrible plague. The name given to this place was Kibroth-ha-Taavah, because it was there that they buried the people who had indulged their greed' (Num. 11).

— 123 —

Lie bag! – God 'detests a lying tongue' (Prov: 6:17). Ananias and Sapphira were killed for being economical with the truth (Acts 5), and Ezekiel was warned that God would exterminate lying prophets (Ezek. 14).

Under such circumstances it ought not to be necessary to enquire if God himself ever lies. Thomas Aquinas rejected the possibility, baldly stating that 'God Himself cannot lie' (*Summa Theologiae*, 2:2:4). What he can do, however (something that is freely admitted in the Bible), is make *other* people lie. 'Behold,' Micaiah said to the kings of Israel and Judah, 'the Lord has put a lying spirit in the mouth of all these thy prophets, and the Lord hath spoken evil concerning thee' (1 Kings 22:23). In a perverse twist to the same game, God sometimes chooses to make prophets lie *in order* to punish them, just as he commands cities to sin so that he may destroy them (Qur'an 17:16). 'I will turn against this man,' he told Ezekiel of the false prophet:

> I will make him an example and a byword and I will cut him off from the midst of my people and he will learn that I am God. And if the prophet is deceived when he speaks, it is because I, the Lord have deceived that prophet, and I will stretch out my hand upon him and will destroy him from the midst of my people Israel. (Ezek. 14:9–10)

All examples of God telling direct lies in the Bible are arguable. Did he lie, for instance, when he told Adam that he would surely die on the very day that he ate the apple (Gen. 2:17)? Or was he lying when he said to the Israelites (after he had put them into the hands of their enemies, half starved them in the desert and struck 14,700 of them dead with a lethal virus) that: 'The Lord your God has blessed you in all you do; he has watched over your journeying through this vast wilderness: The Lord your God has been with you these forty years and you have never been in want' (Deut. 2:7)?

Priestly wisdom rejects the suggestion that God is a liar and flatly denies that he ever makes mistakes. But if God never lies, nor does he err, several passages of the Bible are rendered incomprehensible by his actions; unless of course *truthfulness* does not mean what we *think* it means when it is predicated of God.

— 124 —

Musically speaking. – Music opens the mind to transcendent reality, to the world behind the world of sight, touch, smell and other mundane phenomena, drawing the listener away from himself and, some will claim, closer to God. But this is not proof that God likes music, only that some humans do.

Although he ordered Moses to make trumpets (Num. 10:2) and possibly played the trumpet himself (Judg. 6:34) there is no direct evidence that God enjoys listening to music. As Spinoza pointed out: 'Those things that act through the ears are said to make a noise, discord or harmony, and this last has caused men to lose their heads to such a degree that they have believed God himself is delighted with it.' The Bible leaves the question open, muddled and doubtful.

At the consecration of the Temple of Solomon (2 Chron. 5.12) an orchestra and chorus of 4000 is described. Heman, Asaph and Ethan are appointed chief conductors, crashing their cymbals to keep everyone in time. God's reaction is not recorded but the Temple was destroyed in 586 BCE. When the Ark of the Covenant was moved from Abinadab's house, David 'and all Israel danced before God with all their might, singing to the accompaniment of harps, lyres, tambourines and trumpets'. So raucous were they that the Ark tilted; God lost his temper and killed the man who had put out his hand to steady it (1 Chron. 13:8–9). David's own music-making was a regular cause of divine irritation. God put 'an evil spirit on Saul while he was sitting in his house with javelin in hand: David was plucking the harp and Saul tried to pin David to the wall with his spear' (1 Sam. 19:9–10).

Some Christian reformers believed music to be the work of the devil while others viewed it as a mild impediment to worship. The Prophet Muhammad pushed his fingers into his ears when he heard a musical pipe, while Cecilia, the patron saint of music, has been mischievously associated with that art only because she refused to listen to the organ at her wedding, protesting vehemently that its horrid piped sound might seduce her to accept her husband, Valerian, and renounce her cherished ambition to die *virgo intacta*.

— 125 —

Stop listening to that, and look at me. – Is it pure chance that mystical revelations so often occur when the victim is listening to music? Two examples will suffice. H. Warner Allen, growing tired of life in London between the wars, dragged himself out to a concert. In his book, *The Timeless Moment*, he recalled what happened next:

It flashed up lightning-wise during a performance of Beethoven's Seventh Symphony at the Queen's Hall, in that triumphant fast movement. The swiftly flowing continuity of the music was not interrupted, so that what T. S. Eliot calls 'the intersection of the timeless moment' must have slipped in between two demi-semi-quavers.

What was it that slipped in there? Warner tried his best to recollect:

Rapt in Beethoven's music, I closed my eyes and watched a silver glow which shaped itself into a circle with a central focus brighter than the rest. The circle became a tunnel of light proceeding from some distant sun in the heart of the Self. Swiftly and smoothly I was borne through the tunnel and as I went the light turned from silver to gold. There was an impression of drawing strength from a limitless sea of power and deepening peace. The light grew brighter but was never dazzling or alarming. I came to a point where time and motion ceased. In my recollection it took the shape of a flat-topped rock, surrounded by a summer sea with a sandy pool at its foot. (p. 251)

In the second example a man who bore the name of Watkins was singing a *Te Deum* at his local parish church, bluish smoke puffed from chinks in the floor and a luminous haze engulfed him:

All around me became transformed into golden glory, into light untellable. The golden light of which the violet haze seemed now to have been as the veil of outer fringe, welled forth from a central immense globe of brilliancy. But the most wonderful thing was that these shafts and waves of light and even the central globe itself, were crowded to solidarity with the forms of living creatures, like a single coherent organism filling all place and space, yet composed of an infinitude of individuated existences. Those beings were, moreover present in teaming myriads in the church I stood in: and they were intermingling with, and passing unobstructedly through both myself and my fellow worshippers. The Heavenly host drifted through the human congregation as wind passes through a grove of trees; beings of radiant beauty and clothes in shimmering raiment. (from Wilmhurst, *Contemplations*)

When all these miracles were over and the vision vanished away Watkins, returning to himself, rejoined the *Te Deum* for its last three bars.

— 126 —

Smoke without fire. – The Lord, according to Moses, 'came from Sinai' (Deut. 33:2), though it has been hotly debated whether the modern-day mountain of that name (a 7000 foot granite peak in the South Sinai Peninsula) is the *same* Mount Sinai on which Moses is described having received the Law from God. Christians and Jews accept it as genuine, without proof, but the name *Sinai* is known to have been given to the mountain long after biblical times, for the purposes of establishing it as the holy site where tourism now abounds.

One reason for scepticism is that the modern mountain is not a volcano and yet in the Bible (especially when God comes by) it assumes a distinctly volcanic attitude:

Now at daybreak two days later there were peals of thunder and flashes of lightning, dense cloud on the mountain. The people in the camp were all terrified and kept their distance . . . Mount Sinai was entirely wrapped in smoke, because God had descended on it in the form of fire. The smoke rose like smoke from a furnace and the whole mountain shook violently. (Exod. 19:16–18)

In other passages God's original involvement in the ancient pagan practice of volcano worship is more startlingly revealed.

The prophet Enoch once described God as 'like iron made burning hot by a fire, it emits sparks and it is incandescent' (*2 En.* 39:5).

When God addressed the Israelites from Mount Horeb, 'the mountain flamed to the very sky, and the sky was darkened by cloud, murky and thunderous. God spoke to you from the heart of the fire' (Deut. 4:11–12). Psalm 18 paints a picture of God like a mighty volcanic eruption:

> Then the earth shook and trembled; the foundations also of the hills moved, shaken by his wrath. Smoke billowed from his nostrils and a devouring fire shot from his mouth, so hot that coals were kindled by it. Thick clouds issued from the radiance before him. The Lord thundered in the heavens and his voice shot hail-stones and coals of fire. (Ps. 18:7–12)

God is not the only deity to behave like this. What about that pagan fire fiend, Vulcan, and his Greek equivalent Hephaestus? They too had smoke and sparks blasting from their nostrils.

— 127 —

His smell. – God (or at least his glory) is sometimes reported as exuding a delicious fragrance. We know that much, though the exact nature of the smell is not always carefully described. In the Greek *Apocalypse of Ezra* (a manuscript of unknown provenance, believed to have been written by Greek Christians sometime between 150 and 850 CE) Ezra is found debating with some angels which of his orifices should do the honour of relinquishing his soul at the moment of his death: 'We can bring it out through your nostrils?' suggests a helpful angel. 'No,' replies Ezra, 'for my nostrils have smelled the glory of God' (*Gk. Apoc. Ezra* 6:8).

The same idea recurs in the 2000-year-old Syriac *Odes of Solomon*: 'And the Lord is like the sun upon the face of the land. My eyes were enlightened and my face received the dew; and my breath was refreshed by the pleasant fragrance of the Lord' (*Odes Sol.* 11:13–15), a sentiment that is also echoed in the Armenian *Life of Moses* in which Moses revealed that his 'mouth spoke with God and my eyes saw the light of the Godhead and my nostrils smelt the fragrance of sweetness'.

Not many of the prophets, in their encounters with God, bothered to mention smell, but those that did, hint that it may not have been an entirely natural odour, more like a created perfume. In the first-century Slavonic *Apocalypse of Enoch* God orders Michael: 'Go and extract Enoch from his earthly clothing and anoint him with my delightful oil and put him in the clothes of my glory, for the appearance of that oil is greater than the greatest light, and its ointment is like sweet dew, and its fragrance myrrh' (*2 En.* 22:8–9).

A 4-year-old girl from Irving, Texas, called Danae Lu Blessing told her mother that the smell of an approaching thunderstorm reminded her of 'the smell of God, when you lay your head on his chest'. Danae had been born prematurely and nearly died in her first few months. Her revelation, recorded on an Internet site called 'Encounters with God', was so moving that her proud, fond mother could not contain her tears: 'During the first two months of her life,' her mother bewailed, 'when her nerves were too sensitive for them to touch her, God was holding Danae on his chest – and it is His loving scent that she remembers so well' (www.all-creatures.org stories/rain.html).

— 128 —

Celestial laughs. – Most references to laughter in the Bible allude not to hearty mirth but to the laughter of scorn and derision. Laughter in the modern sense (engendered by embarrassment or a sudden realization of the absurd) is alien to God. On the few occasions that he laughs it is in an angry, derisive vein, not a happy one. Typically, as in Psalm 2, God's laughter begins as mockery and ends in temper: 'He who is enthroned in the heavens laughs, God makes a mockery of them, then in his anger, rebukes them, in his rage he strikes them with terror' (Ps. 2:4–5).

Sometimes God's laugh is so terrible that it kills all those who hear it: 'They shall see him, and despise him; but God shall laugh them to scorn: and they shall hereafter be a vile carcase, and a reproach among the dead for evermore' (Wisd. of Sol. 4:18–19).

Tertullian described God shaking with laughter at the sight of worms popping in and out of Job's flesh as the poor man sat for forty-eight years on a dung heap (*De patientia*, 14:2). When Abraham's wife, Sarah (barren when young and, at ninety, well past her menopause), overheard God telling Abraham that she would bear a child, she chuckled salaciously to herself: 'Is pleasure to come my way again?' God bristled, turned to Abraham and asked him why Sarah had laughed. She protested: 'I did not laugh,' lying because she was afraid. God replied, "Oh yes you did"' (Gen. 18:13–15). Sarah got off lightly, since she had lied to God, but others fared less well. Lot's future son-in-laws were left to burn at Sodom because they thought God was 'only joking' about his intention to destroy that city.

Some Christian scholars, to account for Jesus' oddest behaviour (as when he beat a fig tree with a stick for failing to produce fruit out of season), have ventured to suggest he was attempting to be funny, demonstrating a uniquely gnomic sense of humour, but the gospels do not record anyone laughing at Jesus' jokes, which is just as well: 'Alas for you who are laughing now,' Jesus said, 'for you shall mourn and weep' (Luke 6:25).

The view that laughter is sinful was once an accepted creed of the Jewish, Christian and Islamic religions. Old handbooks and catechisms used to ask: 'Will sport and pleasure make you happy? No, for the wise man said of laughter, it is mad, and of mirth, What doth it?' (Matthew Henry, *Shorter Catechism*, A:4).

In conversation with the American writer Neale Donald Walsch, God has recently objected to the popular belief that he is humourless. He talked to Walsch over a period of several years, 'directly, personally, irrefutably', making him write down answers to all sorts of questions which were put to him by the insatiably curious author. These have been published in three books called *Conversations with God*. In the first, God told Walsch that he is 'the up and the down. The hot and the cold. The left and the right. The reverent and the irreverent. Think you that God cannot laugh? Do you imagine that God does not enjoy a good joke? Is it your knowing that God is without humor? I tell you, God invented humor' (*Conversations with God*, p. 60).

— 129 —

Talking to God. – Many of the prophets found it irksome talking to God, often having to whip themselves up into a trance-like state, sweating and foaming at the mouth in order to do so. Muhammad the Prophet, who was reckoned by the enemies of Islam to be an epileptic, used, when receiving divine messages, to be seized with fits of violent trembling followed by swoons and convulsions. According to one of his earliest biographers 'perspiration would stream from his forehead in the coldest weather; he would lie with his eyes closed, foaming at the mouth and bellowing like a young camel'.

Long before Muhammad's time it was reckoned that a good show-ing of foam from the mouth was a sure sign of a prophet's integ-rity. Lucian, the Greek writer who pursued impostors with satirical gusto in the second century CE, was not impressed by Alexander the Paphlagonian, a bogus prophet whom he had witnessed amassing a fortune by duping gullible pilgrims. 'Alexander was a man of mark and of note,' wrote Lucian, 'affecting as he did to have occasional fits of madness and causing his mouth to fill with foam. This he easily managed by chewing the root of soapwort, the plant that dyers use; but to his fellow countrymen even the foam seemed supernatural and awe-inspiring' (Lucian, *Alexander the False Prophet*, 12).

When Isaiah spoke with God his outward appearance was highly theatrical:

And while he was speaking with the Holy Spirit he became silent

159

and his mind was taken up from him and he did not see the men who were standing before him. His eyes indeed were open but his mouth was silent, and the mind of his body was taken up from him, for he was seeing a vision. (*Mart. and Asc. Isa.*, 6:2.9)

St Teresa of Avila believed that she could only talk to God properly if she was suffering terrible agonies so she tied bracelets of stinging nettles round her arms. When communications remained unclear she prayed that she might receive oozing sores upon her stomach. Nowadays attitudes such as these require psychiatric treatment.

— 130 —

Connection protocol. – When God wishes to start a conversation he will call a name twice in succession, 'Abraham, Abraham!' (Gen. 22:11); 'Jacob, Jacob!' (Gen. 46:2); 'Moses, Moses!' (Exod. 3:4); 'Samuel, Samuel!' (1 Sam. 3:10); 'Esdras, Esdras!' (2 Esd. 14:1). On the other hand, he may just ask, 'Where are you?' (Gen. 3:9). In every case, the proper response is 'Here I am', spoken in a clear, loud, unironic tone. You are now connected. Your conversation may continue. There is no protocol for disconnection. God never says 'Goodbye', 'Have a nice day!' or 'Missing you already', and you must not do so either. Allow the conversation to end naturally and leave it at that.

— 131 —

Divine voice. – Jesus told the Jews who were pestering him at Jerusalem that nobody had heard God's voice 'at any time' (John 5:37), but his view is contrary to a great many other passages of scripture. Adam, for instance, told God, 'I heard your voice in the garden!' (Gen 3:10) and he was not contradicted.

Several prophets have attempted to describe the divine voice. Enoch revealed that it is 'multiple' (*2 En.* 22:5), suggesting a combination of pitches and tones sounding simultaneously. Daniel confirmed: 'the voice of his words is like the voice of a multitude' (Dan. 10:6), while to John of Patmos it was 'as the sound of many waters' (Rev. 1:15). Ezekiel heard the flapping of cherubim wings in it (Ezek. 10:5), while Jeremiah thought he had detected the sound of people shouting while treading out the vintage: 'God roars from on high,' he observed, 'he thunders from his holy dwelling place, shouting like those who tread the grape at all the inhabitants of the land' (Jer. 25:30); to Adam, God's voice was simply 'frightful' (*Apoc. Adam* 8:1).

But God's voice is nothing if it is not versatile. He can make it thunder, he can make it boom (Job 37:2), he can imitate the screeching of a woman in labour (Isa. 42:14) or reduce it to the 'still, small voice' with which he spoke to Elijah. When he wishes, his voice can be 'powerful' and 'majestic' (Ps. 18:13); with his vocal cords alone God is able to strip whole forests bare and cause deer to calve (Ps. 29:8), break cedar trees in half (Ps. 29:5), shake the wilderness (Ps. 29:8) and melt the earth (Ps. 46:6).

God can also throw his voice like a ventriloquist, and better still, he can turn it into a separate, disembodied hypostatic presence. In the book of Deuteronomy Moses informs his people that 'out of the heavens He let you hear His voice to discipline you; and on earth He let you see His great fire, and you heard his words from the midst of the fire' (Deut. 4:36). When John heard a voice behind him like a trumpet, he turned around but saw only seven golden candlesticks (Rev. 1:10–12). Much earlier Noah's oldest son, Shem, described how 'a voice bent toward me, calling from the throne and coming forward, took my right hand and lifted me' (*Apoc. Shem*, Cologne Mani Codex 57:12), and similarly in the third century *Apocalypse of Sedrach* a voice, which Sedrach twice addressed as 'Lord' was sent to raise the good man up: 'And he heard a hidden voice in his ears, and the voice said to him "I was sent to you so that I may carry you up to heaven"' (*Apoc. Sed.* 2:1).

By contrast, when God wished Samuel to serve him as a prophet he called out to him 'Samuel, Samuel', but the voice he used was so ordinary that Samuel mistook it for the voice of his master, Eli, and ran three times into Eli's bedroom in the middle of the night, shouting 'Here I am!' Eli told him to go back to bed.

— 132 —

Einstein's blunder. – When Einstein tried to refute quantum physics with his now famous dictum 'God does not play dice' he revealed his ignorance of scripture, for God does indeed play dice in the form of a game called *urim* and *thummim*. These flat stone dice are mentioned many times in the Hebrew Bible. Although *urim* and *thummim* actually belonged to God (*Ps.-Philo* 47:2) they were jealously guarded by the high priest either in his *ephod* (an oracular pouch) or in a pocket by his chest. The exact manner in which *urim* and *thummim* was played has been lost to the mysteries of time, but it is thought they provided the same function as a coin when it is flipped for heads or tails. When Saul wished to establish a question of blame he set up the *urim* and *thummim* asking: ' "Lord God of Israel, if fault lies with me or my son Jonathan give *urim*: if the fault lies with your people Israel, give *thummim*." Jonathan and Saul were indicated and the people went free. Saul then said: "Cast the lot between me and Jonathan," and Jonathan was indicated' (1 Sam. 14:41–2).

After a while it dawned on the people of Israel that *urim* and *thummim* did not always give reliable results (*Ps.-Philo* 47:2) and so God ceased to be addressed through this medium, probably as early as the seventh century BCE. The whole matter might well have been forgotten had it not been for God lending his *urim* and *thummim* nearly two thousand years later to Joseph Smith in order to help the prophet interpret the 'revised Egyptian' squiggles of the *Book of Mormon*. Smith had to return them to the angel, Moroni, and regrettably failed to make accurate drawings before handing them back. However, in a bewildering twist, God later informed Smith (2 April 1843) that he (God) was now living inside a giant *urim* and *thummim*.

> The place where I reside [said God] is a great *Urim* and *Thummim*. This earth in its sanctified and immortal state, will be made like unto crystal and will be a *Urim* and *Thummim* to the inhabitants who dwell thereon, whereby all things pertaining to an inferior kingdom, or all kingdoms of a lower order, will be manifest to those who dwell on it; and this earth will be Christ's. Then the white stone mentioned in Revelation 2:17, will become a *Urim* and *Thummim* to each individual who receives one, whereby things pertaining to a higher order of kingdoms will be made known. (*Doctrine and Covenants*, 130:8–10)

And Einstein thought that the cosmological constant was his 'biggest blunder'!

—— 133 ——

What to pray about. – If God is omnipotent and people talk to him through prayer how do they resist the temptation to ask for earthly things: money, sweets or the gift of flight? Instinctively people assume that to petition God for money will not earn his favour. According to Enoch, God punishes sloppy praying by shooting the petitioner with flame from his little finger (*3 En.* 40:3). There are risks involved in prayer, for God is not easily pleased. The safest position is to assume that people should never pray for their own benefit, not even for virtues like piety, honesty or fair play; prayer is a mechanism for praising God, that is all.

Augustine (who famously prayed for 'chastity and continency – but not yet!') held that Christians *could* pray for anything so long as it was *legal*, but Thomas Aquinas countered that since God has already decided what everyone will or will not receive, all that a

163

praying person can hope to achieve is a sense of co-operation with God's pre-ordained will, but no amount of praying will ever succeed in changing God's mind.

There is a story in the Jewish Talmud (*Berachoth*, 33b) about a rabbi who overhears a man praying to 'God that is great, powerful, awesome, strong, forceful, firm courageous, reliable and revered'. The rabbi thinks that the man has insulted God and, to illustrate his point, asks him to imagine a king, the proud owner of billions of gold coins being praised for owning a few copper pennies as well. Would the king not be insulted by this praise?

Moses Maimonides (alias Rambam, the most influential Jewish thinker of the Middle Ages) believed that worshippers should resist the temptation to think that God is good, clever or even interesting: 'It is not necessary for you to enter into positive assertions about God in order to glorify Him according to your own understandings,' he wrote.

Is there, then, any point in praying at all? If praying for things does not get them delivered and if God is not susceptible to any praise that is lavished upon him, why bother? For prayer to have any purpose, or any reward, it must be a personal or communal activity, from which God is effectively excluded.

The Jewish Mishnah claims to the contrary that God 'longs for the prayer of the righteous'. Thérèse of Lisieux (as righteous as righteous can be) described her own praying as 'a surge of the heart, a simple look turned towards heaven, a cry of recognition and of love, embracing both trial and joy'. Prayer, then, for the super-righteous is not about asking for things, or even a matter of praising God. Its purpose is to gain knowledge and understanding of the nature of God; to which end it is silent, wordless, ecstatic and perfectly selfish.

—— 134 ——

Posture. – What shape should people's bodies assume when they pray to God? Is it better to kneel with hands together, or to lie prostrate, face down, clasping the forehead? Will God listen more attentively to those whose head is bowed or to those looking upwards, to a bottom sticking up or an elbow tucked away? If one position had been proven to work better than any other, it would surely, by now, have been adopted as universal. God insisted to the Second Isaiah that 'all shall bend the knee to me' (Isa. 45:23) but the bent knee remains only one of many positions in use today.

In the Qur'an God insisted that he would turn a deaf ear to prayers offered up by dirty people. Those who have just been to the lavatory or enjoyed sexual intercourse must, at very least, wipe themselves with 'wholesome dust' before praying (Qur'an 5:9). Elsewhere he desired that prayers be intoned at a moderate volume (Qur'an 17:110) and that they be at all times addressed in the direction of Mecca (Qur'an 8:55), but as to the exact physical attitude of prayer God, in the Qur'an as elsewhere, is not specific.

The elaborate routine of physical posturing that currently accompanies Muslim prayer cannot be traced to a divine command. A devout Muslim is required to raise his hands to his ears for the *takbir*, bow in an attitude of sincere reverence in order to recite the *fatihah*, bow several more times for the *ruku*, repeat the *takbir*, prostrate himself on his knees with both hands flat on the ground for the *sajdah*, sit back on his heels and ask for mercy, prostrate himself once again, then stand up and repeat the whole process. This cycle must take place five times a day.

Christian and Jewish prayer position is less strict and consequently more shambolic. The Bible sanctions standing (Gen. 18:23), kneeling (Ps. 95:6), prostration (Num. 16:4; Matt. 26:39) and sitting (2 Sam. 7:18). When Elijah prayed for rain he went up a mountain and 'put his face between his knees' and the heavens opened (1 Kings 18:42). The

'Elijah position' has since been adopted by groups of Jewish mystics and Muhammad often used it before entering into an ecstatic trance.

— 135 —

Calling all prophets. – When God called certain upstanding men to be his prophets they were not always willing to come. The life of a prophet was tough, they had to lie in huts naked and in ecstasy for days on end (1 Sam. 19:24); political enemies abounded and God did little to protect them. Jeremiah, who loathed being a prophet more than anything, felt he had been raped by God (Jer. 20:7) and consequently staggered about like a broken-hearted drunk (Jer. 23:9). At his initiation Isaiah had his lips purified with white-hot coals (Isa. 6:6); it is no wonder that Jonah tried to run away when called by God to prophesy. Nor did God reward his prophets once they had signed up to his cause. Isaiah was sawn in half with a wood-saw, Jeremiah was stoned to death at Taphnai, Balaam was shredded with swords, Joad was eaten by a lion, Amos died from a club blow to his forehead and Micah was tipped over a cliff.

When God approached Jeremiah, the Judaean pretended he could not speak properly in order to avoid conscription '*Ah ah, ah, ah,* Lord God; you see, I do not know how to speak' (Jer. 1:6). Ezekiel was 'bitter and angry' when he was called up (Ezek. 2:14) and Samuel refused three times to accept that God was calling him (1 Sam. 3:1–9). To get Muhammad to prophesy, God had to send the Angel Gabriel to coerce him in the middle of the night on top of Mount Hira. Gabriel's approach was unsubtle. He woke Muhammad, shouting in his ear '*Iqra!*' (Recite!). Muhammad protested (like Jeremiah) that he did not know how to recite, but Gabriel, who was never going to accept a negative answer, crushed Muhammad in a pythonesque embrace shouting again even louder, '*Iqra!*' Amazingly the brave Arabian declined once more, but after Gabriel had nearly squeezed the life from him for a third time, Muhammad consented, opening his mouth to splutter the first *ayat* of the ninety-sixth *sura* of the book now

known to the world as the Qur'an. 'Recite!' he gasped, 'In the name of the Lord who created man out of a blood clot.'

Afterwards Muhammad was so disgusted at what had happened and by what he had said that he tried to jump off the mountain, but Gabriel blocked his path. Shaking like a leaf, the prophet crawled on all fours, into the lap of his wife, Khadija. In the end, he had no choice but to take up his destiny, for, as the prophet Amos had long ago forewarned, 'When the lion roars; who is not afraid? When God has spoken; who dares not to prophesy?' (Amos 3:8).

—— 136 ——

Fantastic offer ignored. – 'Oh Lord, if you give me plenty of food and clothes,' said Jacob, 'and if you manage to get me safely home, I will let you be my God, furthermore as a gesture of my goodwill, this bit of stone which I used last night as a pillow and have since smeared with grease can be your house and, if you are really decent, I will even let you have 10 per cent of everything that you give to me in the future' (paraphrase of Gen. 28: 20–22). God's reaction to Jacob's offer was not recorded – perhaps he wasn't listening.

—— 137 ——

Nasty incidents. – A Levite from Ephraim was a guest in the house of an old man at Gibeah, a small settlement in the heart of the land of the tribe of Benjamin. The Levite had with him his concubine, and at night-fall, just after they had finished supper, some rowdy Benjaminites came bashing on the door demanding of the old man that he release his guest so that they might rape and molest him. Now guests, in those days, were regarded as sacred animals, so the pious man flatly refused to hand the Levite over but offered his daughter instead: 'Here is my daughter,' he pleaded, 'She is a virgin. I will bring her out to you. Ill-treat her, do

what you like with her, but do not commit such an infamy against this man who is a guest in my house.' But the Benjaminites wanted the man and would not settle for anything less, until, that is, the Levite himself stepped forward and suggested they take his concubine. All that night they raped and abused her, only releasing her in the early hours. Gravely beaten she staggered back to the house of the old man and collapsed on his threshold.

In the morning her husband got up and found her lying there.

'Get up,' he said. 'We must leave.'

But she did not reply. Heavy-hearted the Levite strapped her dead body to his donkey and took it home. Then, with a knife, cut it, limb by limb, into twelve pieces and sent a morsel to each of the tribes of Israel to alert them to the horror of the Benjaminite orgy. At this, encouraged by God, eleven of the tribes of Israel advanced against the House of Benjamin. From a tribe of 25,000 members only 600 Benjaminites survived the slaughter. But the conquering tribes suddenly felt sorry for Benjamin and hurriedly devised a rescue plan for the vanquished. It went like this:

When the girls of Shiloh come out to dance in the vineyards, the Benjaminite men can hide among the vines, leap out and take one each to himself and rape her. By this happy expedient the tribe of Benjamin will avoid extinction.

God, who destroyed Sodom and Gomorrah for behaving exactly as the Benjaminites at Gibeah, lay conspicuously low during this whole affair 'But in those days, there was no king in Israel, and everyone did as he saw fit' (Judg. 19:1 – 21:25).

— 138 —

He of the peak. – God, according to the Bible, lives somewhere high up. He is described as 'coming down' to inspect the Tower of Babel (Gen. 11) and 'coming down' to find out whether the rumours reaching him about the sinfulness of Sodom and Gomorrah are correct (Gen. 18:21).

God told Moses that he would 'come down' to rescue his people from the clutches of the Egyptians (Exod. 3:8). It might be assumed that each time God 'comes down' he is descending from heaven but at the time of Moses God lived not in heaven but on top of a very high mountain.

The name El Shaddai with which God revealed himself to Abram (Gen. 17:1) derives from the Accadian word *shadu* and means 'God of the Mountain', a divine name that is used predominantly in the first five books of the Hebrew Bible and in the book of Job. In Exodus, El Shaddai orders Moses to 'worship God on his mountain' (Exod. 3:12) and to 'Come up to me on the mountain' (Exod 24:12), to receive the Law. Mount Sinai, which is described as 'the mountain of God' (Exod 3:1; 1 Kings 19:8), is also given as the Lord's address in Deuteronomy (33:2), Judges (5:5) and the book of Psalms (68:17), though, according to one minor prophet, Habakkuk, God's favoured peak was Mount Paran in Edom (Hab. 3:3) – but Habakkuk was often muddled.

— 139 —

Mobile home. – In the days of Moses God was not omnipresent, he was a local God, a god of the mountain, particularly of his own mountain, Sinai. When the Israelites left Sinai for the conquest of Canaan they could not take their mountain with them but the prospect of leaving God behind was unthinkable. How could they expect to win any battles without him? In the end they decided to construct a moveable dwelling which could be carried from place to place with God inside it. A plan was agreed. God appointed himself chief architect and instructed Moses on all the details for building, specifying measurements, materials, construction, finance, function and artistic design (Exod. 25).

At the bottom there was to be a small box, known as the Ark of the Covenant, made of *shittim* or acacia wood, covered in gold. Into this God required Moses to place the Ten Commandments – and later to add a pot of manna as well as Aaron's rod (Heb. 9:4). Above the Ark, God required a gold 'mercy-seat' (being a plate or lid) over which he could hover and, from time to time, issue proclamations to the Israelites. This seat was to be protected by the wings of two vast model creatures (possibly cherubim) between which God intended to have his dwelling (1 Sam. 4:4; 2 Sam 6:2).

This Ark, which became the most sacred shrine of ancient Israel, had an unusual history. Originally it was vaunted on poles, carried about wherever the Israelites wandered and treated as a lucky mascot in battles against the Gentiles. At one point it was captured by the Philistines but was eventually returned and moved for safekeeping to Jerusalem where it was held in Solomon's Temple until the Babylonians ransacked it in 587 BCE. The Ark has not been seen since then.

One legend from the first-century *Lives of the Prophets* relates how Jeremiah rescued the Ark *before* the Temple was destroyed and hid it in a rock in the wilderness somewhere between Mount Hor and Mount Nebo. 'In the rock,' we are told, 'with his finger he set as a seal the name of God, and the impression was like a carving made with iron, and cloud covered the name and no one knows the place nor is able to read the name to this day' (*Liv. Proph.* 2:14). The same story is also found in the Second Book of Maccabees (2:4–8) though Jeremiah himself hotly denied it when he declared in his own book that Jerusalem shall in future be called the 'Throne of the Lord' and that the Ark of the Covenant is an anachronism, an irrelevance, best forgotten (Jer. 3:16–17).

— 140 —

God's extraordinary love of the ark. – Even though the Ark of the Covenant was only 115cm x 69cm x 69cm in size (Exod. 25:10–11) – a tiny box-like dwelling – the Lord adored it and was prepared to go to any lengths to protect it from the grubby touch and peering gaze of his people. When it accidentally tipped sideways on a journey to Jerusalem, a man called Uzzah put out his hand to steady it and prevent a catastrophe. God was so enraged that he struck Uzzah dead (2 Sam. 6:1–8).

When the Philistines captured the Ark in battle they developed terrible haemorrhoids (swollen veins in the lining of their anuses) and, assuming the Ark to be responsible, decided to return it to the Israelites. At the border town of Bethshemesh, the Israelites were overjoyed to see their holy shrine returned, but celebrations were short-lived, for a couple of jubilant Israelites peeped inside the Ark and God in his fury, annihilated 50,000 of them.

To God the Ark was far more important than any number of human souls. In *Lives of the Prophets* it is revealed that on the Day of Judgement, 'the Ark will be the first to be resurrected and will come out of the rock [where Jeremiah hid it] and be placed on Mount Sinai and all the saints will be gathered to it' (*Liv. Proph.* 2:15).

—— 141 ——

House proud. –

God went to Moses and said: 'Speak to Aaron and tell him when he sets up those lamps to make sure they light up the front bit of the lamp-stand.' Aaron did this. He set up the lamps to the front of the lamp-stand as God had ordered. The lamp-stand was worked in beaten gold and its stem and petals were also of beaten gold. This lamp-stand had been designed according to a pattern that God had given Moses. (Num. 8:1–4)

—— 142 ——

Home in heaven. – Although God is supposed to be everywhere, he is especially omnipresent in heaven. Jesus advised his followers to pray to

'Our father which art in heaven', filling them with joyful hope that one day they might have a chance to visit and behold for themselves, a vision of God, up there, sitting in radiant splendour on a golden throne.

Traditionally heaven is located somewhere above the clouds. An upward view from the earth nowadays reveals only the sky, but to ancient eyes it was not the sky they saw when they looked above them, it was the *firmament*, a dome-like canopy stretching from one horizon to the next, with the sun, moon, stars and planets stuck to this side of it. Out of sight the firmament was thought to rest, at its ends, on granite pillars sunk into the peaks of distant mountains, while punctured in its surface were the millions of invisible holes through which celestial water was thought to drop onto the earth in the form of rain. On the other side, where the water comes from, there is a glorious lake of sapphire blue (Exod. 24:10; Ezek: 1:26) and this is the floor of the kingdom of God.

The Hebrew Bible divides the heavens into three sections, though most of the pseudepigraphical Hebrew scriptures insist there are seven heavens with God's dwelling in the seventh. To see God, visitors must pass through the six lesser heavens first. In the *Third Book of Enoch* the seventh heaven is itself divided into seven concentric palaces, each made of pure marble or sapphire. Different things are found in each, some of them are store rooms where snow and lightning are held, others contain records and archives or spirits like Wisdom, Peace and Fear of Heaven.

The central palace where God lives, known as the *Merkabah*, is like the centre of a beehive. God sits on his throne in radiant splendour surrounded by his fans, 'a thousand thousand waited on him, ten thousand times ten thousand stood before him' (Dan. 7:10); under his throne flows a great river of fire, symbolising the creative and destructive forces of God's divine judgement.

Other heavens are different and not all of them pleasant. Slavonic Enoch was given a guided tour. First he saw the storehouses of snow, ice and dew. In the second heaven he saw weeping angels. A hundred chirpy angels, delicious fruit and rivers of milk and honey were in the third, called Paradise, but in the northern region Enoch saw only torture and despair:

'Woe, woe! How very frightful this place is!' he cried, and his guiding angel explained:

> This place, Enoch, has been prepared for those who do not glorify God, who practice on the earth the sin which is against nature, which is child corruption in the anus in the manner of Sodom, of witchcraft, enchantments, divinations, trafficking with demons, boasting, stealing, lying, insulting, coveting, resentment, fornication, murder and seizing the poor by the throat. (*2 En.* 10:4)

The *Grigori* (two hundred lusty angels that had fornicated with human women) were found utterly dejected in the fifth heaven.

Rabbinic sources describe the first heaven, *Vilon*, as empty, while *Rakia*, the second, holds the sun, moon and stars; the third, *Shechakim*, is a food factory where the milling of manna takes place. In the fourth heaven, Jerusalem (splendidly rebuilt) is guarded over by Michael the archangel; *Maon*, the fifth heaven, is filled with hosts of angels, praising God by night and keeping silent by day so that God can hear the prayers of Israel; the sixth contains the snow, and *Aravoth*, the seventh heaven, is where God sits on his shining throne.

— 143 —

Hell on Earth. – The Jewish word for hell is *Gehenna*. It is derived from *Ge Hinnom* (the Valley of Hinnom), an eerie place to the south-west of Jerusalem. It was here that for six centuries rebellious Israelites hurled their children into the fires of Molech as a form of appeasement to a deity they feared. God tried to stop the practice in the fourteenth century BCE:

And thou shalt not let any of thy seed pass through the fire to

Molech. Whosoever he be that giveth any of his seed unto Molech; he shall surely be put to death: the people of the land shall stone him with stones. And if the people of the land do anyways hide their eyes from the man, when he giveth of his seed unto Molech and kill him not, then I will set my face against that man, and against his family, and will cut him off, and all that go a whoring after him, to commit whoredom with Molech. (Lev. 20:2–5)

Sacrificing one's own children must be a habit that is hard to break for seven hundred years later the fires were still blazing in the Valley of Hinnom. It took all the resource of a brave leader like Josiah (*c.* 640–609 BCE) to put an end to the evil once and for all. He turned the place into a rubbish tip. The putrid smells arising from the valley were so repulsive that no one dared go near. *Gehenna* became hell, while the modern concept of 'hellfire' was born from the memory of terrified children combusting.

— 144 —

God and the human sacrifice. – While the sacrificing of children to the Ammonite god, Molech, was frowned upon by Moses and eventually stamped out by Josiah, it is by no means certain that God disapproves of human sacrifice *per se.* After all he instructed Abraham to offer his son, Isaac, on a sacrificial pyre to prove that his fear of God was greater than the love of his son. That particular rite did not, in the end, take place, but others did. During a famine David allowed seven of Saul's descendants to be dismembered and sacrificed in order to appease God: 'After that God took pity on the country' (2 Sam. 21); Jepthah sacrificed his only daughter to God as a burnt offering, in gratitude for his help in defeating the Amonites (Judg. 11:29); and God, through an unnamed prophet, threatened to sacrifice priests on the altar at Bethel (1 Kings 13:2).

According to the Christian tradition, God sacrificed his only son,

174

Jesus Christ, upon the cross. But given that (according to the same tradition) Jesus is 'of one substance with the Father', and that after his death he 'ascended into heaven where he is seated at the right hand of the Father' from whence he will 'come again to judge the quick and the dead' (Nicene Creed), it is hard to understand how God, in this instance, can be said to have 'sacrificed' anything at all.

— 145 —

Which is bigger, heaven or hell? – At the Last Judgement it is said that God will choose only the 'elect' to join him in eternal life. 'Straight is the gate and narrow is the way', Jesus said (Matt. 7:14) and 'Many are called, but few are chosen' (Matt. 22:14). This theology presents a problem. If only a few super-righteous people manage to make it to heaven, most souls will presumably end up in hell. This means, not only that hell must be *bigger* than heaven, but that God (though omnipotent and infinitely good) has somehow managed to create a universe which is predominantly bad.

Drexelius (1581–1638), a German spiritual writer, argued that hell was not nearly as big as it seemed because the damned are packed into it at a rate of one billion to the square mile. This may solve the dispute about the relative spatial dimensions of heaven and hell, but not the question of numbers – the devil still appears to have more subjects in his dominion than God has in his. Is Satan therefore more powerful than God? Unthinkable!

SOLUTION: Reclaim the babies!

Until the twentieth century infant mortality accounted for at least 50 per cent of all deaths. Augustine declared that the souls of unbaptised babies were tainted with original sin and consequently damned the lot of them to the eternal torments of hell. But not everybody was happy about this. Part of the fun of going to heaven is that you can peer down from your lofty perch and gloat over the fate of the damned

175

(Isa. 66:22–4; Rev. 14:9–11), but most Christian parents are filled with horror at the prospect of watching their unbaptised offspring boiling in vats of white-hot excrement. Enough objection to Augustine's doctrine was thereby raised for it to be decided that the souls of unbaptised babies should be excluded from hell. Even then, some Christians still objected.

'Why should we goodly ones who have striven all our lives to follow in the ways of Our Lord, why should *we* have to share *our* eternal bliss with unbaptised babies? It's not fair! and what about Jesus' words "only a *few* are chosen"?'

A compromise had to be found. The babies could go to Limbo instead (or *limbus infantium*) which for Dante was within the walls of hell, but would later be moved to become a province of heaven – not the best part of course, that (Paradise) would still be reserved for the elect. In Limbo, unbaptised babies would miss out on God's 'beatific vision' but otherwise enjoy full and natural happiness.

So all is resolved. The divine dominions are indeed bigger and better populated than Satan's hell. If the vast majority of those in heaven are babies, who cares? At least they will be confined to the nursery wing, a safe distance, thank God, from the eternal pleasures of the chosen few.

— 146 —

Peter's hell (the highlights). –

There were those who were hanging by their tongues; they were the blasphemers, and under them was laid fire, blazing and tormenting them. And there was a great lake full of burning mire in which were fixed certain men who had turned away from righteousness, and tormenting angels were placed over them. And there were women hanging by their hair over that boiling mire. These were they who had adorned themselves for adultery. The men who had united with them were hanging by their feet with their heads in the mire, crying out with loud voices, 'We did not believe that we would end up here.'

And I saw the murderers and their accomplices cast into a gorge of venomous reptiles, snakes and worms tormenting them in their torture. And near that place I saw another gorge in which the piss and shit of the tortured had run down the edge and formed a lake of stinking excrement. And there sat women and the filth came right up to their throats; and opposite them sat many children, who were born prematurely, weeping. And from them shot forth rays of fire that smote the women in their eyes. These were the women who had conceived children outside marriage and who procured abortions. And the milk of the mothers oozes from their breasts, congeals and smells foul, and from it come forth beasts that devour flesh.

Near to these are other men and women who chew their tongues and are tormented with red hot irons which are poked into their eyes. These are the slanderous, those who doubt my righteousness. And beside them were other men and women who had glowing rods and smote one another and had no rest from this torture, and near to them others who were burned and turned in the fire and were baked. These were those that had forsaken the way of God. (drawn from the Greek and Ethiopic versions of the *Apocalypse of Peter*, c. 135 CE)

— 147 —

Favourite number. – It took God six days to create the universe and everything in it. On the seventh day he rested. The seven-day creation period has led millions to suppose that 7 must be a sacred number, favoured by God. It is also the most likely reason why there are seven days in a week. But why did the creation take seven days? If God is truly omnipotent he could surely have accomplished the task in less than a second if he really wanted. The answer has deep roots which may require concentration. Follow this:

Ancient Sumerians (some 6000 years ago) invented a system of counting using (instead of Base 10, the decimal system), Base 60 (the sexegisimal system). The reason they preferred 60 to 10 has to do with their ancient way of counting. Using the fingers of the right hand they counted the joints, or phalanges, of each finger by pointing with the thumb. Thus the Sumerian was able, on market days, to haggle his way up to 12 using only his right hand. If a higher number were required he could raise the fingers of his left to count off the twelves. In this way, the number 39, for instance, could be shown by waving 3 fingers of the left hand (36) while the thumb of the right indicated the third phalange of his little finger (3), making a total of 39. The highest number of the system, represented by all 5 fingers of the left hand, was 60 and the symbol for 60 was the raised clenched fist of the left hand.

Thus the number 60 became associated with wholeness and physical unity. Sooner or later, the Sumerians would attach divine significance to this number. Anu, their Creator God, was represented by the number 60 while lesser gods were allotted lesser numbers, with precedence given to those whose numbers divided into 60. The first sacred numbers were 1, 2, 3, 4, 5 and 6, but 7 was deemed to be 'evil' since it would not divide into 60 – so evil in fact that the Sumerians refused to lift a finger or do any work at all on the 7th, 14th, 21st and 28th days of each month in case it brought them bad luck.

This whole system was inherited, lock, stock and barrel, by the Babylonians, who occupied the same territory as the Sumerians (an area of southern Iraq between Baghdad and the Persian Gulf) and may even have been their descendants. In the Babylonian *Epic of Gilgemesh*, Hell (Hades) is divided into seven sections, the pit of the interior was the seventh. In 597 BCE, the Babylonian King, Nebuchadnezzar, captured Jerusalem dragging thousands of Jews (Judaeans) back to Babylon. For several generations Jews were held there and forced to work on seventh days. Not surprisingly they detested the Babylonians, dreaming ruefully of one day smashing their babies' heads against the rocks (Ps. 137:9).

Perhaps they blamed their ill-fortune on the very fact that they were made to work on the cursed 'seventh' days.

'When we get out of here,' they told themselves, 'we shall make the seventh day a holy day. No one shall be made to toil on the seventh day again. In fact it shall be strictly forbidden to do so.' Most of the book of Genesis was written during the period of Babylonian exile (586–538 BCE) and possibly after that. To highlight the differences between themselves and their Babylonian oppressors, Jewish scribes reversed the significance of the number seven. From being the 'evil' number to the Babylonians it became a holy number to the Jews.

The Babylonian concept of seven hells was inverted, and Jews proclaimed a belief in seven heavens. In this spirit of rebellion the Law of Deuteronomy was written: 'Thou shalt not do any work, thou, nor thy son, nor thy daughter, nor thy manservant, nor thine ox, nor thine ass, nor any of thy cattle, nor thy stranger that is within thy gates' (Deut. 5:14). The framework of the story of the creation (Gen. 1–2) was borrowed, in part, from Babylonian myths to which the captive Judaeans added a significant extra line of their own. The line had played no part in the Babylonian original. Perhaps it was put there as a snub: 'And on the seventh day God ended his work which he had made; and he rested on the seventh day. And God blessed the seventh day, and sanctified it: because in it he had rested from all his work which God created and made' (Gen. 2:2–3).

— 148 —

Word of caution. – It has been suggested (both by Jewish and Gentile scholars) that many of the laws, customs and beliefs of ancient Judaism have their roots in a wilful desire to establish a religion that would be seen as the diametric opposite of all other existing religions. *Profana illic omnia quae apud nos sacra*, wrote the Roman historian Tacitus, *rursum concessa apud illos quae nobis incesta* – 'Everything we hold sacred, they [the Jews] judge to be profane while they approve everything which to us is prohibited.' 'The Egyptians worship many animals and monstrous images,' he continued 'the Jews conceive of one god, and with the mind only: they regard those who make representations of god in man's image as impious.' Tacitus claimed that the Jews started sacrificing bulls only to ridicule the Egyptian worship of the bull-god, Apis; similarly they sacrificed rams *in contumeliam Amonis* – to mock the god Amun.

God dictated the Law to Moses on Mount Sinai, and it is remarkable that so many of his admonitions were consciously opposed to practices of neighbouring tribes. The prohibition against cooking a kid in its mother's milk, for instance (Exod. 23:19), was probably motivated by a desire to stamp on a dish favoured by the archrivals of the Israelites, the Canaanites. Goat kid in milk is, to this day, a special treat for the Lebanese gourmet who calls it *laban 'ummu* ('milk of its mother'). The milk stews with the fat of the kid to produce a sauce of magnificent nut-brown clusters that was believed, at one time, to enhance human fertility.

God may not have wished this excellent food to be proscribed at all. We must be cautious here, for often, when we think we are learning important and interesting things about God, we are actually focusing on something entirely different – in this case the contrariness of a handful of ancient Jewish priests.

V

Justice

Squabbles concerning the virgin birth. – In the early centuries of Christianity arguments and counter-arguments were batted back and forth to prove or disprove Mary's virginity; at times it appeared that the very survival of Christianity was dependent solely on its outcome. Groups – long since extinct – with names that mean nothing to us now, argued till faces were purple and voices hoarse with shouting. Apollinarians denied even that Mary was Jesus' mother. The Cerinthians and the Ebionites swore that Joseph was Jesus' father while the Antidocomarians insisted on the virgin conception but denied the virgin birth and flatly rejected the doctrine of perpetual virginity that is still espoused by Catholics today.

Reaction against the Antidocomarians led to a vicious backlash from the Collyridians who, in defence of Mary, set up an idolatrous practice offering to her statue little cakes called *collyrides* which afterwards they ate themselves. The Collyridians were one of many sects that were judged guilty by the established churches of the heresy of Mariolatry ('the sin of rendering to the Blessed Virgin Mary that worship which is due to God'). Meanwhile the issue of Mary's virginity (perpetual or otherwise) has never been concluded to the satisfaction of all parties.

The Muslim conception of Jesus. – While Christian theologians have battled to prove Mary's virginity in order to show that Jesus was the son of God, Muslims (who revere Jesus as a Prophet of Islam) have contented themselves with the view that Jesus was born of a virgin and that was a miracle, but steadfastly reject the inference that he was therefore the son of God or that he was in any way divine.

In the Qur'an, God sent Gabriel to Mary 'in the shape of a perfect man', some say to raise an emotion that would aid her in conception. In the event, Gabriel 'blew into the bosom of her shift' which he opened with his fingers while his breath floated down to her womb and caused her to conceive.

— 151 —

Ubiquitous slander. – In the early days of Christianity, when every cult and every sect of every religion was anxious to do the other down, it was common practice to dish the dirt and receive it back with interest. This was not just a matter of Christians slandering Jews or ancient pagans insulting the new religions, there was infighting too, as Celsus reported in 178 CE:

> Christians, it is needless to say, utterly detest each other, they slander each other constantly with the vilest forms of abuse, and cannot come to any sort of agreement in their teaching. Each sect fills the head of its own with deceitful nonsense and makes perfect little pigs of those it wins over to its side.

The Jews meanwhile bitterly complained of the 'Blood Libel', a common slander which accused them of using the blood of Christian children to bake *Matzah* for their Passover feasts. Jews were also falsely suspected of using Christian blood to anoint rabbis, to soothe sore eyes, to prevent menstrual flow and to conceal their own body odours. The Christians were similarly slandered. Marcus Cornelius Fronto, a Roman rhetorician (*c.* 100–166), described one particularly nasty Christian rite:

A young baby is covered over with flour, the object being to deceive the unwary. It is then served before the person to be admitted to the rites. The recruit is urged to inflict blows onto it which appear to be harmless because of the covering of flour. Thus the baby is killed with wounds that remain unseen and concealed. It is the blood of this infant – I shudder to mention it – it is the blood that they lick with their thirsty lips; the limbs they distribute eagerly; this is the victim by which they seal the covenant.

Epiphanius was similarly disgusted by an early Christian sect called the Phibionites:

The woman and the man take the fluid of the emission of the man into their hands, they stand, turn toward heaven, their hands besmeared by uncleanness, and pray saying: 'We offer to thee this gift, the body of Christ,' and then they eat it, their own ugliness . . . Similarly also with the woman when she happens to be in the flowing of the blood, they gather the blood of menstruation of her uncleanness and eat it together and say, 'This is the blood of Christ'.

—— 152 ——

Jesus' three possible fathers. – The question of Jesus' paternity has been hotly debated through the ages. There are three main candidates: Joseph (Mary's husband), Joseph ben-Pandera (a lusty soldier) and God. If either Joseph (Mary's husband) or Joseph ben-Pandera (the soldier) had been Jesus' father it would stand to reason that Mary could not have been a virgin as Christians and Muslims believe. However, if the miracle of the virgin conception and birth of Jesus could be *proved*, then, of the three, God would be the most likely to have fathered him – for it is conceded by all (is it not?) that God is the best at miracles.

— 153 —

The case for Joseph ben-Pandera. – Celsus, in a mock challenge to Jesus asked:

Is it not true, good sir, that you fabricated the story of your birth from a virgin to quiet rumours about the true unsavoury circumstances of your origins? Is it not the case that far from being born in David's royal city of Bethlehem, you were born in a poor country town, and of a woman who earned her living by spinning? Is it not the case that when her deceit was discovered, to wit, that she was pregnant by a Roman soldier called Pandera she was driven away by her husband the carpenter – and convicted of adultery? Indeed is it not so that in her disgrace, wandering far from home, she gave birth to a male child in silence and humiliation?

Celsus was writing in 178 CE, not long after (or possibly at the same time) as some of the evangelists were writing their gospels. It is not known how long before that, the rumours of Mary and ben-Pandera might have started. The Jewish Talmud contains scattered references to a Jeschu ben-Pandera (sometimes Panthera or Pandira) as well as to a Jeschu ben Strada, both names, it has been suggested, signify 'son of a whore'. Scholars, however, have pointed out that Jeschu (Jesus in its Hellenized form) was an extremely common Jewish name. For Jesus ben-Pandera and Jesus ben-Strada to be the same persons as the Jesus favoured by the Christian world would require revising the accepted date for Christ's birth back a hundred years to about 102 BCE.

Whatever the truth, it seems certain that the Jewish *Toldoth Jeschu* (History of Jesus), purporting to be about Jesus of Nazareth, has its roots in the Talmud stories and is therefore likely to have been built on the foundations of mistaken identity. In a *Toldoth Jeschu* manuscript held at the library of the University of Strasbourg, Jesus' conception is described thus:

His mother was Miriam [Mary] a daughter of Israel. She had a betrothed of the royal race of the house of David, whose name was Jochanan [Joseph]. He was learned in the law and feared heaven greatly. Near the door of her house, just opposite, dwelt a handsome man; Joseph ben-Pandera cast his eye upon her. It was at night, on the eve of the Sabbath, when drunken he crossed over to her door and entered in to her. But she thought in her heart that it was her betrothed Jochanan; she hid her face and was ashamed. He embraced her; but she said to him: 'Touch me not for I am in my separation.' He took no heed thereat, nor regarded her words, but persisted. She conceived by him.

Although Mary is portrayed as reluctantly taken against her will (not as a whore), it is clear that the intention of this passage is to mock the Christian belief that Jesus was miraculously conceived by the Holy Ghost in the womb of the virgin Mary. Adding details of Pandera's drunkenness, Mary's menstruation and the fact of her being married to another man, are carefully aimed slanders against Jesus. But there is a flaw – Mary should not have been able to conceive 'in her separation'. Is the writer suggesting that she lied to avoid sexual intercourse? Is he confused or might he be lying himself? What do you think?

— 154 —

The case for God. – Jesus' virgin birth (which more correctly should be termed his virgin conception) was, according to the Christians, foreseen by the prophet Isaiah when he wrote: 'Therefore the Lord himself shall give you a sign. Behold a virgin shall conceive, and bear a son, and shall call his name Immanuel' (Isa. 7:14). The evangelists Matthew (1:18–25) and Luke (1:26–38) seized on this passage as hard evidence that Jesus was indeed born of a virgin, but they overlooked two crucial points. First, Isaiah said that his name shall be Immanuel, not Jesus; second, the Hebrew word *almah* which so many Bibles have mistranslated as 'virgin' literally means 'young woman' not 'virgin'. Even if the Hebrew word for virgin had been used, the term might have applied only at the moment when the prophet spoke. In other words, what Isaiah may have been saying was, 'A babe called Immanuel shall be born of a girl who is presently a virgin.'

Luke, however, had further details to add regarding Jesus' conception. The nature of the act itself, he said, was revealed to Mary by the angel Gabriel: 'The Holy Spirit will come upon you, and the power of the Most High will cover you with its shadow' (Luke 1:35).

According to the Odists, Jesus was conceived when Mary drank a concoction of milk from the two breasts of the Father, mixed together in the open bosom of the Holy Spirit, who is traditionally female (*Odes Sol.* 19:4). *The Protevangelium of James*, an ancient infancy gospel, once held to be the work of Jesus' brother, is less explicit preferring a view of the conception akin to that of Luke, but the book provides interesting evidence, which does not appear elsewhere, to show that Mary remained *virgo intacta*, even *after* the birth of Jesus. In James' version of the tale Mary gave birth in a cave. A midwife was present and a lady called Salome hovered nearby. At first a dark cloud overshadowed them, but this was soon followed by a bright light. When the light subsided the infant Jesus was revealed.

'Salome, Salome,' yelled the midwife 'I have a new sight to tell you. A virgin has brought forth a thing which her nature does not allow.'

Salome was suspicious: 'Unless I put forward my finger and test her condition, I will not believe that a virgin has brought forth,' she said.

And the midwife went in and said to Mary: 'Make yourself ready for there is no small commotion concerning you.' And when Mary heard this, she made herself ready. And Salome put forward her finger to test her condition. And she cried out, saying, 'Woe for my wickedness and my unbelief; for I have tempted the living God, and behold, my hand falls away from me, consumed by fire!'

Using miracles to prove a point is an ancient religious manoeuvre. Some may be convinced that God is the father of Jesus on the strength of this testimony; others, like the philosopher Denis Diderot, were less impressed: 'If the religion which you proclaim is true,' he argued, 'its truth can be demonstrated by unanswerable arguments. Find these arguments. Why plague me with miracles when you only need a syllogism to convince me? Do you find it easier to make a cripple stand upright than to enlighten me?' (*Pensées Philosophiques*, 50).

— 155 —

The case for Joseph (Mary's husband). – The main evidence that neither God nor ben-Pandera, but Joseph (Mary's husband) was the natural father of Jesus is provided by the gospels and Paul's letter to the Romans. Matthew stated that Joseph 'took his wife, but knew her not until she had borne a son' (Matt. 1:24–5). 'Knowing' in this sense means 'having sexual intercourse with' – the word is used many times in this context throughout the Bible. While Matthew's evidence does not conclusively prove that Joseph was Jesus' father it does at least *imply* that Mary had sexual relations with Joseph after the birth of Jesus and was not therefore a 'perpetual virgin' as she is held to be by the Catholic Church. This same point was underpinned by Luke who stated that when Jesus was born, Mary gave birth to 'her first-born son', leaving the reader to assume that she went on to have more children afterwards – presumably by Joseph.

If all the brothers and sisters of Jesus referred to in the New Testament (1 Cor. 9:4–5; Mark 3:31–5; Mark 6:3 and Matt. 12:46–50) are indeed the children of Mary by Joseph, then Joseph's paternity of Jesus looks ever more likely. The fact that both Luke and Matthew print genealogies in their gospels to prove Joseph's descent from King David (Matt. 1:1–17 and Luke 3:23–38) is also revealing.

The evangelists wanted to show that Jesus' birth fulfilled an ancient scriptural prophecy – a promise made by God to David: 'I will set up

189

thy seed after thee, which shall proceed out of thy bowels, and I will establish his kingdom. He shall build an house for my name, and I will establish the throne of his kingdom for ever. I will be his father and he will be my son' (2 Sam. 7:12–14). Matthew and Luke were determined to prove that Jesus was the 'seed that proceeded out of David's bowels' and was therefore the fulfilment of God's promise.

Paul, who is thought to have sent his letter to the Romans long before the gospels were written (possibly as early as 55 CE) insisted that Jesus was 'descended from David according to the flesh' (Rom. 1:3–4). This seems unequivocal. The following scriptural quotations should also be taken into account:

- 'Is not this the carpenter's son?' (Matt. 13:55)
- 'Is not this Joseph's son?' (Luke 4:23)
- 'Is not this Jesus, the son of Joseph, whose father and mother we know?' (John 6:42)
- 'We have found him of whom Moses in the Law and the prophets did write, Jesus of Nazareth, son of Joseph.' (John 1:45)
- 'His father was a carpenter and made at the time ploughs and yokes . . . the child Jesus said to his father Joseph.' (*I.S. Thom.* 13:1)

It would seem that at the time when these scriptures were being written, Jesus was decisively held to be the natural and legitimate son of Joseph by Mary his mother. Cerinthus, a Gnostic who flourished around 100 CE, agreed with this claiming that Jesus' magical powers had come about through the descent of the Holy Spirit at his baptism. The Gospel of John is thought by some to have been written as a refutation of Cerinthus, in the event John was beatified while Cerinthus was dismissed as a heretic.

— 156 —

Divine paternity. – In the olden days unexplained pregnancies were blamed on fertile lavatory seats or otherwise deemed to be the acts of gods. Modern wisdom teaches us to dismiss the lavatory seat option as nonsense but the question as to whether gods are capable of producing offspring by acts of sexual union with mortal human beings remains open. Tertullian, Josephus, Philo and other distinguished figures of the past, believed that certain devils, attracted by beautiful hair, were able to impregnate young girls through their ears, which was possibly why St Paul advised all women to cover their heads (1 Cor. 11). In the past, experts on this delicate subject have all agreed that a male god has a greater chance of conceiving with a mortal female than does a male human with a female goddess, as the historian Plutarch once observed: 'The fact of the intercourse of a male god with mortal women is conceded by all, but it is not believed that mortal man can occasion pregnancy and birth in a goddess, because the stuff of which gods are made is air and spirit, lacking vital forms of warmth and moisture.' The book of Genesis reveals that 'the sons of God came in unto the daughters of men, and they bore children to them' (Gen. 6:1–2).

In the Christian religion there is only one god who has only one son – namely Jesus Christ – but this notion is blasphemy to the Jews and Muslims who accuse the Christians of worshipping more than one god, counting the Christian Trinity of Father, Son and Holy Ghost (or Mary, according to the Qur'an), as three. The Jews deny any possibility that Jesus might be a son of God citing in particular God's words to Isaiah (Isa. 44:6): 'I am the first; I am the last and beside Me there is no God,' which is interpreted by the Rabbis as meaning 'I am the first' since I have no father, 'I am the last' since I have no son, 'And beside me there is no God' since I have no brother. Islam is equally opposed to the Christian blasphemy: 'It is not meet for God that he should have any son: God forbid!' (Qur'an 19:36).

— 157 —

In good company. – Any self-respecting list of celebrities miraculously born of a virgin mother ought to include the following: Jesus, Krishna, Buddha, Horus, Ra, Romulus and Remus, Lao-tze, Confucius, Zoroaster, Bacchus, Attis, Adonis, Mithra, Mahamaya, Quirinus, Julius Caesar, Alexander the Great, Plato and Pythagoras. Of these, Attis, Buddha, Bacchus, Horus, Krishna, Mithra, Adonis and Jesus all celebrated their birthdays on 25 December. This should tell us something about God's most fertile time of year.

— 158 —

Trial. – First witness: God.

WISDOM: Do you have a son?

GOD: 'Israel is my son, my first-born' (Exod. 4:22).

WISDOM: Yes, but is there another?

GOD: 'When Israel was a child, then I loved him, and called my son out of Egypt' (Hos. 11:1).

WISDOM: Which son do you mean? We know that Israel was in Egypt and that Israel, as you say, was your child, but *Jesus* went to Egypt too, don't you remember? He went there with Joseph and his mother to escape the slaughters of Herod. The evangelist thinks Jesus is the 'son you called out of Egypt' (Matt. 2:14). Is that right? I repeat my question: Do you have another son?

GOD: David, yes: 'David is my son. I told him so the day I begat him' (Ps. 2:7).

WISDOM: OK, David, yes, there's David, and there's Israel, your first-born, but what about—

GOD: 'Ephraim is my first-born son' (Jer. 31.9).

WISDOM: Ephraim? You just said *Israel* was your oldest son, not Ephraim!

GOD: 'Is Ephraim my dear son? Is he a pleasant child? For since I spake against him, I do earnestly remember him still: therefore my bowels are troubled for him' (Jer. 31:20).

WISDOM: Listen, I am not interested in Ephraim or your bowels right now. I am trying to find out if you have another son. You know, the one that also went to Egypt. Oh come on. Do you have another son – yes or no?

GOD: Oh, you mean Joseph?

WISDOM: [*exasperated*] I do not mean Joseph, no. He was the son of Jacob.

GOD: Only there was an Egyptian virgin, Asenath was her name. Oh what a bore she was! Wanted to marry Joseph, but he was an Israelite so naturally he wouldn't touch her at first. I think his rejection gave her anorexia. Anyway, she started praying to *me*, she was blubbing her head off, burning with shame; said she had sinned against me. 'I have fallen in error unwittingly' she jibbered 'and spoken blasphemous words against my lord Joseph, for I did not know (the miserable one that I am) that he is *your* son. People told me that Joseph is the shepherd's son from the land of Canaan and I, the miserable one, have come to believe them and fall in error' (*Jos. Asen.* 13:14).

WISDOM: Well? Was Joseph your son then?

GOD: Of course he bloody well wasn't. I told you, she was hysterical. The people were right. He was the shepherd's son from Canaan. Perhaps he misled her, I don't know! His father, Jacob, was a terrible liar too (Gen. 27:24), so was his great-grandfather, Abraham (Gen. 12 and 20) and his sons (Gen. 34:13) – lying obviously runs in the family.

WISDOM: What about *Jesus*, though? Was he, or was he not your son?

GOD: Some people say he was.

WISDOM: And you? What do you say?

GOD: I have not spoken.

WISDOM: Oh yes you have. You told Jesus at his baptism – and

I quote – 'You are my son, the Beloved; my favour rests with you' (Mark 1:11).

GOD: That was a voice from heaven. You cannot prove it was me.

WISDOM: Why did you subsequently tell the Prophet Muhammad that Jesus was definitely not your son (Qur'an 19:36)?

GOD: Did I?

WISDOM: Did you?

GOD: Ask him yourself.

WISDOM: Call for the Prophet Muhammad!

CLERK: He cannot be found, m'Lady.

WISDOM: Well, where the hell is he then?

DANTE: Precisely, Madam, in hell.

WISDOM: How do you know?

DANTE: I saw him there a few moments ago. 'From the chin down to the fart-hole split as by a cleaver. His tripes hung by his heels; the pluck and spleen showed with the liver and the sordid sack which turns to dung the food it swallows in—' (*L'Inferno*, 8:22)

WISDOM: Yes, yes. Spare us the details. Why is the Prophet in hell?

DANTE: For claiming that Jesus was not the Son of God, m'Lady.

WISDOM: I see. Get Jesus then.

—— 159 ——

Second witness: Jesus. – Then said they unto Jesus, 'Art thou then the Son of God?' And he said unto them, 'Ye say that I am' (King James Bible, Douay-Rheims Bible; Darby Bible); 'It is you who say I am' (New Jerusalem Bible); 'You say it, because I am' (Young's Literal; World English Bible); 'It is as you say, I am He' (Weymouth New Testament); 'Yes, I am' (New American Standard Bible) (Luke 22:70).

Thank you, thank you. You may stand down.

— 160 —

Philip's scientific opinion. –

WISDOM: Some say that Mary conceived by the Holy Spirit, do you agree with them?

PHILIP: They are in error! They do not know what they are saying! When did a woman ever conceive by a woman (*Gos. Phil.*, Log. 17a)?

WISDOM: So you believe the Holy Spirit is a woman, but what about God, *the Father?* As one of the disciples of Jesus, what can you tell us about his paternity?

PHILIP: The Lord would not have said 'My Father who art in heaven' if he had not also another father; but he would have said simply, 'My Father' (*Gos. Phil.*, Log. 17c).

WISDOM: So you think that God is *one* of Jesus' fathers? One among many perhaps?

PHILIP: 'All who are begotten in the world are begotten of nature – The perfect conceive through a kiss and give birth. Because of this we also kiss one and other. We receive conception from the grace which we have among us' (*Gos. Phil.*, Log. 30 and 31).

WISDOM: Yes, thank you. That is quite enough of that. You may stand down.

— 161 —

What the centurion said. – Among the Evangelists there is much disagreement as to who was present at the crucifixion. According to John, Mary (Jesus' mother) was there, as was Mary Magdalene and Mary (wife of Clopas). Matthew, on the other hand, mentions only Mary Magdalene and Mary, mother of James and Joses. It has been debated whether Mary (the mother of James and Joses) was the same

195

Mary as Mary (mother of Jesus) or another Mary altogether. Those who claim they are one and the same, cite Mark 6:3: 'Is this not the carpenter, the son of Mary and brother of James and Joses and Judas and Simon?' If they are indeed the same person why then did Matthew and Mark not describe her simply as 'Mary, mother of Jesus'?

According to one theory Matthew and Mark were trying not to trivialise the words of a centurion who three of the four evangelists suppose to have witnessed the crucifixion. Mark claimed that this same centurion later reported Jesus' death to Pilate (Mark 15:45). We know nothing else about this man, who he was, or where he came from. Perhaps he was put into the story simply to please the Romans. All that is written is what he was supposed to have said on seeing Jesus crucified: 'Truly this man was the son of God' (Mark 15:39; Matt. 27:54). Hardly proof, but something to chew on. John, in his version, makes no record of a centurion being present at all, while Luke quotes him only as saying, 'Truly, this was an upright man' (Luke 23:47).

— 162 —

What the madmen said. – There were some unattractive men who, according to the gospel of Mark, were possessed by demons and knew Jesus to be the son of God. One of them, a Gerasene demoniac called Legion, howled and gashed himself with stones and, when he saw Jesus coming, shrieked at him: 'What do you want with me, Jesus, son of the Most High God? In God's Name do not torture me!' (Mark 5:7). There were other 'uncleans' too who would prostrate themselves whenever they spotted Jesus shouting enthusiastically after him: 'You are the Son of God; you are the Son of God.' Many may feel that the testimony of mad demoniacs is not worth presenting, but as Mark Twain once observed: 'When we remember that we are all mad, mysteries disappear and life stands explained.'

—— 163 ——

Thomas Paine's point (1794). –

When I am told that a woman called the Virgin Mary, said, or gave out, that she was with child without any cohabitation with a man, and that her betrothed husband, Joseph, said that an angel told him so, I have a right to believe them or not; such a circumstance required a much stronger evidence than their bare word for it; but we have not even this – for neither Joseph nor Mary wrote any such matter themselves; it is only reported by others that they said so – it is hearsay upon hearsay, and I do not choose to rest my belief upon such evidence. (*Age of Reason*, I)

—— 164 ——

The summing up. –

WISDOM: There are those who believe that Jesus was the son of God, and there are those who say he was not. We seem to have ignored the fact that Jesus referred to himself at least forty times in the New Testament as 'Son of Man'. Nevermind, as Horace Walpole wrote of genealogy, 'who begat whom, is the most amusing form of hunting' and, that being so, we have to concede, on this occasion, that the fox has got away but we have all had a good time on the field, have we not?

Unfortunately, no one was actually holding the candle at Jesus' conception and so we are left to untangle an impenetrable knot of contrary evidence with no hope whatsoever of obtaining a clean, clear result. It is, as Mr Paine rightly points out, nothing but hearsay upon hearsay.

I would like to put it on record that God himself was a singularly unhelpful witness and were it not that he is Supreme Ruler of the

Universe I would have him up for contempt of court. As it is we are left only to guess who really fathered Jesus. Was it her husband all along or did the angel Gabriel have anything to do with it? Did that old rogue ben-Pandera break into Mary's chamber and force himself upon her? Or was it all done in some mysterious way by the Holy Spirit? God only knows!

Case dismissed!

VI

Pipes and Whistles

Three in one. – On 20 May 325 CE, the Christian church officially acknowledged that God was one substance consisting of three emanations or manifestations, an indivisible Trinity, made up of the Father, the Son (Jesus or the Word) and the Holy Ghost. The discovery of God's tripartite structure was made by a wily Alexandrian bishop's secretary called Athanasius, at Nicea (now Iznik, North West Turkey) and introduced into the dogma of Christendom with the full support of Emperor Constantine I.

The only serious objections came from Arius, a Libyan presbyter, whose opinion that Jesus could not possibly be eternal is now pilloried as the heresy of Arianism. Arius's point, though, was that if Jesus *had* been the son of God, he must, by definition, have been born *after* his father and therefore, at some time or other, he did not exist at all. Arius stuck to his logic, stubbornly refusing to endorse the Trinity and was promptly dismissed into exile.

As it happened the trinity idea was not exactly 'revealed' to Athanasius, nor did he glean it from the scriptures, where it is never mentioned; rather he, and his boss, Bishop Alexander, worked it out as the best solution to a seemingly irreconcilable problem: 'How can we claim to believe that there is only one god if we go about saying that Jesus was also divine? And what about the Holy Ghost? Surely we shall be accused of worshipping three gods if we carry on like this?' Everything was resolved in Athanasius's famous creed:

I believe in one God, the Father Almighty, maker of all things visible and invisible, and in one Lord Jesus Christ, the son of God, the only-begotten of the Father, that is, of the substance of the Father, God from God, light from light, true God from true God, begotten not made, of one substance with the Father . . . And I believe in the Holy Spirit.

The Athanasian solution was sublimely simple and uniquely belligerent. Instead of renouncing belief in the divinity of Jesus (as Arius had) Athanasius boldly asserted, 'I believe in all three, and all three are one.' The statement, of course, is meaningless; but was ratified, nevertheless, at the Council of Nicea and, with a few delicate reinterpretations, has endured as a central plank of the Christian message ever since. From the Christian point of view, the holy Trinity is not supposed to be a logical structure. It is a poetic and mysterious procession, consciously reflecting the infinite, ineffable nature of God. To Jews and Muslims, however, the Trinity is not monotheistic, it reveals nothing about the true nature of God and is profoundly blasphemous.

— 166 —

Understanding the Trinity. – Bernard, twelfth-century Abbot of Clairvaux, asked himself about the Trinity: 'How can plurality consist with unity, or unity with plurality? To *examine* the fact closely is rashness, to *believe* it is piety, to *know* it is life, and life eternal.' Very well, but how are we supposed to *know* it, if we are not allowed to *examine* it in the first place? The answer is *faith,* blind faith engendered by transcendental meditation of the kind which inspires ecstasy and reaps divine knowledge.

The only people who have ever claimed to understand the Trinity are of course *Christian* mystics. Jewish and Muslim mystics (however deep and ecstatic their trances) have so far failed to glimpse the Trinity, for God refuses to reveal his three-in-one secret to those who do not believe in it in the first instance. Those that *have* succeeded in grasping the ungraspable, have not been helpful in explaining their discoveries to others. Thus Teresa of Avila recounts:

Our Lord made me comprehend in what way it is that one God can be in three persons. He made me see it so clearly that I remained as extremely surprised as I was comforted; and now, when I think of the holy Trinity, or hear it spoken of, I understand how the three adorable persons form only one God and I experience an unspeakable happiness.

Leaving us none the wiser!

— 167 —

Thinking in threes. – The Assyrians believed that male children were produced by the sperm of the right testicle (*Anu*) while sperm from the left was responsible for females (*Hoa*). Asher was the male god in the middle, heroically symbolised by the stiff penis, and thus *Asher-Anu-Hoa* became a three-in-one God of fertility. Nobody knows for certain if the divine Hindu trilogy, *Trimurti*, predates the Assyrian fertility triad or not. The *Trimurti* comprises Brahma, the father and creator; Vishnu, the Son and preserver; and Siva, the Holy Spirit and destroyer, 'In those three Persons the one God was shown/Each first in place, each last, not one alone/Of Siva, Vishnu, Brahma, each may be/First second third among the Blessed Three.'

Three-in-one-Gods were discovered by Christian explorers in Peru in 1610. 'It is strange that the Divell after his manner hath brought a trinitie into idolatry,' reported Father Joseph de Acosta, a Catholic missionary, on finding a tribe of Peruvians worshipping Churunti, Apomti and Intiquaoqui as one god. Little did he realise that by 1610 there had been hundreds of divine trinities all over the world – Egypt, Persia, Greece, India, Phoenicia, Mexico and Scandinavia all had them – his was probably one of the last.

— 168 —

The Holy Spirit explained. – Understanding the Christian trilogy is hard enough, but has not been made any easier by the presence in it of the Holy Spirit. God the Father is not literally a 'father' in the human sense, he is a *spirit* and a *holy* one at that. So in what ways is God the Father (holy spirit) different from *the* Holy Spirit?

DICTIONARY DEFINITION: Holy Spirit: The Third Person of the Holy Trinity, distinct from, but consubstantial, coequal, and coeternal with the Father and the Son, and in the fullest sense God. It is held that the mode of the Spirit's procession in the Godhead is by way of 'spiration' (not 'generation') and that this procession takes place as a single principle. (*Oxford Dictionary of the Christian Church*)

Still not clear? You will be! The Catholic Catechism is extremely helpful:

Now God's Spirit, who reveals God, makes known to us Christ, his Word, his living Utterance, but the Spirit does not speak of himself. The Spirit who 'has spoken through the prophets' makes us hear the Father's Word, but we do not hear the Spirit himself. We know him only in the movement by which he reveals the Word to us and disposes us to welcome him in faith. The Spirit of truth who 'unveils' Christ to us will not speak on his own. (*Catechism of the Catholic Church*, 687)

Good, that explains that! Now we may progress from the *whats* to the *whys*:

Now God's Spirit, who reveals God [*why?*] makes known to us

204

Christ, his Word, his living Utterance [*why?*], but the Spirit does not speak of himself [*why?*]. The Spirit who 'has spoken through the prophets' makes us hear the Father's Word [*why?*] but we do not hear the Spirit himself [*why?*]. We know him only in the movement by which he reveals the Word to us and disposes us to welcome him in faith [*why?*]. The Spirit of truth who 'unveils' Christ to us will not speak on his own [*why?*].

Answers on a postcard please!

—— 169 ——

Fatal divisions. – In the fifth century CE a man called Nestorius, patriarch of Constantinople, had a quarrel with a man called Cyril, patriarch of Alexandria. Nestorius was convinced that Jesus was two persons (God and man) miraculously joined as one – Cyril wasn't. Nestorius should have known better than to argue with Cyril, for not long before a philosopher and mathematician called Hypatia had suggested that Cyril was talking rubbish only to be greeted by Cyril's lynch-mob in the street. According to Gibbon she was 'torn from her chariot, stripped naked, dragged to the church and inhumanely butchered by Peter the Reader and a troop of savage and merciless fanatics: her flesh was scraped from her bones with sharp oyster shells and her quivering limbs were delivered to the flames' (*Decline and Fall of the Roman Empire*, 47).

Nestorius's fate was not as gruesome as Hypatia's, but he was branded a heretic nonetheless and sent into exile where his tongue was eaten by worms. Cyril, on the other hand, was canonised by the Catholic Church.

— 170 —

Angels. – At the same time as God created heaven and earth he produced a whole lot (by some accounts many millions) of angels. At first they were wingless males, born with circumcised penises (*Jub.* 15:27), a pleasing odour (*Test. of Levi* 3:6) and full of sexual desire (*1 En.* 6:2). God created them to praise him as he sat upon his throne gleaming in all his glory. And this they did, and still do, singing, blowing trumpets, ever reminding God of his ineffable greatness.

Unfortunately, like men, angels are easily corrupted and many of them end up in hell. After God had created man, he decided that some of his angels should divert their attention from praising him to lauding his new creation. This, according to the Muslim faith, is what caused Iblis (the Devil) to fall out with God in the first place. Some of the more obedient angels have been offered a chance, not only to protect individual human beings (as 'guardian angels'), but, in exceptional circumstances, to act as go-betweens, passing messages from God to his mortal servants on earth.

God uses the courier service that angels provide and has consequently (since the days of Job) made fewer and fewer personal appearances on earth, preferring to send his angels instead. To the prophets Muhammad and Joseph Smith God sent respectively Gabriel and Moroni, two loyal and responsible archangels whose commission was to institute the new religions of Islam and Mormonism.

— 171 —

Seraphim. – As El Sabaoth (Lord of Hosts) one of God's earliest tasks was to organise his angels into ranks for the purposes of good singing, good fighting and good discipline. There has been much theological haggling as to how exactly he stratified his angels and various angelogists have, through the ages, proffered different lists of rank. One of them, an anonymous mystical writer, known for convenience only as Dionysius the Pseudo-Aeropagite, succeeded in controlling the debate with his own list which was collated from two New Testament sources (Eph. 1:21 and Col. 1:16). Some Christian denominations have declared the Pseudo-Aeropagite's list to be the 'definitive' order of angelic rank. First published in his book *The Celestial Hierarchy* at the beginning of the sixth century CE, Dionysius's angelogy reveals that by far the most important order of angels are the *seraphim*. Why God loves these great brutes above all others is a mystery. Enoch, who saw some in heaven, testified to their appearance:

How many *seraphim* are there? [he asked rhetorically] Four, corresponding to the four winds of the world. How many wings have they each? Six, corresponding to the six days of creation. How many faces have they? Sixteen, four facing in each direction. The measure of the *seraphim* and the height of each of them corresponds to the seven heavens. The size of each wing is as the fullness of a heaven, and the size of each face is like the rising sun. (*3 En.* 26:9)

Isaiah spotted a seraph floating above God's throne and explained the purpose of its having six wings: 'Two to cover its face, two to cover its feet [a euphemism for sex organs] and two for flying' (Isa. 6:2–7). Some have identified the seraphim with the fiery serpents of the book of Numbers (21:6) and the flying dragons of Isaiah (14:29). God is drawn not perhaps by their physical appearance, but because of their certain love – they adore him. Day and night they sing a cantata of psalms, hymns and eulogies extolling his majesty and defining his glory. The main function of the seraphim, however, is to burn all the books which Satan and his side-kick Sammael write every day itemising the iniquities of the Israelites. These books, Satan hopes, will turn God against his chosen people, but the seraphim are quick to destroy them, ensuring that God never gets to see what the devil has written.

— 172 —

Not cherubic. – The popular image of a cherub as a delightful 2-year-old winged infant is erroneous. The cherubim, like their senior angels, the seraphim, are not a sight for sore eyes, in fact they are said to burn the eyes of humans from their sockets due to the dazzling light they emit from their persons. Ezekiel saw them and miraculously preserved his vision: 'Each cherub had four faces,' he said 'the first face was the face of the cherub itself, the second face was that of a man, the third of a lion and the fourth was the face of an eagle' (Ezek. 10:14).

The cherubim's bodies have wings, backs, hands and wheels (where they keep their souls) which appear to be made of chrysolite. When not singing the praises of their Lord they are employed as drivers of his chariots and sometimes even allowed to bear him on their backs (Ps. 18:10). In Genesis God set them to guard the entrance to Eden (Gen. 3:24), while in the *Slavonic Enoch* they are used by God to reflect his wisdom and knowledge and maintain his celestial library in neat order.

Maimonides inferred that God himself might look like a cherub, explaining the reason that there are two carved cherubim on the Ark of the Covenant because, 'had there been only one, people might have confused it with a representation of God!' (*Guide of the Perplexed*, 3:45).

— 173 —

Not furniture. – Thrones are angels, not pieces of furniture. God gives them the third most elevated rank in the celestial hierarchy and they stand in the highest triad of the heavenly host. They look a bit like wheels with thousands upon thousands of eyes ogling out of them, which is why they are sometimes called 'the many eyed ones'. God is not put off by their looks, but attracted above all to their humility, which, in his view, allows them to dispense his justice without fear of their succumbing to the destructive forces of pride and ambition.

— 174 —

Dominations, virtues and powers. – God needed to keep all of the lesser angels in check, having the time, but not necessarily the inclination, to do it himself, and so he created a second tier of angels employing the bossiest of them to take control of celestial discipline. Offering them each a sword and sceptre he told them to report to the cherubim. The cherubim informed them they were to be called *dominations,* a suitable job title, since their primary task was to harness their bossiness to keep the whole of the cosmos in working order. Dominations are, in effect, glorified housekeepers, but God does not put it quite like that, preferring instead to bolster their sense of self-worth by giving them control over a large staff of *virtues* and *powers.*

In the Hebrew Bible God is directly responsible for punitive weather conditions, sending flood (Gen. 6:17), drought (Hag. 1:11), hail (Exod. 9:18), earthquake (Num. 16:30) and hurricanes (Jon. 1:4) to deter human beings from apostasy, but he is noticeably less interested when it comes to the everyday weather of mild sunshine, intermittent cloud and light drizzle. For these effects he uses a celestial chain of command, ordering the cherubim to ask the dominations to tell the virtues to produce another day of moderate effects.

The virtues go flat out on the weather and if there is time will help with miracles and human morality too. With the *virtues* abide the *powers* whose principle task is to help God in defeating evil demons. When there are no battles to be fought they sweep the paths between heaven and earth and police the traffic thereon. In their own way, *powers* save God from a great deal of extra work.

— 175 —

Third-class angels. – The lower echelon of angels is concerned with humanity more than anything else. It is divided into three distinct strata: *principalities,* which work for the welfare of continents, countries, cities etc.; *archangels,* who are dignified with personal names and intercede in special cases on behalf of individuals; and, at the very bottom of the celestial heap, plain *angels* which do all the chores associated with round-the-clock praising and serving God, with, according to John Henry Newman, 'keen, ecstatic love', as well as tending to the needs of humans.

Each human is sent a guardian angel and it is through these that God is able to communicate with mankind. He instructs each angel to accompany his allotted human wherever he or she may go. The Jewish Talmud teaches that a guardian angel must stop at the lavatory door where strict Jews are required to pause and offer their apologies to the angel before proceeding with their ablutions.

The surreal question as to whether angels themselves need to defecate has been hotly debated by theologians of the Middle Ages. The answer, based on evidence of colossal appetite (*1 En.* 7), is probably 'Yes'.

— 176 —

Where angels dwell. – Until the nineteenth century nobody knew where angels lived. Philosophers, like Thomas Aquinas, hoped to bury the issue, by describing them as pure spirit: 'Angels exist anywhere their powers are applied,' he wrote, 'So they are not measured by places or positioned in them or contained by them. Rather they can hold and contain places and their contents, just as soul holds body together rather than body soul.' Voltaire rejected Thomist sophistry

and continued to press the point, writing in 1764: 'It is not known precisely where angels dwell – whether in the air, the void, or the planets. It has not been God's pleasure that we be informed of their abode' (*Philosophical Dictionary*).

God must have taken Voltaire's criticism to heart for no fewer than eighty years later he revealed all to the prophet Joseph Smith: 'The Angels', he told him, 'do not reside on a planet like this earth, but they reside in the presence of God, on a globe like a sea of glass and fire, where all things for their glory are manifest, past, present and future, and are continually before the Lord' (*Doctrine and Covenants*, 130:6–7).

— 177 —

Angelic puzzles. – Thomas Aquinas was interested to know how much space an angel's body takes up, whether it can transform itself into something else and what substance it is made from, but Isaac d'Israeli (father of the British Prime Minister, Benjamin) wrote critically of such enquiries in his *Curiosities of Literature* (1791), complaining that:

Aquinas could gravely debate whether Christ was not an hermaphrodite and whether there are excrements in Paradise – The reader desirous of being merry with Aquinas's angels may find them in Scriblerus, in Ch. VII, who enquires if angels pass from one extreme to another without going through the middle? And if angels know things more clearly in a morning? How many angels can dance on the point of a very fine needle without jostling one and other?

And so the phrase was born, 'How many angels can fit on the head of a pin?' – another way of saying, 'Don't ask silly questions that cannot be easily answered.'

Martinus Scriblerus is the name of a fictional author invented by Alexander Pope, John Arbuthnot, Jonathan Swift, John Gay, Thomas Parnell and Robert Harley, Earl of Oxford, founders of the Scriblerus Club whose purpose was to ridicule pedants and 'all the false tastes in learning'. They were co-authors of the *Memoirs of the Extraordinary Life, Works and Discoveries of Martinus Scriblerus* (1741), a book which does indeed lampoon Aquinas's discussion on angels in the seventh chapter, though the exact joke about them dancing on pin heads is not there. The Prime Minister's father must have invented it.

—— 178 ——

Fallen angels. – There are three angelic crimes which God punishes severely. If any member of the heavenly host praises God sloppily he will be shot to pieces (*3 En.* 40:4), if he jealously refuses to admire human beings (*LAE* 14:3) he will be cast out of heaven, and the same thing will happen if he admires human beings too much and has sexual intercourse with them (Gen. 6).

There once was an angel called Semyaza who, with two hundred lusty friends, descended one day onto the summit of Mount Hermon taking human women for their sexual gratification. All the women became pregnant and gave birth to a new race of violent, unattractive giants, three hundred cubits high. The giants consumed the produce of all the people who naturally resented feeding them. In retaliation the giants started to eat the people themselves and when stock ran low they even ate each other, drinking blood by the gallon and fornicating madly with birds, wild beasts, reptiles and even fish.

One of their number, Azazel, taught male humans to work with metal, showing them how to make weapons of war and teaching the women how to adorn themselves with 'bracelets, ornamentation, the beautifying of the eyelids with antimony and all colouring tinctures and alchemy' (*Book of the Watchers*, 7–8). Who should be witnessing this great betrayal but the three upright archangels, Michael, Gabriel and Raphael, who ran immediately to God and told him, in the most lurid detail what had been going on.

God ordered Raphael to 'bind Azazel hand and foot and throw him in the darkness'. Raphael accordingly dug a whole in the desert and chucked Azazel into it, piling sharp rocks on top of him. Other fallen angels were enclosed in the darkness too but many of their giant offspring continued to cause havoc on earth, until, that is, Noah, hearing that his grandchildren were being daily bound and raped by giants, prayed to God for assistance. The giants were represented by their chief, Mastema, who pleaded with God that at least some of his demons should be allowed to continue despoiling the earth: 'O Lord Creator,' he craved, 'leave some of them before me, and let them obey my voice. And let them do everything which I tell them, because if some of them are not left with me, I will not be able to exercise the authority and corrupt the children of men' (*Jub.* 10:7–9).

To God this seemed a capital plan. He bound nine-tenths of the angels in darkness and allowed Mastema to run riot on earth with the remaining tenth at least until the Day of Judgement.

—— 179 ——

Portrait of Satan. – Angels do not have childhoods and Satan is no exception. He first appeared at the creation jealously refusing to show any interest in God's new toy, Man. At one time Satan was thought to be God's favourite. He was the second being of creation and the highest angel that stands before God's throne. In the Rabbinic scripture his name is Sammael, in the Qur'an it is Iblis, and elsewhere, in apocalyptic texts, he is Sataniel.

Whatever his name, it was always his idea to send the serpent to Eve in the Garden of Eden. He found Eve curiously attractive and, after the Fall, it is written that he had intercourse with her (Bereshith, *Mishnah* 42) and that Cain was the product of this union. During his squabble with God he had the idea of building himself a throne higher than the clouds above the earth, so that he might be equal with God. God claimed to have thrown him out of heaven: 'Then I hurled him out from the height,' he said, 'together with his angels. And he was flying around in the air ceaselessly, above the Abyss' (*2 En.* 29:6).

Why then was Satan on such good terms with God in the book of Job? Here, as in the story of Balaam (Num. 22–24), he is not God's adversary but a useful messenger whose task it is to test, obstruct and accuse mankind on God's behalf. There is no question of Satan being punished for the harm that comes to Job, far from it. He is described in the book of Job as one of the 'sons of God' and they talk together like close friends:

'Where have you been?' God asked him at a council meeting.

'Oh just roaming about on earth, here and there,' came the relaxed reply (Job 1:7).

Something must have gone awry, offstage. Isaiah satirised the fall of the King of Babylon: 'Your pride has been flung down to hell with the music of your lyres; under you a mattress of maggots, over you a blanket of worms. How did you come to fall from the Heavens, Day Star, son of Dawn' (Isa. 14:11–12). From this poetic reference the Morning Star (Lucifer) came to be associated with the Devil as well. He was fallen, but through God's patronage, is still allowed to spoil human life on earth. God allows him to command the air (Eph. 2.2), to make people do evil things (Luke 22:3) and to make them violently sick (Matt. 15:22; Luke 11:14).

Eventually, Satan is destined to be cast into a lake of fire where 'his torture will not come to an end for ever and ever' (Rev. 20:10–15), but in the meantime Tobit, the apocryphal prophet, suggests that the best way to ward him off is to burn ashes of incense together with the heart and liver of a vicious river fish: 'And the devil shall smell it, and flee away, and never come again any more' (Tob. 6:17).

Modern Christian theologians, like Father Gabriele Amorth of Modena, who is employed as an exorcist by the Roman Catholic Church, reject such primitive methods: 'The Devil is wary of talking and must be forced to speak,' he told an English newspaper reporter.

The word ISRAEL may have derived
from a compound of divine Egyptian
names – Isis, a moon deity (*top left*),
Ra, the sun god (*above*), and El or Ali
(*left*), the lesser gods identified with
the stars.

Titian's interpretation of
the Trinity. God the Son is
sitting to God the Father's
right, while God the Holy
Ghost hovers in the image
of a dove between them.

God appears to Moses as a
burning bush in a
watercolour by Blake.

Wearing a hat in a fifteenth-century painting by Baco and Rexach.

Like Father, like Son – The Creator in a painting by Jacobo Torriti.

World weary in a Spanish painting of the sixteenth century.

Father Major Jealous Divine – 'I am God'.

Joseph Smith, to whom God gave the
Book of Mormon.

Moses, to whom God gave the Torah.

Neale Donald Walsch, who recorded his
conversations with God.

God sends bears to kill forty-two children for teasing Elisha.

Mary is pregnant but is God the Father?

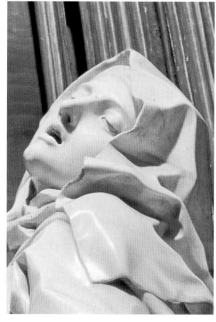

Teresa in ecstasy: 'The pain was so great that it made me moan.'

Jews at the Western ('Wailing') Wall in Jerusalem.

Muslims in different attitudes of prayer.

God's message is passed through the hands of one charismatic Christian into the head of another.

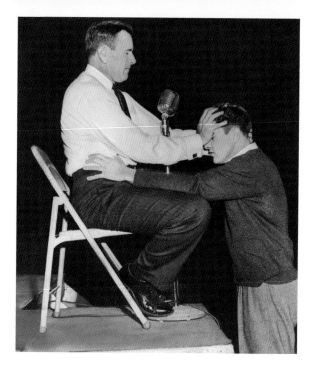

A Victorian family kneels on the dining room floor as paterfamilias reads from the Good Book.

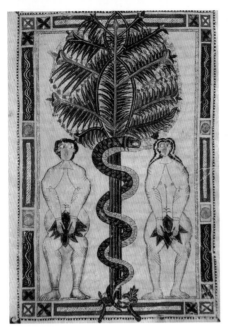

God made Adam and Eve 'in His own image'. Two artists show how they might have looked.

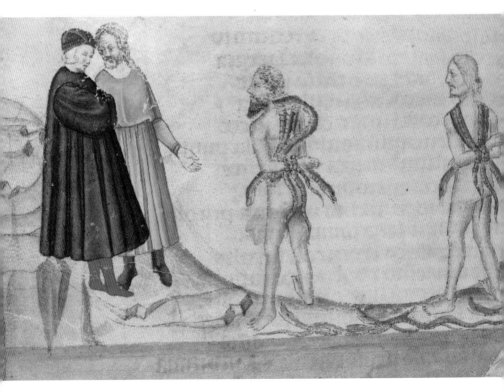

Dante and Virgil look on as thieves are punished by serpents in Hell.

'When he is voluntarily chatty it is a trick to distract the exorcist. Experience has taught me that using oil, holy water and salt can be very effective.' In the traditional exorcism, Father Amorth and other priests of the Society of St Paul touch the neck of the possessed person with the hems of their stoles and hold their hands on his head. Then, one of them, taking up a crucifix, shouts with all his might in the Latin language: '*Ecce crucem Domini*' ('Behold the cross of the Lord!').

Why the Devil should bother to wince at Father Amorth's crucifixes is a mystery. Normally Satan is delighted by the symbols of torture and especially one to which his principal adversary was once so gruesomely appended. When Jesus, on the other hand, returns to earth for his warmly anticipated 'second coming' the last thing *he* will wish to see is a cross.

—— 180 ——

Four of the best. – Of the seven archangels, named as Uriel, Raphael, Michael, Gabriel, Raguel, Suriel and Remiel (*1 En.* 40:71), the first four are regarded (by humans, if not by God) as superior in rank to the others. That their names invariably end with the suffix *el* is no coincidence, for these were once the little gods of the *elohim*, the sons of El. Michael is championed above all as the guardian of the Jewish nation. He is by nature a warrior, pitting himself with relish against the forces of evil; overthrowing them all in the apocalyptic clash of Revelations, chapter 12. Until the battle of Armageddon, God will use Michael as his chief librarian and heavenly scribe (*3 En.* 90) or hire him as an undertaker at important funerals such as he did at the deaths of Adam, Abel and Moses.

Gabriel is God's chief messenger. It was he who announced the birth of Jesus to Mary (Luke 1:19), and, in the Qur'an, helped her to conceive the child. He is the special friend of Islam, the interlocutor between God and Muhammad. For God, Gabriel has many uses. He ushers people into his presence (*2 En.* 21:3) and interprets the divine message to mankind (Dan. 8:16–26). At the destruction of Sodom and Gomorrah, Muslim tradition has it that he scooped up both cities under his wing and took them so high that even the angels of lower heaven could hear the cocks crowing and dogs barking, then, turning his wing upside-down, he allowed both cities to crash back down to earth.

God's admiration for Raphael stems from the archangel's unique ability to cure people of diseases and purge them of diabolic spirits (Tob. 3:17); his name means 'God has healed.' Uriel, on the other hand, appears to have no obvious talent and consequently no obvious brief. Once he gave Enoch a guided tour of the tortures of hell (*2 En.* 20:2) and cut Esdras down to size by telling him how pathetic he was compared to God (2 Esd. 5). In the *Life of Adam and Eve* Uriel acts as the under-undertaker helping Michael to bury the bodies of Adam and Abel in Paradise.

— 181 —

God's Moronic messenger. – On 21 September 1823, God (who had had little to do with his servant Joseph Smith Jnr since their last meeting four years earlier in a wood outside Manchester, Vermont) decided that his American prophet should be put to use. He had many interesting new things to tell mankind – titbits concerning the whereabouts of the lost tribes of Israel and news of a trip that Jesus had made to America shortly after his ascension. The time was right and Smith was the man.

It was evening and the prophet had retired to his bedroom for the night where he 'betook [himself] to prayer and supplication to Almighty God for forgiveness of all [his] sins and follies':

While I was thus in the act of calling upon God, I discovered a light appearing in my room, which continued to increase until the room was lighter than at noonday, when immediately a personage appeared at my bedside, standing in the air, for his feet did not touch the floor. He had on a loose robe of most exquisite whiteness. It was a whiteness beyond anything earthly I had ever seen; nor do I believe that any earthly thing could be made to appear so exceedingly white and brilliant. His hands were naked, and his arms also, a little above the wrist; so, also, were his feet naked, as were his legs, a little above the ankles. His head and neck were also bare. I could discover that he had no other clothing on but this robe, as it was open, so that I could see into his bosom. Not only was his robe exceedingly white, but his whole person was glorious beyond description, and his countenance truly like lightning. The room was exceedingly light, but not so very bright as immediately around his person.

When I first looked upon him, I was afraid; but the fear soon left me. He called me by name, and said unto me that he was a messenger sent from the presence of God to me, and that his name was Moroni; that God had a work for me to do. He said there was a book deposited, written upon gold plates, giving an account of the former inhabitants of this continent, and the source from whence they sprang. He also said that the fullness of the everlasting Gospel was contained in it, as delivered by the Saviour to the ancient inhabitants; Also, that there were two stones in silver bows – and these stones, fastened to a breastplate, constituted what is called the Urim and Thummim – deposited with the plates; and the possession and use of these stones were what constituted *seers* in ancient or former times; and that God had prepared them for the purpose of translating the book. (*Joseph Smith History*, 30–35)

Having said all this Moroni launched into a sea of scriptural recitation, some of it recognised by Smith, other bits altered from the King James translation of the Bible:

After this communication, I saw the light in the room begin to gather immediately around the person of him who had been speaking to me, and it continued to do so until the room was again left dark, except just around him; when, instantly I saw, as it were, a conduit open right up into heaven, and he ascended till he entirely disappeared, and the room was left as it had been before this heavenly light had made its appearance.

What, if anything, Moroni said to God on his return is not recorded, but he had delivered the right message to Smith and so there was no reason to suppose that God was in any way dissatisfied with Moroni's achievement. However, nobody understands – not even Smith – why Moroni insisted on returning two minutes later and repeating the whole message *verbatim* to him all over again. That was odd enough, but no sooner had he disappeared for the second time, than the pestering angel was back once again and, 'without the least variation', went through his whole wretched speech for a third time. In this way Moroni managed to keep Smith awake all night long. The next day Smith was exhausted and collapsed in a heap while climbing a fence at his father's farm. When he regained his consciousness who should be hovering above the fence and what should he be saying? – you've guessed it!

— 182 —

Betting on the races. – Popular myth ascribes to Lord Alfred Douglas (Oscar Wilde's young companion) and to Hilaire Belloc the corny rhyme, 'How odd of God to choose the Jews', to which a soothing riposte was later added, 'But not so odd as those who choose a Jewish God and spurn the Jews.' The head was in fact by William Norman Ewer and the tail by Cecil Browne – alas, nothing but names to us now. American author Leo Rosten has offered an alternative tail: 'Not odd of God, *goyim* annoy him' – a joke which is lost to those who have not learned that *goyim* means non-Jews or Gentiles in Hebrew.

In any event God did not exactly *choose* the Jews. The word 'Jew' originally applied to any member of the tribe of Judah resident in Judaea and it was not until the second century BCE that the term 'Judaism' was used in scripture (in 2 Maccabees 2:21 or Esther, whichever was written first). Before that, both 'Jew' and 'Judaism' were terms used predominantly by Gentiles, while the 'Jews', whether from Palestine or the scattered Diaspora, referred to themselves as 'people of Israel'.

Who then are the chosen people? To answer this question we must go back to the moment that God made his choice. But when was that? Many cite the calling of Abram (who was not a Jew) when God said to Abram: 'Leave your country, your kindred and your father's house for a country which I shall show you; and I shall make you a great nation, I shall bless you and make your name famous. You are to be a blessing' (Gen. 12:1–2). But if Abraham and all his descendants are 'the chosen people' then the term must nowadays be expanded to cover a great deal more of the population than that which is currently deemed to be 'Jewish'. The Arabs, for instance, are said to descend from Abraham through Ishmael (his bastard son by the Egyptian concubine Hagar).

Israelites take their name from Abram's grandson Jacob, who changed his name to Israel on God's command (Gen. 32:28) and when God addressed the 'Children of Israel' in the desert he said to them, 'The Lord your God has chosen you out of all the peoples on earth to be his people, his treasured possession. Not because you were so numerous, for indeed you were the smallest of all, but because he loved you and meant to keep the oath which he swore to your ancestors' (Deut. 7:6–8). If then, the Chosen People are to be defined as the descendants of Jacob, an estimated 12,000,000 Gentiles in Britain and America (those who are able to trace their descent from Jacob using *Burke's Peerage, Royalty for Commoners* by R. W. Stuart, and the New Testament, Matt. 1.1–16 or Luke 3:23–38) must be part of the 'chosen race' as well.

Others have maintained that God's Chosen People are not just the descendants of Jacob or Abraham but the descendants of Adam and Eve. Why 'chosen' if Adam and Eve's descendants are all there are to choose from? 'Not so!' said Isaac La Peyrère (1596–1676), whose theory of the pre-Adamites, based on a detailed study of Genesis and Paul's Letter to the Romans (5:12–14), made him a cause célèbre in his lifetime. To La Peyrère, Adam was not the first man on earth, nor the ancestor of all people, only the 'first Jew'. La Peyrère is no longer famous.

Paul, the inventor of Christianity, was keen to point out that blood had nothing to do with it, forcefully arguing that there is 'no distinction between Jew and Greek' (Rom. 10:12) and that 'all who are led by the Spirit of God are sons of God' (Rom. 8:14). It was Paul's considered opinion that the Chosen People were not literally the blood descendants of Abraham and Isaac:

> For not all who are descended of Israel belong to Israel, and not all are children of Abraham because they are his descendants; but 'Through Isaac shall your descendants be named.' This means that it is not the children of the flesh who are the children of God, but the children of the promise are reckoned as descendants. (Rom. 9:6–8)

Tradition alone defines the Chosen People as those descendants of Jacob, who identify themselves with one of the tribes of Israel and who traditionally adhere (in principle at least) to the Law of Moses, that is, the Jews. Nowadays Liberal Jews prefer not to use the term 'chosen race', believing that it breeds bigotry in Jews and anti-Semitism in Gentiles. On the other hand, Orthodox Jewry, which still affirms the dogma, stresses its belief that *being chosen* is an arduous responsibility, not a meal ticket.

— 183 —

The chosen slut. – Israel 'the chosen people' are given a rough ride by God, rougher than any god has ever given his people. The Hebrew

Bible reveals a staggering onslaught against a struggling race the likes of which have never been read in literature before or since. Perhaps the writing was always on the wall. God would not protect his people for ever: 'My spirit', he said, 'cannot be indefinitely responsible for human beings who are only flesh' (Gen. 6:3). In the tense deteriorating relationship between Israel and God as it is described from the book of Isaiah to the end of Malachi, God repeatedly refers to his people, Israel, in terms of violent and unrestrained hatred. Particularly gruesome is God's analogy of himself as a nurturing father/lover/husband while Israel is the baby daughter, turned attractive virgin, turned whore, who rebels and finally betrays her father's love. God supplies this lewd metaphor to several of his prophets. Perhaps the most dramatic version of it is Ezekiel's, regarded by many, as pornographic.

First God finds baby Israel deserted on the day of her birth: 'There was no one to cut your navel string, or wash you in water to clean you up, or rub you in salt or wrap you in swaddling clothes, I saw you kicking in your blood as I was passing and I said to you "Live!"' As Israel grows older God's attitude changes: 'Your breasts became firm and your hair sprouted. You were stark naked when I saw you time for love had arrived, so I spread my robe over you and covered your nakedness and I entered into a covenant with you by oath, declares the Lord God, thus you became mine. I bathed you in water and washed the blood off you, I anointed you with oil.'

Then he dressed her in finery and gave her a nose-ring, but Israel became vain and conceited and was soon to incur the wrath of God by 'fornicating with the big-cocked' Egyptians and masturbating with lewd phallic objects.

'Very well, whore,' snarls the Lord 'for having squandered your money and let yourself be seen naked with your lovers I shall strip you naked in front of *all* of them. I shall pass on to you the sentence that murderesses and adulteresses receive; I shall submit you to their jealous fury' (Ezek. 16).

Five biblical pages on and God's blind rage is still not abated:

You were hankering for the debauchery of your girlhood, when they used to rub your nipples in Egypt and fondle your young breasts and so the Lord God says this: 'I shall set all your lovers against you. I shall direct my jealousy against you and they will treat you with fury, they will cut off your nose and ears, and what is left of the family will fall by the sword, they will slaughter your sons and daughters and what is left will be burnt. I shall hand you over to those you hate. They will treat you with hatred, they will rob you of the entire fruit of your labours and leave you stark naked.' Thus saith the Lord to his chosen one. (from Ezek. 23:21–31)

— 184 —

Betrayed. – God was so outraged by the infidelity of his chosen people that on many occasions he betrayed them. He 'handed them over to muggers who plundered them; he delivered them to the enemies surrounding them, and they were not able to resist them. In every warlike venture the hand of God was there to foil them, as God had warned, as he had sworn to them; so he reduced them all to dire distress' (Judg. 2:14–15).

God delivered the people of Israel into the hands of the cruel King of Edom where they were enslaved for seven years. He rallied a large army of Amalekites, Moabites and Amonites, to march against them, to capture the city of Jericho and enslave his people for eighteen years (Judg. 3:14). Then he put them all at the mercy of a Canaanite king called Jabin, the proud owner of 900 iron-plated chariots. Jabin violently oppressed God's people for twenty years (Judg. 4:3), and when they had escaped from the tyranny of Jabin, God handed them straight to the Midianites.

God wanted to punish his people, that was all, not to destroy them utterly. On occasion, though, he sailed dangerously close to the wind. In 721 BCE, for instance, God put ten of the twelve tribes of Israel into the merciless hands of the Assyrians; they were dragged off by their captors and have never been seen since.

—— 185 ——

Unchosen. – And the Lord said: 'You are not my people, and I do not exist for you!' (Hos. 1:9).

—— 186 ——

Who needs God anyway? – When the Persian king Ahasuerus (possibly Xerxes) asked his wife to do a twirl and vaunt her beauty for his chamberlains, she refused. Furious, the king chucked her out and found himself another wife, a plain Jewess called Esther. Now Mordecai (who, some say, was Esther's uncle, others her cousin and is claimed in the Talmud to be her husband!) happened to have offended the king's favourite, Haman, by not bowing to him. Purple with indignation, Haman planned a retributive slaughter of all the Jews in Persia. Queen Esther, hearing the news, ran to the king, her husband, and told him what Haman had planned.

Sick with fear, Haman begged Esther to persuade the king to forgive him, leaping (in desperation to put his case) onto her bed. When the king walked in to find Haman on top of his wife he was beside himself with rage: 'What!' he cried, 'Is he going to rape the queen in my own palace?'

Haman was hanged. The Jews of the land who had been bemoaning their imminent demise were given a reprieve by the king and, as a special treat, allowed to slaughter as many non-Jews as they wished. Ecstatic for joy, they butchered 75,000 Gentiles in a single day and have celebrated the anniversary of that achievement ever since.

And what has this to do with God? Nothing.

Nothing?

That's just it. The book of Esther, as it appears in the Hebrew Bible, does not even mention God once. It is a fairy tale about a proud new race – not Israelites but Jews – not buffeted, cursed, abused, raped, betrayed, chosen and unchosen by a jealous God, but able now to stand on its own two feet. The Jews in Esther do not plead with God to extricate them from the threat of Haman, nor do they ask for his assistance in slaughtering 75,000 Gentiles. They manage it all by themselves. Oh happy day! – it is called the Feast of Purim.

—— 187 ——

Send in the fish. – When God asked a sleepy Hebrew prophet called Jonah to run an errand, the prophet tried to run away by jumping on a ship headed for Tarshish (the furthest end of the world). In the course of his voyage Jonah was caught in a storm, thrown into the sea, swallowed by a giant fish (sometimes described as a whale) and vomited, after three days repenting in the fish's stomach, back onto dry land. The story has often been criticised as unrealistic, childish and almost certainly untrue, but in 1891, God may, or may not, have had a hand in a similar episode concerning a fisherman called James Bartley. Bartley was a crewman on the whaler *Star of the East* when he fell overboard seven miles off the coast of the Falkland Islands. After a considerable tussle with a gigantic sperm whale, Bartley was swallowed. Next day, the same whale was harpooned and flensed to the side of the ship. When the fish's stomach was dragged on deck, Bartley was found unconscious but still alive inside it. For several days he was a 'gibbering maniac' but eventually returned to normal life except that his face and hands were for ever bleached by the whale's gastric juices. Krishna spent three days inside a crocodile before being spat out onto dry land and Hercules spent a similar period in the stomach of a dog.

— 188 —

Holy shit! – From the earliest times people have worried about what will happen to their bodies at the resurrection. Both the *Gospel of Philip* and Paul's letter to the Corinthians express anxieties about being caught with their trousers down at that all-important moment (*Gos. Phil.* 23a and 2 Cor. 5:3). Both Philip and Paul believed it was necessary to be both spiritually and physically prepared for the event whenever it should happen. But what of Michael Edwards, the Australian fisherman whose head was retrieved in September 2000 from the stomach of a 96lb, 5ft 10in black spot cod at a 'A Fine Kettle of Fish', a food processing plant in Cairns? The rest of his body has never been found. How is he to prepare for the resurrection?

In *A Companion for the Festivals and Fasts of the Church of England* (1717), a theological guide once described by Dr Johnson as 'a most valuable help to devotion, which has, I understand, the greatest sale of any book ever printed in England, except the Bible', this very problem is rigorously addressed:

> How can Bodies that have been devoured by Cannibals, who chiefly live on Human Flesh, or Bodies eaten by Fishes, and turned to their Nourishment, and then those Fishes perhaps eaten up by Other Men, and converted into the Substance of their Bodies, how should both these at the Resurrection recover their own Body?

The book's solemn answer stresses that a body is always changing, 'spending and renewing itself, losing something of the matter it had before and gaining new'. God does not mind what state your body is in at the exact moment that he calls you to the resurrection, even if, at that time, 99 per cent of you has been transformed into a ribbon of fish shit. The *Companion* continues:

This doth clearly solve the forementioned difficulties, since any of those Bodies he had at any time before he was eaten, are every whit as good, and as much his own as that which was eaten. It hath been moreover observed, that scarce the hundredth part of what we eat is digested into the Substance of our Bodies, that all the rest is rendered back again into the common Mass of Matter by sensible and insensible Evacuations; therefore what should hinder an Omnipotent Power from raising the Body a Cannibal hath devoured, out of the ninety-nine Parts which return into the common Mass of Matter? (*Companion*, 27)

—— 189 ——

War Lord. – In the first seven books of the Bible God serves his people, principally, as a lucky mascot God of war. He is the Israelites' field-marshal. They consult him on tactics and weaponry, giving him dispensation to pick their enemies and decide when, where and how to eliminate them. Occasionally he joins the battle himself, throwing hailstones (Josh. 10:11), rallying the stars to action (Judg. 5:20), or stopping the sun from setting to give the Israelites more time to pulverise their adversaries (Josh. 10:12).

'God goes forth like a mighty man, like a man of war he stirs up his fury: He cries out, he shouts aloud, he shows himself mighty against his foes' (Isa. 42:13). But at Gaza, Ashkelon and Ekron the 'mighty man of war' was unable to rout the enemy armies 'because their chariots were made of iron' (Judg. 1:19). Elsewhere God's military tactics led to ignominious defeat. When the Israelites consulted him as to which of their tribes should go first into battle, he confidently asserted, 'Judah is to go first.' The Judaean regiments duly marched forward and 22,000 men were massacred. Wiping tears from their eyes, the other soldiers went back to God and asked him, 'Are you really sure we should continue this battle?'

'March against them!' God ordered, and so the Israelites marched for a second time into battle. Once again they were defeated and 18,000 of them met their deaths (Judg. 20:14–28).

His method of picking soldiers was no less eccentric. During Gideon's campaign against the Midianites, God decided that the army had far too many soldiers in it.

'Take them down to the waterside,' he told Gideon, 'and I will sort them out for you there.' So Gideon took his men to the water and God said to him, 'All those who lap the water with their tongues, like dogs, put on one side, and all those who kneel down scooping the water in their hands to drink, put them on the other side.' God chose the scoopers to fight against Midian and dismissed the rest (Judg. 7:4–8).

— 190 —

Trying to kill the Amalekites. – God had harboured a grudge against the Amalekite tribe ever since it had refused permission for Moses and his 600,000 followers to tramp across its territory *en route* to the Promised Land. At that time God swore to Moses, 'I will utterly put out the remembrance of Amalek from under heaven' (Exod. 17:14).

Nothing was done at the time, but a thousand years later God ordered Saul to 'Go and utterly destroy those sinning Amalekites, and fight against them until they are consumed' (1 Sam. 15:18). Saul killed every one of them (man, woman, infant and suckling) except the Amalekite king, Agag. In the next generation, David, Saul's successor, found that the Amalakites had not been so thoroughly destroyed after all, and attacked them himself, 'leaving neither man nor woman alive' (1 Sam. 27:9). But no sooner had he done this than an Egyptian servant informed him the Amalekites were still alive, singing and dancing after a victory against the Philistines.

David found the dancing Amalekites and fought with them all day, killing everyone, except 400 youths that managed to escape on camels (1 Sam. 30:17). The Amalekites were 'completely' destroyed for the third time by Simeonites in the first book of Chronicles (1 Chron. 4:43). Even this was not the very end of them.

'If you cannot beat 'em, join 'em,' goes the old saying, so 'God gathered unto him the Amonites and the Amalekites and went and smote Israel' (Judg. 3:13).

— 191 —

Animal weapons. – God has always had a fiendish 'capability' of animal weapons at his disposal. Against the Egyptians he sent frogs, mosquitoes, horseflies and locusts (Exod. 8–10); to sting the Hivite, Canaanite and Hittite tribes, hornets (Exod. 23:28; Deut. 7:20); the Philistines were plagued with rats (1 Sam. 6:5), while poisonous snakes were used against his own people: 'The Lord sent fiery serpents among the people, and they bit the people; and many people of Israel died' (Num. 21:6).

'I will send wild beasts among you,' God threatened, 'and they shall rob you of your children, and destroy your cattle, and make you few in number' (Lev. 26:22). People who did not worship or regard him highly enough were prime targets for such attacks, as were some foreigners who had been forcibly resettled by the King of Assyria, into Samaria: 'When they first came to live there, they did not worship God, and so God sent lions on them which killed a large number of them' (2 Kings 17:25). Earlier God had despatched a 'man of God' who had eaten a meal against God's wishes also by sending a lion to maul him to death (1 Kings 13:26).

When Elisha, the bald prophet (son of Shagpat), was on his way to Carmel some cheeky little children teased him, shouting, 'Hurry up, baldy! Up you go bald one!' Elisha was beside himself and looked to the heavens for help. God sprang to the prophet's aid sending two savage bears out of the woods. Forty-two children were killed (2 Kings 2:23–5).

—— 192 ——

Conventional warfare. – In the Bible, when not using animal or other natural weapons God resorts to standard military hardware. Habakkuk saw him threatening the sun and moon with a 'glittering spear' (Hab. 3:11). 'I will render vengeance to mine enemies,' God said, 'and will destroy those that hate me. I shall make my arrows drunk with blood and my sword shall devour the flesh of the slain and the skulls of the enemy' (Deut. 32:41–2).

God boasted to Amos that he would use his sword 'to cut them in the head' (Amos 1:9), meaning those who were not loyal to his religion, while the prophet Nahum suggested that God enjoyed hurling rocks onto peoples' heads (Nah. 1:6). At the Battle of Badr (624 CE) God helped Muhammad to victory by throwing gravel into the faces of his enemies (Qur'an 8:16), and afterwards rebuked Muhammad for failing to cut off the fingers of his captives.

—— 193 ——

Dangerous pets. – God had two pets, Leviathan and Behemoth. Biblical exegetes have long argued that Behemoth (who 'lies under the lotus, hides among the reeds in the swamps with the water up to his mouth' and 'feeds on green stuff like an ox, with great strength in his loins') is meant to be a hippopotamus, and Leviathan (who is praised for his 'matchless strength, and a breastplate of double armour') is a crocodile, but careful examination of the texts reveals them to be more sinister than a common croc and hippo.

'Who dares to open the gates of his mouth?' God asked Job. 'Terror reigns round his teeth! His back is like rows of shields sealed with a stone seal.' To God, Leviathan, who breathes fire from the mouths of his seven heads, is a pet (Job 40:29) and was created in the first instance 'for his sport' (Ps. 104:26), while Behemoth, who God describes as 'a great monster' (2 Bar. 29:4), is held in special affection as the first of God's creations (Job 40:19).

When God described his pets to Job, the man of virtue was quite overawed, completely humbled and at a loss for words. 'I have nothing to say,' Job conceded to God. Afterwards, when God restored Job to his fortunes, he presented the hapless farmer with 280 pet dogs (*T. Job*, 9:3).

— 194 —

Happier Hunting Ground. – Technically pets do not have souls and cannot therefore go to heaven, but many pet owners, especially in America, continue to appeal to God to make their pets welcome in his kingdom after they have died. In Evelyn Waugh's Anglo-American tragedy, *The Loved One*, a Hollywood pet funeral service called 'The Happier Hunting Ground' offers (for the price of its 'Grade A Service') an urn for the ashes, a niche in the company's columbrarium while, 'at the moment of committal, a white dove, symbolising the deceased's soul, is liberated over the crematorium'. Without further charge the owner may also receive a card of remembrance on the anniversary of his pet's death: 'Your little Arthur is thinking of you in heaven today and wagging his tail.'

God's relationship to his own pets is not so sentimental. No niche in the columbrarium for Behemoth and Leviathan. When God has finished playing with them his intention is to crush their heads and feed their flesh to the wild beasts of the wilderness (2 Esd. 6:52; Ps. 74:14).

—— 195 ——

Imaginative rewards. – Faithful obedience to the voice of God and observing his commands will reap rewards. 'He will make you abundant in possessions: in offspring of your body, in the yield of your cattle and in the yield of your soil' (Deut. 28:11–12).

For the pious is prepared a place of bliss: gardens planted with trees and vineyards and virgins with swelling breasts all of the same age. They shall have a certain provision in paradise, namely delicious fruits and they shall be honoured: they shall be placed in pleasure gardens, leaning on couches face to face; a cup shall be passed among them, filled with a limpid fountain for the delectation of all those who drink: it shall not oppress the understanding, neither shall they be inebriated by it. And near them shall lie the virgins of paradise, with restrained glances, large black eyes and skin like ostrich eggs covered in dust. (Qur'an 78:30, 37:40 and 37:40–48)

—— 196 ——

Imaginative punishments. – If you do not obey the voice of the Lord your God and do not keep and observe all his commandments and laws:

God will strike you down with consumption, fever, inflammation, windy bowels and gangrene. He will plague you with Egyptian ulcers, with swellings in the groin, with scurvy and the itch, for which you will find no cure. He will hit you hard with madness, blindness, distraction of mind, until you grope your way even in the sunlight like a blind man groping in the dark, and your steps will lead you nowhere. The Lord shall smite you in the knees, and in the legs, with a sore botch that cannot be healed, from the sole of your foot unto the top of your head. (from Deut. 28:15–40)

— 197 —

Divine justice. – King David was strolling on his roof one day and spotted, through a neighbour's window, a tantalisingly beautiful woman, splashing naked in her bath, so he sent a strong man round to pick her up and, having impregnated her in his bedroom, sent her home again. When he discovered that she was married to Uriah the Hittite, David ordered Uriah to join the army and sent a letter to his general, Joab, instructing him to 'put Uriah out in front where the fighting is fiercest and then fall back so that he gets wounded and killed'.

Uriah was killed and David married his widow. A son was born to them, but God was so disgusted by David's behaviour he decided to punish him. 'Before your very eyes,' he told David, 'I shall make your wives have sexual intercourse in broad daylight with all your neighbours.' And 'God struck down the child, which Uriah's wife had born to David, and it was very sick indeed. And it came to pass on the seventh day that the child died.'

God's plan – killing the boy with painful sickness and humiliating David's wives – certainly succeeded in humbling David. As soon as his son was dead he annointed himself in oil, put on some clean clothes and prostrated himself in the Temple. After that David ate a large meal and consoled his grieving wife with more sexual intercourse (2 Sam. 11:1 – 12:25).

— 198 —

God goes for Jehoram's bowels. – Jehoram was a minor king of Judah, the eldest son of Jehoshaphat, who killed his brothers to increase his own power and allowed idolatry to thrive. One day, a letter dictated to Isaiah by God himself somehow found its way into Jehoram's hands. It read: 'Since you have done all these terrible things, God is going to afflict your people, your sons, your wives and all your property with a great calamity, and you yourself with a severe disease affecting your bowels, as a result of which, you will suffer protrusion of your bowels.' God raised an army of Philistines and Arabs who stormed into Judah, ransacking Jehoram's palace, abducting his wives and children, and 'after all this, God afflicted him with an incurable disease of the bowels; in due course, after about two years, his bowels fell out as a result of this disease and he died in acute pain' (2 Chron. 21:8–20).

— 199 —

Story time. – Once upon a time, God had a relationship with someone who is not named in the Bible, though, according to the Jewish historian Josephus, was called Jadon ('Antiquities', 8:9:1, *Whiston's Josephus*). He was a prophet and a 'man of God'. When the King of Bethel invited Jadon to dinner, the invitation was reluctantly declined: 'Were you to give me half your palace I would not go with you, for God has ordered me saying I am forbidden to eat or drink anything.' Thus Jadon dutifully set off on an empty stomach. But on his way home, Jadon met a man who invited him to supper: 'I cannot go back with you,' answered Jadon, 'for God has expressly told me not to eat and drink.' But the other man lied: 'I am a prophet too,' he said, 'and an angel told *me* by God's command: "Bring that man back with you to your house and give him supper."' Believing him to be telling the truth, Jadon accepted the man's hospitality, eating and drinking his fill.

During supper, God whispered into Jadon's ear: 'Since you have defied your God, your corpse will never reach the tomb of your ancestors.' After the meal Jadon saddled his donkey and set on his way, but a few miles down the road was confronted by an angry lion. And the people said: 'That was the man of God who defied the Lord's command! God handed him over to a lion, which has mauled and killed him, just as God had foretold it would' (1 Kings 13:1–30).

— 200 —

Diabolic bet. – One day Satan, disguising himself as a beggar, came to the land of Uz where there dwelt a rich farmer called Jobab (whose nickname was Job) and his wife Sitis. Satan knocked at Job's door but was sent away with a burnt loaf of bread. Injured, he turned to God.

'What have you been up to?' asked God.

'Oh, just prowling about on earth, roaming here and there.'

'Did you pay any attention to my loyal servant Job? There is no one like him on the earth, a sound and honest fellow who shuns evil.'

'Ay,' said Satan, 'But the only reason he is so honest is because you protect him all the time. Take away all his possessions and he will curse you to your face.'

Thus a wager was born.

'Very well,' said God, 'you can take all Job's things away from him. 'Let's see if he curses me then?'

So Satan torched 7000 of Job's sheep, 300 camels, 500 donkeys, 500 yoke of oxen and allowed the remainder to be stolen or eaten by wild beasts. Disguised as a Persian, he smashed Job's house down, massacred his seven sons and three daughters, persuaded some local hooligans to go to Job's ruin and loot whatever of his possessions remained.

But Job was a tolerant man and he did not curse God. Satan was furious.

'The only reason Job didn't curse you,' he said to God, 'was that he was scared for his own life. I bet you if I attack his body so that he is in so much pain as he no longer wishes to live, he will curse you to your face then – double or quits.'

'You're on!'

Job relates what happened next:

'I was sitting, mourning the loss of my children, when Satan came like a great whirlwind and tipped up my chair. I was trapped under it for three hours unable to move. And then he struck me with a revolting disease which spread from my toe-nails up to the top of my head. In great distress I went and sat on a dung heap, where my body got riddled with worms. Pus exuding from my body made moist puddles on the ground. Many worms were inside me and if one ever sprang out, I would take it up and return it to its original place, saying: "Stay in the same place where you were put, until you are directed otherwise by your commander."'

The worms' commander was, of course, God. 'How God laughed!' reported Tertullian. 'How what was already lacerated was the more mangled when, with laughter, he would call the little worms breaking forth back into the pits and pastures of Job's furrowed flesh!' (*De patientia*, 14:2).

Despite all these hardships Job still refused to 'curse God to his face', though he was perilously close at times to doing so. Why, he asked, was God treating him in this disgusting way and where *was* God when he was needed? Impossible to find, deaf to his prayers, yet seemingly blind to all the sin that each day passes unpunished.

'God', said Job, 'has wronged me and enveloped me in his net. If I protest against his violence I am not heard, if I appeal against it, judgement is never given. He has built an impassable wall across my path and covered my way with darkness. He has deprived me of my glory and snatched the crown from my head. He attacks me from all sides at once, he uproots my hope as he might a tree. Inflamed with anger against me he regards me as his foe. His troops have come in force, directing their line of advance towards me. They are now encamped around my tent.'

How long would it be before Job would do as Satan hoped and curse God to his face? We shall never know, for in the nick of time God swooped down offering restitution. To compensate for his suffering, he offered Job a new farm, but it was overwhelmingly large (130,000 head of cattle, 140,000 donkeys, 9000 camels and 180 dogs) and

Job complained: 'Those who milked my cows grew weary, since milk flowed from the mountains. Butter spread over my roads, and from its abundance my herds bedded down in the rocks and mountains because of the births. So the mountains were washed over with milk and became as congealed butter.'

Job never saw his sons and daughters again, but God presented him with a new set to replace them. By his second wife, Dinah, he fathered seven sturdy boys and three angelic daughters whose names were Turtledove, Cassia and Mascara. (This story is taken from the book of Job and the *Testament of Job*.)

— 201 —

His finest hour. – Half way through the Bible God disappears. From the book of Psalms to the end of the Christian New Testament he speaks only through the mouths of his prophets or his angels. No more does he descend in a mighty whoosh of divine person, no more talking to his friends, strolling through his gardens, wrestling with patriarchs or leading his people from the midst of a whirling pillar of cloud. It is as though he has given up with humans altogether as once he had forewarned: 'My spirit cannot be indefinitely responsible for human beings, who are only flesh' (Gen. 6:3).

God's disappearance from the Bible after Job may be connected to the changing theology of the Jewish prophets and priests who wrote those books. Anthropomorphism was out. God now inhabited a world of spirit to which even the prophets themselves were semi-excluded. But his departure from the Bible is in the grandest manner, a whirlwind appearance followed by a rocket of a speech the likes of which have never been heard before or since. This grand despatch (Job 38–41) is the literary summit of the Bible – everything that precedes it is directed to this one climactic point, all that follows is but commentary and spin. It is a speech delivered with glorious eloquence, not to a vast crowd of cheering fans, nor to a celestial assembly of fauning angels, but addressed with all the passion of a Nuremberg rally to one miserable man; a dejected, crumpled, worm-eaten tramp who has been sitting on a dung heap for forty-eight years.

And what does God have to say to this man? Does he comfort him with words of hope? Does he establish a covenant as he had with Noah, Abraham and Moses? Does he pity him in his plight or help to wash the worms from his skin? Not a bit of it. God tramples him underfoot, squashing him deeper into the depths of his dung. The whole speech can be summed up in six words: 'I Almighty Yahweh; You pathetic Job.'

In a devastating series of rhetorical questions God insists that he, and he alone, is the most fearful, the most powerful, the most magisterial force of the universe, while Job is comparatively nothing, a powerless, hopeless, spineless weakling, not worth the shit he is sitting upon. It is a wonderful speech, fraught with anger, conceit and spite, laced with occasional humour, basking and glowing in its own richly poetic language.

Boast piles upon boast, insult upon insult, but through this fabulous rhetoric, this glorious pomp, God reveals more about himself than anywhere else in the Bible. The opening lines were enough to silence Job, perhaps there was no need to go on, but God for once was clearly enjoying himself, and who can blame him? This was his swansong, his ultimate testament and his finest hour.

— 202 —

That speech in full. – From the heart of the tempest the Lord gave Job his answer; and this is what he said:

Who is this darkening my counsel with his ignorant words? Gird up now your loins like a man; for I will demand of you, and you shall answer me. Where were you when I laid the foundations of the earth? Speak, if you can. Who measured it

237

out and stretched the tape across its boundary? Go on, tell me if you know?

Where are the foundations fastened? Who laid the corner stones when the morning stars sang together, and all the sons of God shouted for joy? Who slammed the doors on the breaking sea as it leapt in tumultuous waves from the womb? Who clothed those seas a robe of mist, and gave them their swaddling bands of darkest cloud? Did I not decree a place for them and set them behind these strong bolted gates? 'Come so far,' said I, 'but no further; here shall your proud waves break!'

Have you in all your days commanded the morning; and sent the dawn to its post; that it might take hold of the ends of the earth and shake the wicked out of it? She turns the morning red and stands as a dazzling robe blocking the light of the wicked, and breaking the evil arm as it is raised to strike. Have you been down to the very source of the sea? or walked to the bottom of the Abyss? Have the gates of the dead been opened unto you? Have you seen the way to the shadow of death? Have you any idea of the vast size of all of this? Tell me if thou know it all. Show me where the light is dwelling and where the darkness lives too. Go on, tell me, where is the place for that? Have you beheld the distant boundaries of light and dark and followed all the paths that lead to them? Do you know these things because you were born so long ago? Are you really that old?

Have you been inside the secret places where all the snow is kept? Have you seen where the hail is stored, which I have reserved for times of trouble, against the day of battle and war? Do you know how lightning forks or where the East Wind comes up upon the earth? Who has made holes in the firmament for the outflowing of rain? Who has cleared the way for lightning and thunder, and made it so that rain may pelt on the earth, where no man is; even on the desolate plain, to satisfy the thirst of waste ground; and to cause the bud of the tender herb to spring forth?

Has the rain a father? Who has begotten the drops of dew? From what womb came the ice and the hoary frost of heaven, who has borne these things when the waters grow hard as stone, and the face of the deep is frozen still?

Can you bind the sweet influences of Pleiades, or loose the reigns of Orion? Can you bring forth the shining Crown in each season? or can you show the Bear and its cubs which way to go? Do you really know the ordinances of heaven? Can you apply these celestial laws from down here on earth? Can you raise your voice to the clouds and make the pent-up water bucket down upon you? Will lightning flashes answer to your command and call out to you, 'Here we are'?

Who has endowed the earth with wisdom? Who has given understanding to the heart? Who can number every cloud and tilt the water bottles of heaven so that the very dust turns to fertile soil, and the cracked earth cleaves fast together?

Will you hunt the prey for the lioness? or fill the appetite of her cubs as they crouch in their dens, and abide in the covert lying in wait?

Who provides for the raven his food when his young ones cry up to God craning their necks in search of meat?

Do you know the time when the wild goats of the rock are in labour? or can you mark when the hinds are in calf? Do you know the months of their gestation? or the times when they shall at last give birth, crouching down, bringing forth their young ones, casting out their burdens. When they grow up they go forth, never to return. Who has let the wild ass free? Who has loosened the harness of that wild donkey and given it the wilderness, and the barren land for its dwelling? He scorns the bustle of the city, and ignores the call of the donkey driver, sticking to the mountains in search of green pasture.

Will the wild ox be willing to serve you or abide by your crib? Can you harness this creature to furrow your field? Can you make the wild ox harrow your valleys? Will you trust him (because his strength is great) to do all your work for you? Can you rely on his massive might, to bring home your harvest, and store it in your barn?

Did you give bright feathers to the peacocks? or lend the ostrich its thick plumage? She leaves her eggs in the ground, and warms them in dust, forgetting what foot may crush them, or what wild beast may smash them in, for she is hardened against her young ones, as though they were not hers, little caring if her labour goes for nothing. This is because God has deprived her of intelligence, and given her no share of wisdom. Yet with her great height she can make a fool even of a horse and his rider.

Have you made the horse so bold, and clothed his neck with a flowing mane? Did you make him leap like a grasshopper? The glory of his nostrils is terrible, printing his hooves in the valley, and charging the battle-line in full strength. The horse just laughs at fear, and is not affrighted; nor does he turn from the sword. Arrows fly through the air; the glittering spear and the shield are upon him. He gallops apace with fierceness and anger: when the trumpet summons there is no holding him back. He neighs among the trumpets when he senses the battle from afar, the thunder of the captains, and the shouting.

Is it by your ingenuity that the hawk is able to fly, stretching his wings toward the south? Does the eagle soar up at your command, and make her nest way up on the rock, on the highest crag that is her stronghold? From there she searches her prey, and her eyes behold far off. Her young ones also enjoy the blood: and where the slain are, there is she.

Has God's opponent given in then? Has God's reproachful critic thought up an answer to all this eh?

Then Job answered the LORD, and said: 'Behold, I am vile; what can I say to you? I will lay my hand upon my mouth. I have spoken once. I shall not speak again. I have spoken twice; I have nothing more to say.'

Then the LORD answered Job out of the whirlwind, and said:

Gird up your loins now like a man: I will demand of you and you must answer me. Will you contradict my judgment, hold me to be in error while you put yourself in the right? Does your arm have the strength of God's? Does your voice thunder as the voice of God? Come on then, deck yourself out with robes of shining majesty; array yourself in glory and splendour. Let's see your anger burst forth to humble the proud at a glance, to lay them all low; and to stamp them all down in their place; burying them together in the dust, gagging their conceited mouths for ever. Let me see you do all this and then I shall be the first to pay you homage. Then shall I admit that your own right hand is strong enough to save you.

But first see Behemoth, my creature just as you are; eating grass like an ox. See how his strength is in his loins, observe the power of the muscles in his belly. He slashes his giant tail about, as though it were a cedar: the sinews of his testicles are wrapped together. His bones are like strong rods of brass, like great bars of iron. He is the first of God's creations: I have threatened him with a sword and forced him go up into the mountains in search of food where the other wild animals are. He lies under the shady trees, in the covert of the reed, and wallows in the fen shaded by fine trees; the willows of the brook compass him about. See there, he drinks up a river, for he knows that he could draw up all the waters of the Jordan into his great mouth if that is what he chose. Who is able to grab him by his eyes: or subdue him by piercing those nostrils?

And what about the great Leviathan: can you catch him with a hook? or hold down his flashing tongue with a rope? Can you stick a spear through his nose? or pierce his jaw through with metal? Will he beg *you* for mercy or plead with *you* softly? Will he cut a deal with *you* to take him your slave for ever, to treat him as a pet, taking him about on a lead to entertain your little girls? Will you know how to serve him up to your friends or share his flesh among the merchants? Can you fill his skin with barbed iron or his head with fish spears?

You have only to lay one hand upon him and you will never forget his strength or risk battle with him again. Look now upon that brute, whatever hope you have is all in vain: why, the very sight of him will cast you down. Since no one is fierce enough to dare to stir him up: who then will dare to stand before me? Whatsoever is under the whole heaven belongs to me. I will not conceal his parts, nor his power, nor his comely form. Who would dare to loosen his tunic? or pierce the double-armour of his breastplate? Who can force open those terrible jaws and brave those rows of gnashing teeth? His scales are his pride, shut up together as with a close seal. One is so near to another, that no air can come between them because they are so tightly joined one to another, they stick together, and cannot be sundered.

And when he sneezes, light shines forth, and his eyes are like the eyelids of the morning. Out of his mouth shoots burning light, and sparks of fire leap out. Smoke billows from his nostrils, as out of a seething pot or caldron. His very breath can kindle wet coals, and flame from his aweful mouth devours all before it. But his greatest strength is hidden in his neck, for a violent force is there. The plates of his flesh are joined together: they are firm in themselves and cannot be moved. His heart is also as firm as a rock, as hard as a millstone. When he stands at his height, the bravest are afraid, even the waves themselves cower and retreat. Swords will not stick into him, nor spears, nor darts, nor sharp harpoons. He treats iron as straw, and brass like rotten wood. He will not flinch at the sight of arrows: slingstones just tickle him like hay. Clubs to him are as weak straw and he laughs at the point of a spear.

Meanwhile he fills the depths with sharp stones and spreads pointed things upon the mire. He makes the deep boil like a cooking pot: he makes the sea fume like an incense burner. Behind him he leaves a glittering wake, a white fleece that trails through the deep. There is nothing like him upon this earth, nothing so fearless for he stares the mightiest right in the eye knowing that he is king over all the lordly beasts. (Job 38–41)

VII

Sans Everything

— 203 —

Conflicting extensions. – In affirming God to be supreme in all things, the classical theist describes him in a number of ways. He is perfect, loving, good, infinite, omnipotent, omniscient, eternal, timeless, transcendent, personal, immutable and immanent. But how can this be? Is it really possible to be *both* eternal *and* timeless? Immutable *and* immanent? Personal and at the same time transcendent?

As the Australian philosopher J. L. Mackie pointed out in his famous essay *Evil and Omnipotence* (1955), with God you can only go so far before running into contradictions. Mackie summed up the problem of theodicy in its simplest form like this:

God is omnipotent; God is wholly good; and yet evil exists. There seems to be some contradiction between these three propositions, so that if any two of them were true the third would be false. But at the same time all three are essential parts of most theological positions: the theologian it seems, at once *must* adhere and *cannot consistently* adhere to all three.

Hume confined the conflict to the existence of evil versus God's omnipotence. 'Is God willing to prevent evil, but not able?' he asked, then he is impotent. Is he able but not willing? then is he malevolent. Is he both able and willing? whence then is evil?' (*Dialogues Concerning Natural Religion*).

God is like a computer, the more software you put in, the greater the danger that extensions will conflict. Perhaps this is why Moses Maimonides (1135–1204), the Jewish thinker, rejected any attempt at describing God, however favourably: 'We are only able to apprehend the fact that He is,' he wrote, 'and cannot apprehend his essence. It is consequently impossible that he should have affirmative attributes' (*The Guide of the Perplexed*).

— 204 —

Here, there and everywhere. – The scriptures contain a mass of contradictions concerning God's place of dwelling. On the one hand he chose the Temple of Solomon to be his house (2 Chron. 8:16) and yet the author of Acts (was it Luke?) insisted that God 'does not make his home in temples made by human hands' (Acts 17:24). Moses believed that, most of the time, God was to be found on top of Mount Sinai (Exod. 3:1), while Samuel said that 'he dwelleth on the Ark of the Covenant' (1 Sam. 4:4; 2 Sam. 6:2). Jacob supposed that God's house, or at least the gateway to it, must be at 'the place' where he had his famous ladder dream (Gen. 28:17). Others are convinced he lives in heaven (Ps. 2:4), thereby ignoring the evidence of Chronicles that the 'heaven of heavens cannot contain him' (2 Chron. 2:6).

This extraordinary muddle might at first seem to clear the way for the classical doctrine that God is everywhere all at once; that he is omnipresent, but the concept of God's omnipresence only serves to intensify our confusion. It was first suggested by David:

Wither shall I go from thy spirit? Or wither shall I flee from thy presence? If I ascend up into heaven, thou art there: if I make my bed in hell, behold, thou art there. If I take the wings of the morning, and dwell in the uttermost parts of the sea; Even there shall thy hand lead me, and thy right hand shall hold me. If I say, Surely the darkness shall cover me; even the night shall be light about me. Yea, the darkness hideth not from thee; but the night shineth as the day; the darkness and the light are both alike to thee. (Ps. 139:7–12)

The idea that God is everywhere and will spot you, even if you're hiding in the dark, started as a priestly warning to sinners that they cannot escape divine justice. God is 'nearer to man than his jugular vein', Muhammad threatens in the Qur'an (50:16), or, as Job's young comforter, Elihu observes: 'his eyes are upon the ways of man, there is no place where the workers of iniquity can hide themselves' (Job 34:21–2).

But elsewhere the Bible contradicts this view. Adam and Eve for instance 'hid themselves from the presence of the Lord' (Gen. 3:8), and Cain 'fled from the presence of the Lord' (Gen. 4:16).

If God really is everywhere, posits the cynic, then he must be in disagreeable places as well as in delightful ones. He must be down the lavatory, for instance, in a septic boil, even in the Devil's brain. These are not comfortable considerations. For if God *is* everywhere then he must also *be* everything. How can God claim to exist in every atomic particle of the world's filth and yet deny that he *is* that filth in itself?

Thomas Aquinas the architect of Christian theology spotted this problem in the thirteenth century and tried to argue a solution. 'God', he said, 'causes all existence and therefore exists everywhere as the agent for everything's existence.' This sounds like a complicated wriggle-around, but is, in fact, ingeniously simple. Aquinas contests that God exists everywhere and in everything by *substance*, *presence* and *power*, explaining these three terms with his own comparison: 'A king exists by *power* which extends everywhere in his kingdom. He exists by *presence* everywhere in his field of vision, and by *substance* wherever he is sitting. But God is by *power* everywhere, and by *presence* everywhere (seeing everything), and by *substance* everywhere (causing everything's existence)' (*Summa Theologiae*, 8:3).

All that is meant by God's omnipresence, then, is that he controls, surveys, brings into being and sustains the existence of every atom of everything everywhere – so God is categorically not a lavatory or, as Aquinas himself put it, 'We cannot know what God is, but only what He is not, so we must consider the ways in which He is not rather than the ways in which He is.'

— 205 —

Good God! – God must be gratified, surprised, puzzled even, that he is nowadays so often described as 'good' – especially since the holy scriptures bear a considerable weight of testimony to the contrary. The Roman Catholic Church teaches that 'God is infinitely good and all his works are good' (*Catechism of the Catholic Church*, 385), yet it is written in the same Church's sacred scripture that God killed 14,700 Israelites by spreading a fatal disease among those who had mourned the deaths of Korah, Dathan and Abiram (Num. 17), that he slew 50,000 Israelites because a handful of them had peered into the Ark of the Covenant at Bethshemesh (1 Sam. 6), that he abetted genocidal pogroms to exterminate the Amorites, Hittites, Perizzites, Canaanites, Hivites and Jebusites (Exod. 23:23) and that God himself had said: 'I will dash them one against another, even fathers and sons together, I will not pity, nor spare, nor have mercy, but destroy' (Jer. 13:14).

These actions alone are not ostensibly 'good' in the modern sense of the word; and so we have a problem. Either God is *not* infinitely good after all, or the sacred scripture has misrepresented him and is in error. What can we say? The safest position is surely to retreat behind that philosophical cloud which hovers over the meaning of that word *good*. Here we will soon discover that not one of us knows what *good* really means. Many will argue that *good* indicates nothing more than that which is *desirable*. In which case absolute good cannot exist, for what is *good* [desirable] for one may well be *bad* [undesirable] for another. While it was *good* for Moses to exterminate the Amorites and take over their land, it was obviously *not good* for the Amorites to be exterminated and robbed by Moses.

Ralph Waldo Emerson's definition that 'good or bad, better or worse, is simply helping or hurting' falls into the same trap. The English philosopher John Stuart Mill believed that *good* is best defined by common sense: 'I will call no being good', he wrote, 'who is not what I mean when I apply the epithet to my fellow creatures; and if such a being can sentence me to Hell for not calling him so, to Hell I will go.' In the end neither Mill, Emerson, the Pope, nor anybody else is able to provide an irrefutable definition of what this word actually means. 'The question of good and evil remains an irremediable chaos, for those who seek to fathom it,' volunteered Voltaire. 'It is a mere mental sport to the disputants, who are captives that play with their chains.' Until *good* is satisfactorily defined we had better leave off describing God in this way, for to call him good without knowing what it means might, in some circumstances, be regarded as a blasphemy.

— 206 —

A perfect being. – When Randolph Churchill, son of Sir Winston, was irritating his friends by talking too much, they bet him he could not stay quiet for a week. Churchill, a compulsive gambler, thought he could win the bet by reading the Bible, but after a few pages exploded uncontrollably, 'God! God's a shit!' and promptly lost the bet. Churchill was by no means the first to notice that the God of the Bible was far from perfect. Marcion was complaining about his behaviour in the second century CE. But while the Bible itself remains the principal source for many of God's most dastardly deeds, the book is not elsewhere afraid to speak of his perfection: God's work is perfect (Deut. 32:4), his way is perfect (2 Sam. 22:31; Ps. 18:30), his law is perfect (Ps. 19:7), and, of course, he himself is utterly perfect (Matt. 5:48).

But what does it mean to say that God is perfect? Perfect for what? In normal language it is hard to define anything as perfect unless the idea of perfection is limited to its function. For instance, to talk of a perfect saw, makes no sense, because some saws are good for felling large trees, while others are used to make intricate jigsaw puzzles out of ply. Neither is *perfect* for the other's task. A work of art

251

might be described as perfect, but only as a work of art, exciting aesthetic pleasure, it would be hopeless for felling trees or washing car engines.

Some theologians believe it is possible to argue that God is perfect *per se*, that his perfection is not limited to any particular sense or function but to anything and everything that is good. But is this logically possible? Can God be a perfect square and a perfect circle, perfectly loud and perfectly quiet, perfectly sharp and perfectly blunt, all at one time? Thomas Aquinas says yes, perfections of opposites 'all pre-exist united in God, without detriment to his simpleness' (*Summa Theologiae*, 4:1) – a mystical explanation which needs faith, and lots of it, to understand. Others might find comfort in the idea that God is 'perfect' only so far as he is a 'perfect god'. But, since he is supposed to be the one and only god, can he be both perfect *and* unique? The Eiffel Tower, for instance, might be described as a perfect tower, given that there lots of towers to compare it with, but since there is only one 'Eiffel Tower' does it mean anything to say 'the Eiffel Tower is the perfect Eiffel Tower'?

Theologians run the risk of tangling themselves into knots in their efforts to uphold all of their precarious generalisations about God, but as Emerson sagely recorded, 'God is our name for the last generalisation to which we can arrive' and so we should not be too surprised if nothing that follows makes any sense at all.

— 207 —

Omnipotent being. – When Mark, the evangelist, wrote 'With God all things are possible' (Mark 10:27), he may have been expressing an opinion rather than stating a fact. In either case Matthew and Luke repeated it, probably copying from Mark (Matt. 19:26; Luke 1:37), while both Jeremiah (Jer. 32:17) and Job (Job 42:2) encouraged the notion that God was indeed all-powerful. God himself has not, however, pronounced on the matter except by asking Abraham a rhetorical question to which no response was offered: 'Is anything too hard for the Lord?' (Gen. 18:14).

And so we are left wondering. Is he or isn't he? Time to call on the wisdom of Karl Popper, an Austrian philosopher of the twentieth century, who taught that a scientific theory cannot be shown to be true, only proved to be false. The theory works like this: you cannot *prove* that 'all deer are brown', except by finding every deer in the universe and noting its colour, and how can anyone be sure that he has found every single deer in the universe? However, by finding just one deer that is white it is possible to assert without contradiction that 'not all deer are brown'.

How does this help with God's omnipotence? Matthew, Mark and Luke all claim that God is omnipotent but to prove it they would need to have witnessed God doing *everything* that his omnipotence allows him to do. Since they were mortal, the evangelists never had the time to conduct such a test. However, if they had found just one piece of evidence to show that God was incapable of doing *something* because he did not have the *power* to do it, they could have claimed that God is *not* omnipotent without fear of contradiction. Perhaps none of them had read the book of Judges: 'And the Lord was with the tribe of Judah and he drove out the inhabitants of the mountain; but he could not drive out the inhabitants of the valley, because they had chariots of iron' (Judg. 1:19).

That settles the case – unless, of course the Judges were mistaken.

—— 208 ——

What an omnipotent god can and cannot do. – Can an all-powerful being make a spherical cube? It would be illogical if he could, so most philosophers have taken the line that God's omnipotence is limited to what is logically possible. But even that is not obvious in all cases; can an omnipotent God make a mountain that is too heavy for him to lift? If the answer is 'no' then he cannot be omnipotent, can he? But if it is 'yes', he straight way refutes his omnipotence by being unable to lift the mountain.

The word omnipotent derives from the Latin *omni* (all) and *potens* (powerful), the present participle of *posse* (to be able) and the key to its English use lies in this Latin etymology. He who is *omnipotent* can, in theory, do anything that it is *possible* for him to do and this (in the case of God) happens to include miracles, theophanies and resurrections. He could also make a mountain that is far too heavy for even himself to lift, but having made it, he would no longer be omnipotent – what kind of a fool God would do a thing like that?

— 209 —

Immutable. – Most bewildering of all the classical attributes of God is immutability. Why should it be a good thing that God never changes? The problem comes about because theologians like Aquinas held the very definition of God to be 'that which is the perfection of all perfections'. If God is perfect, the argument runs, then the slightest change would alter his perfection, therefore he cannot possibly change. The notion is upheld by a scriptural passage from Malachi: 'For I am the Lord, I change not.' But God is not claiming immutability in the classical theist sense here, only suggesting that he likes to stick by original intentions – a claim which, incidentally, is not conspicuously upheld elsewhere in the scriptures: 'And the Lord repented of the evil he said he would inflict upon the Ninevites' (Jon. 3:10).

If God were immutable he would be intransigent, unable to adapt to the developing conditions of mankind, unhelpful and fundamentally boring – and that, surely, would refute his perfection. To escape this criticism it has been suggested that God exists outside of time altogether. The reason he is not boring is because boredom requires the passage of time. The trouble now is that to exist outside of universal time means not to exist in the universe at all. At which point why bother with God in the first place? Boethius, a philosopher of the sixth century who was much influenced by Augustine, side-stepped the problem by asserting that 'God beholdeth all things in his eternal present'. But either the eternal present is a self-contradiction or it means 'the present'. Boethius cannot logically have his cake and eat it.

A popular rebuttal to the proposition of God's immutable timelessness holds that he could not have created the world at any given time if he himself has always existed outside of time. The theist philosopher, Keith Ward, attempted to refute this with an analogy: 'Rather as my bodily actions can be caused by my anger, which is not in any spatial relation to my body, so temporal events can be caused by a reality, God, which is not in any temporal relation to them' (*Concept of God*, 154). He is trying to compare 'a reality, God' to 'my anger' as though 'my anger' were also a reality and not just a convenient linguistic definition of effects (i.e. red face, loss of temper, waving fist etc.). At very best, Ward's argument turns God into a timeless creative emotion, but what exactly is that if not *nothing at all*?

— 210 —

How a good god makes evil. – In theory, since he is omnipotent, God can do anything he wants. He can, if he chooses, commit gross acts of evil: 'The Lord made everything for a purpose, even the wicked for an evil day' (Prov. 16:4), but most religious minds refuse to accept that. How can he create evil, they ask, for he is *infinitely good*? Abelard and John Wycliffe were both condemned (respectively at the Councils of Sens and Constance) for suggesting that God's power was *limited* by his goodness and this limitation prevented him, of necessity, from creating evil. To avoid similar condemnations others have found subtler ways round. Augustine, for instance, judged that God 'would never allow any evil whatsoever to exist in his works if he were not so all-powerful and good as to cause good to emerge from evil itself' (*Enchiridion*, 11:3), but this ignores the crucial question: Where did evil actually come from in the first place if it was not created by God?

Augustine looked into it and flunked: 'I sought whence evil comes and there is no solution' (*Confessions*, 7.7:11). One hundred years later the Roman philosopher Boethius thought he had solved the problem by declaring that evil cannot really exist at all: '"Is there nothing that an omnipotent God can not do?"' he asked, '"No." "Then can God do evil?" "No." "So that evil is nothing, since that is what He cannot do who can do anything"' (*Consolation of Philosophy*).

In trying to absolve God in this way, Boethius may have been guilty of the sin of blasphemy, for the Lord himself refutes Boethius in the book of Isaiah: 'I form the light, and create darkness: I make peace, and create evil: I the Lord do all these things' (Isa. 45:7). There is an alternative solution but nobody wants to give it a go: scrap the predicate 'infinitely good' and the problem disappears – jus' like that!

— 211 —

Know all. – If God is omnipotent he must be omniscient too. Since knowing is a form of doing and since he is able to *do* everything that it is possible to do, he must also *know* everything that it is possible to know.

Not true! He might only have sufficient knowledge to do all the things which it is possible for him to do, and no more than that. Even so, it remains an unshakeable pillar of most religious dogma that God does indeed *know* everything. The attribute of omniscience originally came about in two ways. First as a threat: 'Don't think that you can hide your sins from God because he knows everything even your sinful thoughts and will surely punish you for them.' The second source follows from the premise that God is perfect, or, as Aquinas said, 'the perfection of all perfections'. If God is perfect and if ignorance is a fault, God must be ignorant of nothing, hence he must *know* everything. With so many superlatives problems are sure to arise and the one most often associated with God's omniscience is that concerning the future and free will.

Why is there evil in the world? Because God, out of love for his creation, gave human beings free will, which they, or more specifically Adam and Eve, abused. But since God knows everything he must have knowledge of the future. He must have known that Adam was going to take the apple even before Adam was created. So did Adam really have a free choice in the matter, or was it pre-ordained for him by being inscribed, as it were, in God's knowledge *before* the event?

Just because God *knew* that Adam would take the apple it does not mean Adam could not have done otherwise, for if he had not taken it, God would have *known otherwise*, that is all. So it is possible for God to know the future without depriving human beings of their free will.

The real problem of omniscience lies elsewhere. If God knew in advance of creating the world that the first man he created would freely choose to eat a forbidden apple and thereby condemn the rest of humanity to suffer, why did he create that particular world with that particular man in it? If he really had no choice (and now we are chiselling away at his omnipotence) could he not, at least, have placed the tree out of sight of the man? If God knows the future then he must share in the guilt of Adam's crime. If in the very idea of the 'perfection of all perfections' sharing any guilt is an anathema, he should no longer be defined as omniscient.

There are two ways to rid God of the stigma of omniscience. Firstly with the argument that the future does not exist, it is something that has not yet come into being (i.e., nothing), and can therefore never be known, not even by an omniscient being. Secondly (a useful fallback in any theological debate), refer to the scriptures. Two examples will suffice.

God made Abraham go nearly all the way to sacrificing his son Isaac in order to find out if Abraham feared him (Gen. 22). If it were true, as is written in the New Testament, that 'God can read everyone's heart' (Acts 1:24), he would never have needed to put Abraham to the test. In the Garden of Eden God was looking for his sinful creations; 'And the Lord God called out to Adam and asked of him: Where are you, Adam?' (Gen. 3:9).

— 212 —

Eternal source of Light Divine. – God and time is a muddled area of theology, particularly so since human beings have stubbornly refused to understand the idea of time since they started pondering it at the dawn of human civilisation. Most of God's time problems are centred on the idea of eternity. In order to shield God from the humiliation of being *created* and, worse still, from the ignominy of mortality, it was long ago decided that God neither was born, nor shall he ever die, in other words he is eternal, he stretches both backwards into the past for ever and will be everlasting in the future.

We shall dismiss the question of God's *future* immortality since it can never be known by man, nor even by God himself – since it would require an eternity (which of course can never pass) to prove. So the question of God's transcendence of time must be concentrated on his birth (or lack of it) and not the impossibility of his death, which has no meaning. There are three ways to investigate the source of God's eternal existence: the scriptural, the scientific and the philosophical.

In that order:

1. A SCRIPTURAL INVESTIGATION: There is only one biblical passage in which God himself claims to have had no beginning. It is reported *verbatim* by the Second Isaiah: 'I am God, yes, from eternity I am. No one can deliver from my hand; when I act, who can thwart me?' (Isa. 43:13). The phrase 'from eternity' is self-contradictory, for the word 'from' implies a starting point. He would have been better off saying, 'I am God and I have always been in existence,' but before correcting God on his use of English it might be as well to examine the biblical translation. That translation is from the New Jerusalem Bible, a scholarly version, promoted by the Catholic Church, which subscribes to the doctrine of God having no beginning. So what did God really say to the Second Isaiah? The Basic English Bible translates the passage thus: 'From time long past I am God and from this day I

am he,' while The American Standard Bible renders it, 'Since the day was, I am,' which is similar to the Douay-Rheims translation (1582), 'from the beginning I am the same,' a version drawn from the Latin Vulgate which uses the words *ab initio* ('from the beginning').

It is starting to look as though God himself knows that he *did* have a beginning. 'No god', he told Isaiah, 'was formed before me, nor will be after me.' In this, God is unequivocal. He is saying not only that gods are *formed* but that no god was formed *before* him. If he had always existed, the phrase 'before me' would have no meaning. When using that phrase he is clearly implying that there was a time when even he (the first of the gods) had not yet been formed.

2. A SCIENTIFIC INVESTIGATION: For scientific evidence we can turn to the modern consensus among theoretical physicists that the universe was formed from an explosion called (with some understatement) The Big Bang. It has been calculated that this event occurred 15 billion years ago and scientists have pictured what the universe must have been like only 0.0001 second after the moment of creation. It was, they say, very dense indeed (100,000 billion times denser them water) the temperature was a 1000 billion degrees above absolute zero; the universe was a cosmic fireball of super-hot radiation. All well and good, but what was happening, just before that? This unfortunately is where the trail ends. We can only deduce that there existed a 'singularity', by which is meant one invisibly minute point into which all the matter in the universe had collapsed, so small that it took up no space, existed for no amount of time and yet was so dense as to contain all the matter of the universe. Scientists describe it as 'infinitely dense' but this is to confuse mathematics with reality; let us just say it is as dense as dense can be.

The concept of a singularity may to the non-scientist seem as mystic and unreal as the concept of God appears to the atheist, yet there are remarkable similarities between the two. Unity, transcendence of space and time, scorching heat, dazzling light, the power to create the universe; all these attributes are used equally by scientists to describe a 'singularity' as by theists to explain what they mean by God. If God was the singularity itself then sadly he would have died from the divine ejaculation that created our universe 15 billion years ago. If, on the other hand, he was not that unity from which scientists say that everything was made (he is something other, an alternative presence in this universe), then, according to the pervading laws of theoretical physics, neither he nor anything else could have existed *in time* before that singularity 15 billion years ago, and so, God, who ever he is, cannot have been God for ever.

3. A PHILOSOPHICAL INVESTIGATION: In order for any series to be infinite (in spatial, temporal or even numerical terms) infinite time has to pass. This naturally presents a contradiction. No infinite series can be said *presently* to exist, nor can there ever be a time in which an infinite series will exist, for such a series would cease to be infinite (ceasing even to maintain the potential for infinitude) if it were not always *in the process of carrying on.*

In other words the series of numbers 1, 2, 3, 4, 5 . . . cannot go on forever without *infinite time* in which to do so, and since infinite time is infinite, the process can never end, hence the series can never be defined infinite. If the universe really were an infinite number of years old then every event that has ever occurred would need to be preceded by an infinite number of events and we would never have been able to arrive at the present. Since time is the measurement of events moving in one direction only (from past to present) and cannot extend backwards (towards the past) an infinite number of past events is impossible. The universe must therefore have had a beginning.

But where does this leave God? If there was a god before the creation of the universe what was he? With no events, no things, no time and no space, the exact meaning of 'God before the universe' is the same as 'no-God'. In other words he cannot possibly have existed.

— 213 —

Temptation. – When God put the Tree of Knowledge into the Garden of Eden with all its juicy fruit, was he not tempting Adam and Eve to take some? Jesus thought that he was, and asked his congregation at the Sermon on the Mount to plead with God not to 'lead us into temptation' any more (Matt. 6:13). High church instinct declares it is impossible for God to lead anyone into temptation, citing the general epistle of James (once held to be the work of Jesus' brother, now thought to be a later Greek impostor): 'Let no man say when he is tempted, I am tempted by God, for God cannot be tempted, nor will he tempt any man' (Jas. 1:13). Why should the modern Christian churches choose to side with the pseudo-brother of Jesus, rather than the great man himself? They don't.

What is argued is that Jesus and his brother's impostor were actually in agreement. The Catholic answer is that 'it is difficult to translate the Greek verb used by a single English word'. In other words Jesus did not mean 'lead us not into temptation', but, 'do not allow us to enter into temptation', or preferably, 'do not let us yield to temptation'. In Joseph Smith's Inspired Version of the Bible the same passage is translated, 'suffer us not to be led into temptation'.

These sophistical sidesteps cannot conceal the fact that elsewhere in the scriptures, God, contrary to the epistle of James, both tempts others and is tempted himself. He tempted David, for instance, into committing a petty crime against religion (2 Sam. 24:1) and 'God did tempt Abraham' (Gen. 22:1) to sacrifice his son Isaac; he 'hardened Pharoah's heart' in Exodus and put an evil spirit into Saul causing him to lunge at David with a spear (1 Sam. 19). God even admitted to being tempted himself, for 'they have tempted me, the Lord, ten times' he complained (Num. 14:22).

God stated his position clearly to Muhammad: Whomsoever God desires to guide, He expands his breast to Islam; whomsoever he

261

desires to lead astray, He makes his breast narrow and tight. So God lays abomination on those who do not believe' (Qur'an 6:125). But there is a catch; for those who do not believe in Islam are disbelievers through no choice of their own, but because God has willed it that way: 'If the Lord had willed, whoever is in the earth would have believed, all of them, all together. Wouldst thou then constrain the people, until they are believers? It is not for any soul to believe save by the leave of God; and He lays abomination upon those who have no understanding' (Qur'an 10:99–100).

Muslims must wonder then if God is guiding them towards him or leading them in the opposite direction to *Gehenna*, for 'God confirms those who believe with the firm word and God leads astray the evil doers; and God does what he wills' (Qur'an 13:27).

What then becomes of those whom God has lead astray? 'Whomsoever God guides, he is rightly guided; and whom he leads astray – they shall not be protected, except by Him. And we shall muster them on the Resurrection Day upon their faces, blind, dumb, deaf, their refuge shall be *Gehenna*, and whensoever it abates we shall increase the blaze for them' (Qur'an 17:97). If he wishes to destroy a whole city, as he did at Sodom and Gomorrah, God may first tempt its citizens to sin so that he has a good excuse: 'When we desire to destroy a city,' God told Muhammad, 'We command its men who live at ease, and they commit ungodliness therein, wherefore the sentence is justly pronounced against that city and we destroy it utterly!' (*Qur'an* 17:16).

— 214 —

Time warp. – God said to Adam, 'of the tree of the knowledge of good and evil you are not to eat; for the day that you eat thereof you shall surely die' (Gen. 2:17). But this was not strictly true, for Adam, as we know, ate the forbidden fruit and lived for 930 years (Gen. 5:5). In order to avoid the assumption that God had made a mistake, or, worse still, told an outright lie, the author of the first-century BCE *Book of Jubilees* gave this excuse: 'When Adam died, he lacked seventy years from one thousand years, for a thousand years are like one day in the testimony of heaven and therefore it was written concerning the tree of knowledge, "In the day you eat from it you will die." Therefore he did not complete the days of this year because he died in it' (*Jub.* 4:30).

The source for this information was probably the much older Psalm 90, the only psalm which is attributed to Moses: 'A thousand years are to you like a yesterday which passes like a watch in the night,' he says. In the Christian New Testament Peter adds to the confusion by stating that 'there is one thing, my dear friends you must never forget: that with the Lord a day is like a thousand years, and a thousand years is like a day' (2 Pet. 3:8), leaving the reader to wonder if a day to God is like a thousand years to us or vice versa. Whatever Peter meant by this remark, it has been widely interpreted that one thousand years to us is like a day to God. This being so, a new interpretation of the Genesis story of creation may arise. If God created the world in six days, it would seem like six thousand years to us. In which case, to those who believe that the world was created only 4000 years before Christ, is it not possible that the creation is still taking place? Seventh-Day Adventists and many other apocalyptic creeds have based their faith on precisely this premise.

—— 215 ——

Micro-rest. –

If God's days were really the same as 1,000 years to us (i.e. 365,000 days to us), then presumably our days would likewise be 365,000 times shorter when they are experienced by God. When the Book of Genesis says that God created the world in six days it is not stated whether those six days are 'human days'

or 'God days', which, as we have seen, differ in time-duration by a factor of 365,000. If Genesis meant to say that God created the world in six 'God days', then fine, we can, if we wish to stretch our imaginations beyond the horizon and back, interpret this as meaning that he created the world (or intends to create the world) in 6,000 'human years'. If, on the other hand, what Genesis is trying to say (and seems to be succeeding in saying quite clearly) is that God created the world in six 'human days', then as far as God is concerned the act was accomplished in 1.4202 of a second – hardly long enough to justify a rest on the seventh day, especially since his rest would have lasted no more than 0.2367 of a second. (A. Waugh, *Time*, pp. 173–4)

— 216 —

Fancy that! – It took God 40 days to write the Law on 2 tablets of stone using his finger (Exod. 24:18), yet Enoch managed 366 books in only 30 days using a speed-writing pen he had borrowed from God (*2 En.* 23)!

— 217 —

Infallible reason. – In 1869 Pope Pius IX presided over the First Vatican Council. Bishops descended on Rome from all over the world to debate issues ranging from Catholic dogma, faith, discipline, law, to priestly wages and foreign missions. As church councils go it went smoothly enough – the bishops managed to restrain themselves from thumping and buggering each other as they had done in the heated debates of church councils in the first millennium (see *Eusebius: History of the Church*). Even so the pace of Vatican I was slow, speeches were far too long and emergency measures had to be introduced to keep things moving.

Perhaps the most famous upshot of Vatican I was the vote on papal infallibility in which it was agreed that any decision taken by the pope was 'irreformable of itself'. In other words, whatever the pope decreed was eternally correct, and could never be altered. At the same time it was agreed that God could be known, or proven to exist, just by the application of a bit of clever thinking.

'Our holy mother, the Church,' decreed Pope Pius 'holds and teaches that God can be known with certainty by the natural light of human reason.' This caused a sensation. If the infallible pope asserts that we can all know for certain that God exists just by applying a bit of reason, he must be right and we must all be saved. But why did it take until 1869 for the Catholic Church to reveal this all important information? Can it possibly be true?

Unfortunately Pius IX was not concentrating properly when he issued the decree. How can you know anything from reason alone? The most obvious answer is by use of a syllogism; the most famous of these being the 'Barbara' of Aristotle: All men are mortal; Socrates is a man, therefore Socrates is mortal.' The truth of the final statement, 'Socrates is mortal' is drawn inevitably from the first two premises. All well and good, but what happens when a conclusion is taken from a set of false premises? For instance, 'No fish can swim; some seals are fish, therefore some seals cannot swim.' Obvious rubbish! but the internal logic of the syllogism remains intact, that is, if no fish could swim and if some seals were fish, then it would be true to conclude that some seals could not swim. What the syllogism does not address is the external veracity of the first and second premise (i.e., whether it is indeed true in the natural world that fish cannot swim and that some seals are fish). In order to know God 'with certainty by the natural light of human reason' we must agree at least *two premises* which are true. Whoops! We haven't got that, have we? No, the pope and his council of bishops have failed to grasp the first rudiments of elementary philosophy. But the church has declared that the pope is infallible, so now what?

A much later pontiff (Pius XII, who guided the Vatican through World War II) tried a crab-like explanation:

Though human reason is, strictly speaking, truly capable by its own natural light of attaining to a true and certain knowledge of the one personal God, yet there are many obstacles which prevent reason from the effective and fruitful use of this inborn faculty. For the truths that concern the relations between God and man wholly transcend the visible order of things, and, if they are translated into human action, and influence it, they call for self-surrender and abnegation. The human mind, in its turn, is hampered in the attaining of such truths, not only by the impact of the senses and the imagination, but also by disordered appetites which are the consequences of original sin. So it happens that men in such matters easily persuade themselves that what they would not like to be true is false or at least doubtful. ('Humani Generis 561', Pius XII)

And there we must leave it – incomprehensibly dangling at the Vatican.

— 218 —

Wisdom and faith. – When the pope declared in 1869 that 'certain knowledge of God could be attained by the light of reason alone', clever people rejoiced, for traditionally Christian churches have been opposed to reason, rebuffing bright, enquiring minds especially when they ask difficult metaphysical questions. Celsus, author of the earliest surviving attack on Christianity which dates from around 178 CE, criticised the new religion as a lure for dim-wits: 'Taking its root in the lower classes,' he complained, 'the religion continues to spread among the vulgar: nay, one can even say that it spreads *because* of its vulgarity and the illiteracy of its adherents. It thrives in its purer form among the ignorant.'

According to Celsus deliberate targeting of *ignorami* was the only way that Christianity could survive, accusing its leaders of recruiting morons to their cult with the line: ' "Let no one educated, no one wise, no one sensible draw near. For these abilities are thought by us to be evils. But as for anyone ignorant, anyone stupid, anyone uneducated, anyone childish, let him come boldly".'

Schopenhauer showed how nothing changes, even 1600 years later: 'Religion', he wrote, 'is the only means of introducing some notion of the high significance of life into the uncultivated heads of the masses, deep sunk as they are in mean pursuits and uncultivated drudgery.' This, from his *Dialogue on Religion*, published with other essays in 1851, brought Schopenhauer, for the first time, enormous popularity. But does God agree with him? Are the 'uncultivated masses' able to comfort themselves with the thought that if Schopenhauer and Celsus are not on their team, God at least is?

Paul quoted God as saying, 'I will destroy the wisdom of the wise, and will bring to nothing the understanding of the prudent' (1 Cor. 1:19), yet elsewhere the Bible affirms, 'Happy is the man who findeth wisdom' (Prov. 3:13). Paul and the early Christians were instinctively opposed to sceptics asking questions in high Socratic tone for the sole purpose of making them look foolish. What better, then, than to claim that God himself loathes clever questioning and intends to destroy the wisdom of the wise?

Martin Luther, founder of the Reformation, was the most virulent of God's servants in what now seems like an hysterical crusade against reason. Reason seeks out wisdom, which leads in turn to knowledge. All dangerous stuff to Luther! 'Faith', he exhorted, 'must trample under foot all reason, sense, and understanding, and whatever it sees it must put out of sight, and wish to know nothing but the word of God.' Luther accused 'reason' of being a hooker: 'The devil's bride, *ratio*, the whore, comes in and thinks she is clever. Stay at home with your ugly devil's bride . . . It is more possible to teach an ass to read than to blind reason and lead it right; for reason must be deluded, blinded, and destroyed' (*Works Vol. 12*, Martin Luther).

God may have been on Luther's side for he was certainly against the accumulation of knowledge as is testified by the very first words he spoke to any human being: 'Of every tree of the garden thou mayest freely eat,' he said to Adam. 'But the tree of the knowledge of good and evil, thou shalt not eat of it: for the day that thou eatest thereof thou shalt surely die' (Gen. 2:17).

— 219 —

A question of faith. – People often ask one another: 'Do you believe in God?' You may suppose that there is only one intelligent response: 'Sorry, I don't understand the question,' but this marks you out as a pedant. 'Mind your own business!' creates more of a *frisson*.

— 220 —

French joke. –

I supplicated, I demanded a sign, I sent messages to Heaven – no reply. Heaven ignored my very name. Each minute I wondered what could be in the eyes of God. Now I know the answer: nothing, God does not see me, God does not hear me . . . I am going to tell you a colossal joke: God does not exist. (Jean-Paul Sartre, *The Devil and the Good Lord*)

— 221 —

Catch 22 (for Christians). – If faith is not acquired but is a gift of God as is stated by Paul in his letter to the Ephesians (Eph. 2:8), what happens to those who do not receive it? Jesus and Thomas Aquinas respectively taught, 'he that believeth not shall be damned' (Mark 16:16), and 'be cut off from the world by death' (*Summa Theologiae*, 32:11:4–5). Without the gift of faith we perish. With it we are saved. But no one who has not received this gift can pray for it because God (according to Aquinas) has already decided what each person will or will not receive from him, so there is no point in asking for anything else.

— 222 —

Promises, promises. – At some stage in the long millennium before Jesus was born God may have realised that he was not a particularly good god. He had not succeeded in providing prosperity or security for his people; he had not given them either the lands or the multiple descendants that he had covenanted to them; by the middle of that millennium ten of the twelve tribes of Israel had completely disappeared, possibly merged with idolatrous Assyrian races, while the Temple at Jerusalem had been utterly destroyed and all the intelligent, professional members of God's chosen race dragged off into exile at Babylon. God even abhorred those who had been left behind: 'They', he said, 'shall fall by the sword, I shall give them to the wild beasts to be devoured and they shall die from pestilence' (Ezek. 33:27).

God sorely needed to restore credibility; but what could he do? Could he not rescue the ten lost tribes, pull the exiles out from Babylon and resettle them in the land of milk and honey which he had always promised to give them? God had yet to honour his original covenant with the Patriarchs and yet, at Israel's darkest hour, when he was in grave danger of being abandoned by all but a handful of exiled fanatics in Babylon, God devised the cunningest of all cunning plans – another covenant!

This one will be better than all the others. Nay, it will supersede them all. He will guarantee them things that he never guaranteed before; not just land, milk, honey or thriving descendants, much more than that. He will return in person, he will descend to the earth, rid it of everything selfish and evil and make the whole world pleasant, prosperous and peaceful. Furthermore, he will assure all people on earth that he will never abandon them again, that they will be protected for ever under his loving gaze so that no harm will come to mankind again – and that's a promise!

'I will make a covenant of peace with them,' he told the exiled
Ezekiel:

and I will eliminate harmful beasts from the land so that they may
live securely in the wilderness and sleep in the woods. I will make
them and the places around my hill a blessing. And I will cause
showers to come down in their season; they will be showers of
blessing. Also the tree of the field will yield its fruit and the earth
will yield its increase, and they will be secure on their land. Then
they will know that I am the Lord, when I have broken the bars
of their yoke and have delivered them from the hand of those who
enslaved them. They will no longer be a prey to the nations, and
the beasts of the earth will not devour them; but they will live
securely, and no one will make them afraid. (Ezek. 34:25–8)

God also promised to reverse the declining life expectancy of human
beings. People like Adam had lived for 930 years; in the seventh
generation Enoch lasted only 365 and life-spans continued to shrink
with each passing generation:

And the days will begin to increase and grow longer among the
sons of men, generation by generation, year by year, till their
days draw near to a thousand years, and to a greater number
of years than previously they had days. And there will be no old
men who are full of days, for all will be as children and youths.
(*Jub.* 23:27–8)

God vowed that he would bring not only health and prosperity but
peace too. So much peace that all fighting would cease for ever between
living things:

And the wolf will be living with the lamb, and the leopard will
take his rest with the young goat; and the lion will take grass for
food like the ox; and the young lion will go with the young ones

of the herd; and a little child will be their guide. And the cow and the bear will be friends while their young ones are sleeping together. And the child at the breast will be playing by the hole of the snake, and the older child will put his hand on the bright eye of the poison-snake. There will be no cause of pain or destruction in all my holy mountain: for the earth will be full of the knowledge of the Lord as the sea is covered by the waters. (Isa. 11:6–9)

—— 223 ——

The down side. – Of course the coming of God's kingdom is not going to be fun for everyone. God's threat to quake and shake the earth, sending fire and destruction right across it, is clearly intended to encourage good behaviour among the wicked, but with only 144,000 places available in his kingdom for the saved (this according to Revelation), the vast majority will be damned to an eternity of sulphurous hell fire. If God's apocalyptic promises are to be fulfilled in 2050 (by which time estimates claim there will be nearly 9 billion people on earth), each person will stand only a 1:62,500 chance of salvation – 8.9 billion will be damned.

The lucky winners will be identified like cattle with God's and Jesus' names branded on their foreheads (Rev. 14:1) and made to sing hymns of praise for all eternity. If this sounds bad, the fate of the losers will be far worse. God promises to trample over all their lands, crush them under his feet so that their blood squirts even on his own garments (Isa. 63:3). Enemies of Israel and their descendants will be automatically slaughtered. 'Their dead will be thrown away, the stench will rise from their corpses, the mountains will run with their blood, the entire array of heaven will fall apart' (Isa. 34:3). The entire country of Edom (now south-west Jordan between the Dead Sea and the Gulf of Aqaba) will be devastated as a punishment for having taken advantage against the Israelites during the exile: 'Its streams will turn to molten pitch, its dust into fiery brimstone, its country will be ablaze; never quenched, night or day, its smoke rising for ever, the country will lie waste for ever and ever' (Isa. 34:9–10).

On top of this God has promised a pitched battle against the devil and all his forces at Armageddon (Rev. 16:16), a small hill to the south of Mount Carmel, while a mass of earthquakes shall ripple around the globe destroying every single city that man has built.

— 224 —

Crafty ploy. – God's new set of promises to the Jewish prophets had exactly the desired effect, for God, suddenly, was interesting again; he was back in vogue and the 'in thing' was eschatology, a hip doctrine of the last or final things. Eschatology succeeded in invigorating religion from the moment that God made his covenant with Ezekiel in the sixth century BCE, and it continues to this day as the prime cause for all religious observance. If God had not sworn to return some day, had he not promised to judge and to damn and to save, he would have been forgotten a long time ago; for religions thrive on unfulfilled promises – without them, they collapse.

— 225 —

Another bite of the apple. – To Enoch God revealed an interesting detail of his 'kingdom' plan. He intended to plant a tree, he said, 'in the direction of the northeast' whose delicious fruit with magical fragrance and special effects can be enjoyed by the 144,000 righteous people that survive the purgatory holocaust of his coming judgement. Enoch described the tree in all its glory: 'among all the fragrances, nothing could be so fragrant; its magnificent leaves, its handsome blossom and its beautiful wood would never wither; its fruit is delightful and resembles the clustered fruits of a palm tree' (*1 En.* 24:5–6). God promises that this tree will bring long life and spiritual happiness to all who eat from it: 'Then they shall be glad and rejoice in gladness and they shall enter into the holy place; its fragrance shall penetrate their bones, long life will you live on earth such as your fathers lived in their days' (*1 En.* 25:6). This magic tree may have been the method by which he intended to inject his spirit into all good people as he had previously divulged to the biblical prophet Joel: 'It will come about after this that I will pour out My Spirit on all mankind; And your sons and daughters will prophesy, your old men will dream dreams, your young men will see visions. Even on the male and female servants will I pour out My Spirit in those days' (Joel 2:28–9).

God threw Adam and Eve out of Paradise, not because they had disobeyed him by taking the apple from the Tree of Knowledge but because he was worried that they would go on to eat from the Tree of Life and become gods like him; for as he told the *elohim*:

'Now that the man has come like one of us in knowing good from evil, he must not be allowed to reach out his hand and pick from the Tree of Life too, and eat and live for ever!' So God expelled him from the garden of Eden and in front of the garden posted the great winged creatures and the fiery flashing sword, to guard the way to the tree of life. (Gen. 3:22–24)

Originally God was not concerned if they ate from the Tree of Life, telling them: 'You are free to eat of *all* the trees in the garden *except* the Tree of the Knowledge of good and evil' (Gen. 2:16–17). If Adam and Eve had happened to eat from the Tree of Life *before* they took the apple from the Tree of Knowledge perhaps they would have become god-like straightaway and the whole of human history would have been different. As it happens they took the wrong one first.

By declaring his intention to put the Tree of Life at the disposal of mankind God effectively promises to human beings the divine status which he previously denied them in Eden. Would it not have been easier if Adam and Eve had been allowed to eat this fruit in the first place?

— 226 —

The great guessing game. – The idea that God will one day return to earth, performing a magnificent entrance, with 10,000 trumpeting angels on the top of a Middle Eastern mountain is exciting enough; but what if we miss it? Since God declared his new covenant the burning question of the last two and a half millennia has been, 'When will he be coming?'

Jesus was so excited that he started predicting right away: 'There are some of you standing in front of me right now', he said, 'that will be alive when the kingdom comes' (Matt. 16:28). But Jesus was not the only one to get it wrong. A Flemish monk called Roual Glaber said it would happen in the year 1000 CE, but when God failed to materialise on that date he commuted the kingdom to 1033 CE – nothing happened then either.

James Ussher, seventeenth-century Bishop of Meath, predicted 23 October 1997; Nostradamus suggested in the gnomic Quatrain 72, that something spectacular was going to happen in August 1999 involving Ghengis Khan and Mars.

Jason Hommel, an American Latter-day prophet was 'amazed' to find that there are 5760 grains of gold in a Troy pound. Taking this information, together with the 'amazing fact' that the number of faces, sides and vertices of a cube can be multiplied to get 576, Hommel realised that God would fulfil his promises in the Jewish year 5760 (1999). When this prediction was shown to be wrong Hommel defended his work by announcing that 'the associative thought processes that lead one to accomplish rational thinking and figuring were completely absent from this process'.

By far the most prodigious prognosticator of God's intentions is a modern biblical decoder called Marilyn Agee. In 1998 she predicted God's arrival on 31 May. When nothing happened then she changed her prophesy to 6 June, then to 7 June, to 14 June and to 21 June. Eventually the whole of June was abandoned as Ms Agee stated:

There have been a few count-downs this summer and the final one is now counting to 20th September. Many of us have been maybe too eager to accept new dates after pentecost-98 proved to be not the moment. Maybe it is just that about nobody can boast 'I knew the right time' + we are tested.

When 20 September 1998 had been and gone, the Agee camp predicted that the Israel/PLO peace agreement of 23 October 1998 corresponded to the seven-day warning that God gave Noah about the flood and that God intended to put in an appearance *seven months* after October 1998. This too proved to be wrong, but the redoubtable Ms Agee was never one to give up; a new idea occurred: 'It seems that the Lord is showing us by the process of elimination, that the third year in the parable of the barren fig tree (Luke 13:6–9) is the right year. It is the year when the Lord SPEAKS.' This led to a new conviction that 9 or 10 June 2000 was a 'definite date'.

After these passed without incident, Ms Agee's prophetic tone became a little more cautious: 'I wonder if the indwelling Holy Spirit will fly the dove to her rest, Heaven, on Sunday 20th August 2000?' she asked – er? no, wrong again!

Try maths: 'If we count 33.5 as 34, as the Jews would do, June 5, 1967 + 34 = June 5, 2001. That agrees pretty well with the tribulation beginning on the Feast of Weeks in 2001. Sivan 7, 5761, is our May 29, the anniversary of Pentecost in 30 AD on both calendars. I feel that we have to be gone before that' (*Prophecy Corner*: http://home.pe.net/~mjagee).

— 227 —

Posthumous determination. – When Abraham died, God had still not fulfilled the promise of his covenant; but once in heaven the determined patriarch was able to ask God in person what he intended to do about it. As he was brought into the divine presence Abraham was nervous. There was no floor; and instead of prostrating himself as he had on earth (Gen. 18:2) Abraham was forced to bow instead: 'Teach me, show me, and make known to your servant what you have promised me.' But God did not answer. Abraham was scared and started to mumble any old rubbish: 'Accept also the sacrifice which you yourself made to yourself through me as I searched for you . . .'

'Abraham, Abraham!'

'Here I am!'

'Look from on high at the stars which are beneath you and count them for me and tell me their number!'

'When can I? for I am a man!'

'As the number of stars and their power so shall I place for your seed the nations and men of the earth!'

It was the same old promise Abraham had heard many times before – he almost knew it by heart. But what about the land? All his descendants were circumcising themselves down there and still they did not have all the land that God had promised them. WHEN? WHEN? WHEN? – that was all Abraham needed to know.

'Eternal, Mighty One!' he gingerly ventured, 'How long a time is the hour of the age?'

'I decreed to keep twelve periods of the impious age among the heathens and among your seed and what you have seen will be until the end of time. Count it up and you will understand.'

'Er?!?' But Abraham knew better than to press the point and incur the mighty wrath, so he 'accepted the words of God in his heart' and left (*Apoc. Abr.* 17–32).

— 228 —

The commonplace Christian. –

If Christianity were right, with its theories of an avenging God, of general sinfulness, of redemption and the danger of eternal damnation, it would be a sign of weak intellect and lack of character *not* to become a priest, apostle or hermit, and to work only with fear and trembling for one's salvation; it would be senseless thus to neglect eternal benefits for temporary comfort. Taking it for granted that there *is belief,* the commonplace Christian is a miserable figure, a man that really cannot add two and two together, and who, moreover, just because of his mental incapacity for responsibility, did not deserve to be so severely punished as Christianity has decreed. (Friedrich Nietzsche, *Human, all-too-Human,* 116)

— 229 —

Platonic proof by motion. – Plato's 'proof' for the existence of God is not a good one. He was over eighty years old when he wrote the tenth book of Laws in which it appears, and it seems to have been written in defence of an Athenian law which made it a criminal offence not to believe in gods. The reason behind such a law was the belief that atheism led to immorality and that 'no one who believes in gods as the law commands, ever intentionally commits an unholy act or lets an unlawful word pass his lips'.

Plato suggested that in order to uphold such a ruling the existence of gods ought to be proved. Why, after all, should it be *illegal* not to believe in something which the state itself cannot prove to exist? Let's prove it then, said Plato. His argument centred on a discussion of movement. There are ten different kinds of movement, he stated, but one is infinitely superior to all the others. It is 'motion which can move itself'. By this he meant uncaused self-generated motion. Anything which can move itself must be alive. Self-generated motion is, therefore, in effect, *soul*. Furthermore 'the soul, being the source of motion, is the most ancient thing there is'.

How many 'souls' are there? 'More than one. At any rate we must not assume fewer than two: that which does good and that which has the opposite capacity.' Since Plato believed that the sun, moon and stars all contain a 'soul' and that 'this soul provides us with light, every single one of us is bound to regard it as a god. Isn't that right?' Satisfied?

Plato concluded, 'So far as atheists are concerned we may regard our argument as complete.' But just in case – for any atheists who were still not convinced – the philosopher recommended a minimum sentence of five years imprisonment and, on a second offence – death!

— 230 —

The slapdash bish-up of Canterbury. – Anselm, Archbishop of Canterbury (1033–1109), believed that it was logically impossible to conceive of God as non-existent. This line of argument (which came to be regarded as a proof of God's existence) is known to the philosophical community as the *ontological* proof [*ontos* in Greek means 'being']. Anselm's theory started with a mind-bending concept he defined as 'that than which nothing greater can be conceived' (*id quo nihil majus cogitari possit*).

'That than which nothing greater can be conceived' exists, he said, in the mind, and can be understood, even by those who do not believe in God. If 'that than which nothing greater can be conceived' also existed *outside* of the understanding (i.e., in reality) then it would, necessarily, be greater than the version which exists in the mind alone. Therefore 'that than which nothing greater can be conceived' must, by its very definition, exist both in the mind and in reality, for if it only existed in the mind 'that than which nothing greater can be conceived' would, paradoxically, 'be something which a greater *can* be conceived. And this is clearly impossible.' Anselm ended his peroration by concluding: 'That than which nothing greater can be conceived so truly exists that it is not possible to think of it as not existing. This being is yourself, Lord our God.'

All well and good – but no! Anselm's argument is bished, his 'proof' is fatally flawed. What has he done wrong? Simply he has confused the *concept* of something, as it exists in his mind, with the *thing itself*, as it exists in reality. The two are entirely different. If Anselm imagines his home, for instance, the concept he has of it is not the same as the actual house itself and cannot therefore exist (for greater or for worse) *outside* of Anselm's mind. The same applies to 'that than which nothing greater can be conceived'. How Anselm came to such a slapdash philosophy is revealed in the first chapter of his *Proslogion*: 'I do not seek to understand so that I may believe, but I believe so that I may understand and what is more I believe that unless I do believe I shall not understand.' By this expedient Anselm gave birth to a spaghetti-like confusion which has lasted for over a thousand years.

—— 231 ——

What everyone understands to be God (Parts 1 and 2). – Thomas Aquinas, who shared with Plato the wish that heresy be punished by death, also believed that the existence of God needed to be proved and so, in the first part of his colossal *Summa Theologiae*, he set out to do just that.

'There are five ways of proving there is a God,' he stated.

So what are they?

His first and second ways are so remarkably alike (one deals with motion or change and the other with the concept of cause) that they may as well be treated together. Aquinas says, like Plato, that all motion or change is caused by previous motion or change. Go back far enough in the chain and what do you get? 'Now we must stop somewhere,' he argues, 'otherwise there will be no first cause of the change, and, as a result no subsequent causes . . . We arrive then at some first cause of change, not itself being changed by anything, and this is what everybody understands by God.'

There are several problems here. Why should we believe that everything has a cause? And, even if we do believe that, why must the sequence of causes 'stop somewhere' and arrive at a first cause? Either everything is caused, or it is not. Aquinas wants to have it both ways. His argument is not significantly different from Plato's, although he took it from Aristotle, with whom, it might be fair to say, Aquinas had something of an obsession. While Plato's system of first-cause proof resulted in 'no fewer than two' gods, Aristotle's parallel theory from *Metaphysics* produced more than forty 'unmoved movers'. Aquinas does not furnish us with any explanation as to why, in his schema, there might not be a billion causal threads and therefore a billion unmoved movers 'that everybody understands' to be *gods*.

— 232 —

What everyone understands to be God (Part 3). – In his third proof (borrowed from Maimonides' *Guide to the Perplexed*), Thomas Aquinas requires us to understand that most things we come across 'can be, but need not be'. What he means by this is that most things that exist also have had, or will have, a period of non-existence (i.e., before they were born or made and/or after they die or are destroyed). Now, not everything can be like this, Aquinas asserts, 'for a thing that need not be, once was not; and if everything need not be, once upon a time there was nothing'. Before allowing Thomas to conclude it should be noted that his logic has already fallen to pieces. Just because all things which are finite did not exist before they came into being, it does not prove that 'once upon a time there was nothing'. Things do not all come into being and die *at the same time*. That there is no living ant more than ten years old proves to no one except perhaps Thomas Aquinas that 'once upon a time' there were no ants. Even so, he pushes on.

'If nothing was in being, nothing could be brought into being, and nothing would be in being now, which contradicts observation.' In other words, nothing comes of nothing, so how come there are things? He concludes: 'Not everything therefore is the sort of thing that need not be and one is forced to suppose something which must be.' This thing that 'must be' owes its being to nothing outside of itself. Once again Thomas's edifice tumbles. What does it mean to talk of a thing that must be? Must be what? A shape *must be* a triangle if it has three angles, a colour *must be* green if it is made by mixing equal amounts of blue and yellow. In order for the concept of a 'necessary being' to make any sense it must be related to presupposed conditions. 'Because x exists and y exists then God must exist.' This type of argument would make sense, though unfortunately we have no 'x' and we have no 'y'. Thomas doesn't seem to mind; he just jumps to the conclusion ('Therefore God must exist') which, standing on its own, is a nonsense.

—— 233 ——

And this is what we call God. – Thomas Aquinas's fourth proof for the existence of God is 'based on the gradation observed in things':

> Some things are better, truer, more excellent than others. Such comparative terms describe varying degrees of approximation to a superlative; for example, things are hotter and hotter the nearer they approach to what is hottest. Something therefore is the truest and best and most excellent of things, and hence the most fully in being. Now when many things possess some property in common,

the most fully possessing it causes it in the others: fire, as Aristotle says, the hottest of all things, causes all other things to be hot. Something therefore causes in all other things their being, their goodness, and whatever other perfection they have. And this is what we call God.

There must be a thousand ways to blow this fragile edifice of reasoning apart, but most glaring of its faults are the suggestions in it that:

1. Things must exist which are superlatively hot, good, noble etc. etc.; why should they?
2. Even if something *is* hotter than anything else why is it 'hence the most fully in being'?
3. How can that which is the hottest of all things also be that which is the coldest of all things?

Can God be superlatively orange and superlatively yellow? Clearly this needs a rethink. The origins of Aquinas's fourth way lie in a mixture of Plato's philosophy (that all things aspire to an ideal) and ancient Greek polytheism which would of course allow for a god of heat and a god of cold equally to coexist, but with only one god to play with, Aquinas's argument just doesn't work.

— 234 —

The fifth way. – Thomas concludes his 'five ways of proving there is a God', with what Kant would have called a *teleological* argument (from the Greek meaning a 'purpose', 'goal', or 'completion'). This type of argument presumes that nature has been designed by an intelligent being, or else it would not work so well or look so nice. If everything (from birds' wings to fishes' scales, the leaves on a tree, the rising and the setting of the sun) appears to have a beneficial purpose in the great scheme of things then surely they must have been put there by an intelligent benefactor.

As Thomas put it: 'Nothing lacking awareness can tend to a goal except it be directed by someone with awareness and understanding; the arrow, for example, requires an archer. Everything in nature, therefore, is directed to its goal by someone with understanding, and this we call *God.*' But wait! Darwin has taught that the design of all life forms *evolved* over millions of years through evolutionary processes of biological trial and error. Even if giraffes have long necks and *Homo sapiens* has a big brain, we can be sure that they were not originally made that way. When genealogies of giraffes and of human beings are traced back as far as they go, science tells us that we find a common ancestor, a primordial, single-celled globule, without either long neck or a big brain. There is no reason that Thomas Aquinas should have known this for he was dead and buried 500 years before Darwin was born.

— 235 —

Isaac Newton approves the fifth way. –

Atheism is so senseless and odious to mankind that it never had many professors. Can it be an accident that all birds, beasts, and men have their right side and left side alike shaped? (except in their bowels); and just two eyes and no more on either side of the face; and just two ears on either side of the head; and a nose with two holes; and either two forelegs or two wings, or two arms on the shoulders, and two legs on the hips and no more? Whence arises this uniformity in all their outward shapes but from the counsel and contrivance of an Author. Whence is it that the eyes of all sorts of living creatures are transparent to the very bottom, and the only transparent members in the body, having on the outside a hard transparent skin with a crystalline lens in the middle and a pupil before the lens, all of them so finely fitted and shaped for vision that no artist can mend them? Did blind chance know that there was light, and what was its refraction, and fit the eyes of all creatures after the most curious manner to make use of it? these and such like considerations always have and ever will prevail with mankind to believe that there is a Being who made all things and has all things in his power, and who is therefore to be feared. ('Letter', VI:123, *Newton's Philosophy of Nature*)

— 236 —

The divine watchmaker. – William Paley, an Anglican priest, used to advise his pupils if they had to preach every Sunday 'to make one sermon and steal five'. In this spirit he plagiarised an analogy of God as a watchmaker which he used to support the argument from design in a book called *Natural Theology*, published in 1802. He took the idea from the *Religious Philosopher*, by Dutch theologian Bernard Nieuwentyt (1654–1718), which had been translated into an English edition for the first time in 1750.

Whatever its provenance the Divine Watchmaker theory made Paley's name as a philosopher. This is how it started:

In crossing a heath, suppose I pitched my foot against a stone and were asked how the stone came to be there, I might possibly answer that from anything I knew to the contrary it had lain there forever; nor would it, perhaps, be easy to show the absurdity of this answer. But suppose I had found a watch upon the ground, and would be enquired how the watch happened to be in that place, I should hardly think of the answer which I had before given, that for anything I knew the watch might have always been there. Yet why should not this answer serve as well as for the watch as for the stone? why is it not as admissible in the second case as in the first? For this reason and for no other, that when we come to inspect the watch we perceive what we could not discover in the stone, that its several parts are framed and put together for a purpose, e.g., that they are so formed and adjusted as to produce motion, and that motion so regulated as to point out the hour of the day: that if the different parts had been differently shaped from what they are, or placed after any other manner in any other order than that in which they placed, either no motion at all would have been carried on in the machine, or none that would have answered the use that is now served by it.

After several pages in this vein, Paley gets to his point (or is it Nieuwentyt's point?) that the world shows so much evidence of design that it *must* have been designed, by the great watchmaker in the sky, God. His argument is flawed because it relies too heavily on the initial analogy. What Paley is hoping to convince his readers of is that by agreeing that things in nature are like human artifacts (i.e., they are created with intelligent purpose), it will follow that God must have made them and that God must exist.

Put like that the argument is untenable. What happens, for instance, if the analogy is changed to 'things in nature are like organisms', or 'things in nature are like descriptions'? And why, if this universe has been designed by a perfect and intelligent God, are there so many imperfections in it?

'Ah!' Paley might have replied, 'things that appear to be imperfections to us are not necessarily imperfect.'

So what about design? Is everything that *appears* to us to have been designed, definitely and unquestionably designed? Or is the appearance of design just another illusion too?

—— 237 ——

Pure Kant. – Immanuel Kant, revered by many as the greatest Western philosopher since the Greeks, dismissed all of the existing 'proofs' for

God in his masterpiece, *Critique of Pure Reason* (1781). However, when it came to providing his own proof seven years later he failed to distinguish himself.

The argument, which is laid out in his *Critique of Practical Reason* (1788) states that the existence of human moral values (such as right and wrong, good and bad) makes it *reasonable* to assume that there must be a God, the source, as it were, from which our understanding of these values must derive. Given that an ultimate state of goodness exists, then it is *reasonable* that a human being's highest goal should be to aspire to this ultimate goodness; but getting there can only be done by combining perfect virtue and perfect happiness. This Kant concedes must necessarily take for ever. It is therefore *reasonable* he says to assume that the human soul must be immortal. Since, looking around, we can see no obvious way to combine perfect virtue and perfect happiness, it once again *stands to reason* that this combination can only be achieved with some external help from outside the world of human experience. This agency, let us say, is God. When Kant argued that things *stand to reason* or that they are *reasonable* he was referring to *practical* reason (a discredited form of intelligence directed pathologically towards a moral outcome) and not, alas, to the *pure* reason of deductive logic. That is why Kant's argument is of no merit whatsoever.

— 238 —

His existence proved by universal consent. – Christians and Muslims have attempted to uphold the existence of God by using the argument of 'no smoke without fire'. If so many millions of people throughout the world have believed (and continue to believe) in some form of deity then he must exist, musn't he? The majority cannot be wrong. Jews have traditionally rejected this argument, on the basis that idolaters believe in nothing at all, though the eleventh-century poet, Solomon Ibn Gabirol, insisted that even idolaters are inadvertently worshipping the one true God of Israel.

From a philosophical point of view, the argument of universal consent is a non-starter, for even if everyone in the world believed in one God it would not prove his existence. The Christian, C. S. Lewis, thought that the atheist's greatest difficulty is in 'trying to persuade himself that most of the human race have always been wrong about the question that mattered to them most' (*Mere Christianity*); to which the waspish Bertrand Russell would have retorted: 'The fact that an opinion has been widely held is no evidence whatever that it is not utterly absurd; indeed, in view of the silliness of the majority of mankind, a widespread belief is more likely to be foolish than sensible' (*Marriage and Morals*, p. 50).

—— 239 ——

End of proof. – Even theists seem to have given up trying to *prove* that God exists. A familiar position of retreat is to claim that although his existence cannot be proven it is not possible to prove that he does not exist either. Boastful scientists are in the habit of popping up from time to time and claiming to the contrary. But if they could prove the non-existence of God, would that not be counter-productive to the atheist cause? As can be learned from a father's knee: 'Religion would suffer a greater loss of credulity if scientists announced they *had* proved God's existence' (*Daily Telegraph*, 28.12.96).

So what is left? There is, according to some, a middle way. It is true that none of Aquinas's five proofs, nor Anselm's *ontological* argument, nor Kant's *moral* argument are in themselves valid, but taken together do they not add up to some sort of overall proof? The arguments for God's existence have been likened to the firing of a quiver full of arrows. While no single arrow hits the bull's eye, the pattern in which the arrows land, speaks a truth. There is a poetry to this explanation which some may find seductive, but will they be satisfied that by mixing all these defective proofs together, a genuine truth will mysteriously emerge? While children are instilled from birth with the old cliché 'two wrongs do not make a right' they are also asked to accept that in mathematics a minus times a minus equals a plus. There is no possible reason why this should be so, yet we accept it – maybe because it is mysterious, maybe because it descends from a higher authority. Is this the only way to assert that the existence of God has been proven?

— 240 —

Safe bet. – It is a sad thing that Blaise Pascal, brilliant mathematician, inventor of an arithmetic calculator at the age of sixteen and esteemed philosopher of the seventeenth century, should best be remembered for the dismal conceit known to posterity as 'Pascal's Wager'. Pascal did not publish it in his lifetime and probably had no intention of ever doing so. It goes like this:

Even if you cannot prove the existence of God you should bet that he exists by believing in him and leading a devout life. There are four alternatives: if you wager he exists and he does not then you have lost nothing; if he does exist, you hit the jackpot and go to heaven. If, on the other hand, you bet that he *does not* exist and he does, you go to hell where your entrails will be impaled by a ghoul (for ever); if he does not (and you bet that he did not) then, once again, (according to Pascal) you lose nothing.

Pascal himself presented it more simplistically than that: 'Let us assess the two cases,' he wrote, 'if you win you win everything, if you lose you lose nothing. Do not hesitate then; wager that he does exist.' But what are the odds? This, as a mathematician, Pascal believed to be the most persuasive thread of his argument:

There is an infinity of infinitely happy life to be won, one chance of winning against a finite number of chances of losing, and what you are staking is finite. That leaves no choice; wherever there is infinity, and where there are not infinite chances of losing against that of winning, there is no room for hesitation, you must give everything. And thus, since you are obliged to play, you must be renouncing reason if you hoard your life rather than risk it for an infinite gain, just as likely to occur as a loss amounting to nothing. (*Pensées*, p. 418)

If instinct were allowed to have its wicked way most people would tell the Frenchman to get lost – the best thing is not to place any bet at all, but Pascal pre-empts this objection by stating (without explanation), 'You *must* wager. There is no choice, you are already committed. Which will you choose then?'

'All right, if we are forced to play your babyish game then so we shall, but first a better explanation is needed. If I choose to believe in God, because, as you say, it is a far better bet, how do I actually do it? – believe I mean, how can I possibly make myself believe that something exists (which I cannot see, touch or feel) on the strength of a few good gambling odds?'

Pascal might have countered with Thomas Aquinas's point that 'believing is an act of mental assent commanded by will, perfected by dispositions both of will and of mind' (*Summa Theologiae*, 10:4), instead he chose his own words with a similar ring: 'If you are unable to believe it is because of your own passions, since reason impels you to believe and yet you cannot do so. Concentrate then not on convincing yourself by multiplying proofs of God's existence but by diminishing your passions.'

'All right then, let's say that I can believe anything I want as an act of will, and I choose to believe in God. How can I guarantee that if he exists I shall go to heaven for eternity?'

'Well, you cannot exactly guarantee as it is impossible to predict God's will.'

'What are my odds then?'

'That is not the point. The point is this. If you win, your winnings are infinite. If you lose, you lose nothing.'

'If I spend my whole life praying and going to church and it turns out that God does not exist, and life on earth is all that does exist, then I have lost everything, haven't I?'

'No you have not, you have wasted time, that is all. Nothing compared to the eternal reward that you could win if . . .'

'Yes, yes, you've said that. But how can I know that God will not send churchgoers to hell and punish them for their piety? How do I know that he will approve of whatever theology it is that I decide to believe? For instance, each of the different churches holds to beliefs which are regarded as heretical by other denominations and other religions. If I am guilty of heresy then I will surely spend an eternity among the damned. What are the odds, then, out of the thousands of different religions and dogmas on offer, that I choose the one which might bring me eternal happiness and not any of those which are said to guarantee an eternity of hell?'

'Er – I don't know.'

'In that case, we are back where we started and I refuse to bet, goodbye.'

'Boo! hoo! Don't go! blub! blub! sob! sob!'

— 241 —

Plucky God is dead. – Friedrich Nietzsche, to whom posterity has wrongly ascribed the invention of the phrase 'God is dead!' was not, as is popularly assumed, an atheist in the strictest sense of the term. He despised Christianity but that is not the same thing. When he used the phrase 'God is dead!' he was not claiming that God had suddenly ceased to exist or even that people's belief in God had collapsed into nothing. He meant something more specific: that Christianity had castrated God, had shorn him of his dignity, of his power and his vitality. The first we hear of it is from a madman in Nietzsche's collection, *Die Fröhliche Wissenschaft* (*The Gay Science*) of 1882:

Have you ever heard of that madman who lit a lantern in the

bright morning hours and ran about the market place shouting: 'I seek God! I seek God!' – As there were many people standing around who did not believe in God, he caused a great deal of amusement. Has he got lost? one asked. Did he lose his way like a child? asked another. Or is he hiding? Is he afraid of us? Has he gone on a voyage? or emigrated? Thus they screamed with laughter.

The madman jumped into their midst and pierced them with his eyes. 'Where is God gone?' he cried out. 'I shall tell you. We have killed him – you and I. All of us are murderers. But how have we done it? How did we manage to drink up the sea? Who gave us the sponge to wipe away the whole horizon? What were we doing when we unchained this earth from this sun? Where is it heading now? Where are we all heading? Away from all suns? Are we not plunging continually? Backwards, sideways, forwards in all directions? Is there any up or down left? Are we not straying as through an infinite nothing? Do we not feel the breath of empty space? Has it not become colder? Does not the night come on continually, darker and darker? Do we not hear the noise of the grave-diggers who are burying God? Do we not smell the divine putrefaction? – for even Gods putrefy! God is dead! God remains dead! And we have killed him. (*The Gay Science*, 125)

Nietzsche identifies himself, not with the scoffers, but with the madman. So what has happened to make it possible for Nietzsche's God to die? What have the wretched Christians done to him? They have turned God into a transcendent concept of goodness, an expression of eternal love. 'Yuck!' says Nietzsche. 'How disgusting!' For Nietzsche Christianity is full of bullshit, nothing but imaginary *causes* (God, the soul, spirit, free will), imaginary *effects* (sin, salvation, grace, punishment, forgiveness of sins), imaginary beings (God, spirit, soul) and an imaginary teleology (the kingdom of God, the Last Judgement, everlasting life): 'This purely fictitious world distinguishes itself very unfavourably from the world of dreams: the latter reflects reality, whereas the former falsifies, depreciates and denies it.'

The Romans, he argued, needed benign gods to thank for their prosperity and good fortune, just as they needed perverse or bad gods to help them come to terms with rotten luck. Nietzsche's philosophy stresses the need for a god who is both good and bad and deplores the Christian remoulding, the taking of that wonderfully capricious God of Israel, the retributive, warlike, unprincipled God of the Jews, and turning him into something foppish – a mere symbol of 'good'. For God to have any meaning he must be more than that – an *affirmation of life*, of the will to live and more specifically the will to power. But the Christian God has lost his strength: 'He is for ever moralising,' Nietzsche says, 'he crawls into the heart of every private virtue, becomes a God for everybody, he retires from active service and becomes a cosmopolitan. Formerly he represented a people, everything aggressive and desirous of power lying concealed in the heart of a nation: now he is merely the good God' (*The Antichrist*, 16).

'Exactly,' retorts the worthy Christian, 'and what is wrong with that? Who wants aggressive, desirous people anyway? Who wants the will to power? What is wrong with love and peace, and a God that is all good? Surely this is better than what we had before?'

'What is good?'

'It is love.'

'I am experiencing a physiological resistance to your last point.' [NB: Nietzsche means he is about to be sick]. How, he would ask, can anyone argue that the evolution of the concept of God, from the God of Israel, the God of the people, to the Christian God, the quintessence of all goodness, marks a step forward? 'Why, the very contrary stares one in the face,' Nietzsche asserts, 'when the prerequisites of ascending life, when everything strong, plucky, masterful and proud has been eliminated from the concept of God, and step by step he has sunk down to the symbol of a staff for the weary, of a last straw for all those who are drowning; when he becomes the pauper's God, the sinner's God, the sick man's God *par excellence*, and the attribute "Saviour",

"Redeemer", is all that remains over as the one essential attribute of divinity: What does such a metamorphosis, such an abasement of the godhead imply?'

In a nutshell what Nietzsche is saying is that the Christian God is *unnatural.* Nature is 'good' in the philosophical sense, life itself is where everything positive lies, not in morality, not in limp social duty, in pity or in charity. The Christian God is the very opposite of life and of the will to power so evident in all of nature. The madman says that God is dead because the Christian God

is one of the most corrupt concepts of God that has ever been attained on earth. Maybe it represents the low water mark in the evolutionary ebb of the godlike type. God degenerated into the contradiction of life, instead of being its transfiguration and eternal Yea! With God war is declared on life, nature and the will to life! God is the formula for every calumny of this world and for every lie concerning a beyond! In God, nonentity is deified, and the will to nonentity is declared holy! (*The Antichrist,* 18)

There is nothing in this rhetoric to suggest that Nietzsche is in favour of rejecting God altogether – far from it. It is just that he finds the Christian concept of God abhorrent. This is 'the God of Christian mono-tono-theism. This hybrid creature of decay, nonentity, concept and contradiction, in which all the instincts of decadence, all the cowardices and languors of the soul find their sanction!' (*The Antichrist,* 19).

—— 242 ——

Dear Dr Nietzsche. – Contrary to what you believe, the Christian concept of God is entirely natural, certainly every bit as natural as your *Eternal Yea!* (whatever that is supposed to be). You see, Man was made above the animals, this is evident from the scriptures, for

God said to Adam and Eve, 'Be fruitful and multiply, replenish the earth and subdue it, and have dominion over the fish of the sea, and over the fowl of the air, and over every living thing that moveth upon the earth' (Gen. 1:28).

Man's position in the grand hierarchy is therefore *above* all of the nature of which you speak and just below the angels. That Man was created by the breath of God (Gen. 2:7) tells us that he is elevated. God has given him a soul and for this reason Man himself is to some extent unnatural; what is natural for animals is not necessarily natural for Man. Man is unique among all the living creatures of this earth because he understands the difference between right and wrong. You say you value life, and life is in itself your God. But we Christians value life too – more so, I should say, than you do. We are taught to help the dying man in the street, to pity the infirm, to save life, not to destroy it, not to sink as you would to the animal level, acting from your basest instincts, clambering over others, the sick and dying, in your self-centred 'will to power'. And what is at the end of it for you? Nothing; no life whatever. Yet we have the promise of eternal life!

Yours,
with lots and lots of love,
Father M. Goodman sj

— 243 —

Dear Father Goodman. – I do not believe in your eternal life, nor do I believe in your soul. Man is superior to the animals, not because scripture says so, but because man has a greater will to power than the animals and a greater ability to fulfil that will. But since you are so keen to rely on your scripture I shall remind you, for I too know the Bible well and used to read it aloud to my friends at school with so much feeling it brought tears to their eyes and my school mates called me 'The Little Minister'.

You say your god is good but he himself has told Isaiah that he creates evil. Job knew God better than you do, Father Goodman, and he asked his wife, 'Should we accept only good from God and not evil?' Did Job's comforters not say that God was only good and did God not reprimand those comforters for talking rubbish: 'I burn with anger against you', he said, 'for not having spoken correctly about me as my servant Job has done.'

God is not the god of goodness, nor was he ever meant to be, not until the Christians turned up, crusading, torturing, and intolerant. Only then did he become the God of infinite goodness.

And what did the wise Solomon have to say? Eh? Have you forgotten that?

> Consider the work of God. Who is able to straighten what He has twisted? In times of prosperity be happy, but in times of adversity, reflect: For God has made the one just as he made the other, so that man may find no fault with him.
>
> I have seen everything in my futile lifetime; the righteous person perishing in righteousness and the wicked person surviving in wickedness. Do not be excessively righteous and do not be overly wise. Why should you ruin yourself? Do not be excessively wicked and do not be a fool. Why should you die before your time? It is good that you grasp one thing without letting go of the other; for the one who fears God will do his duty by both. (Eccles. 7:13–18).

Mit freundlichen Grüssen,
Herr Dr Friedrich Nietzsche

— 244 —

Postcard from the edge. –

Dr Nietzsche,
St John plainly states, 'Who is the liar but the one who denies the

Father and the Son? For the spirit of the Antichrist is already in the world, from this we know that it is the last hour.' – May the Devil have you!

Goodman

—— 245 ——

Image make-over. – Any one who reads the Christian Old Testament cannot help but notice, as Nietzsche did, that the God of those books is a very different creature from the Christian view of a transcendent being of infinite goodness and pure love. Did all those Israelites who traipsed through the desert with Moses – bossed, half-starved, quite often killed – did they believe that God was Love? Surely not; for them God was the mysterious source of punishment for their sin, he was the source of earthly reward too for their good behaviour, but he was never a wellspring of eternal love.

The Israelites were ordered to 'love the Lord your God with all your heart and with all your strength' (Deut. 6:5), but what of God's love for them? Could they feel it in the same sensitive way that the mystic Julian of Norwich was to feel it in England at the beginning of the fifteenth century? What would Moses or Aaron have made of Julian's extraordinary definition?

'What is the meaning of the Lord?' she asked in her *Revelations of Divine Love.*

Learn it well: Love is his meaning. Who showed it to you? Love. What did he show you? Love. Why did he show it to you? For Love. Hold yourself in that Love and you shall have more of the same. There is nothing else eternal. Thus I learned that Love was his meaning. And I saw as clearly as anything that before God made us He loves us; which love has never slacked, nor ever shall be. And in this love He has done all his works; and in this love he has made all things profitable to us; and in this love; our love is everlasting. In our making we had beginning; but the love with which He made us has been in Him for all eternity, in which love we have our beginning. And all this shall we see in God. (Julian of Norwich, *Revelations of Divine Love*, XI)

But there was clearly more to the God of Israel than just 'love'. Love is not the way Moses spoke of God, he would not have understood it; even less would he have managed to grasp the point of Augustine's fancy definition: 'He that knows the Truth,' he wrote, 'knows what that Light is; and he that knows It, knows eternity. Love knoweth it. O Truth Who art Eternity! and Love who art Truth! and Eternity Who art Love! Thou art my God, to thee do I sigh night and day' (*Confessions*, VII).

This sort of language would never have persuaded Moses, Aaron and their sickly troupe of itinerant Israelites to up-sticks and march through that desert. It was milk and honey they were after, not love and truth and eternity, nor any combination of these incomprehensible effects.

Not all modern Christians are happy either. Some are painfully aware that God needs updating and redefining if he is to continue to be useful to future generations. After all, a punishing, rewarding God was more *useful* to the Israelites in the desert than any amount of Love and Truth would have been. They needed hope and they needed the Torah to get them through. It may come to pass that eternal Love and Truth are not what future generations will want from their god either.

John Robinson, the late Bishop of Woolwich, was one among several prominent modern Christians to recognise this problem and attempt, in the face of fierce resistance, to redefine God:

Traditional Christian theology has been based upon the proofs for the existence of God – they argue from something which everyone admits exists (the world) to a Being beyond it who could or could not be there . . . Now such an entity even if it could be proved beyond dispute, would not be God: it would merely be another piece of existence – Rather we must start the other way round. God is, by definition, ultimate reality. And one cannot argue whether ultimate reality exists. One can only ask what ultimate reality is like – whether, for instance, in the last analysis what lies at the heart of things and governs their working is to be described in personal or impersonal categories. (*Honest to God*)

Bishop Robinson's 'ultimate reality' comes dangerously close to Nietzsche's Eternal Yea! but since the German philosopher gleefully described himself as the Antichrist it is probably not what the Bishop would have liked to hear. Even so, when his book was written in 1963, there were plenty of people calling for him to be indicted for heresy. Robinson had earlier caused a stir by testifying at the famous obscenity trial of D. H. Lawrence's novel *Lady Chatterley's Lover*, in favour of its publication, but *Honest to God* was, for many Christians, the final straw. The *Observer* newspaper ran with the headline: 'Bishop says the God up there or out there will have to go.' Robinson recognised that the plucky Bible god was unworshipable: 'The biblical view of God has been totally eclipsed,' he said, 'we use God as a tool at appropriate moments of need, like a Santa Claus.' Robinson's motivation was not diabolic, far from it, but it was odd. It is as though he were saying it does not matter what God is, so long as people continue to worship him, if the definition of God as provided to us by our ancestors, or by holy scripture, is unattractive and does not persuade us to worship him then what we need is not a new god, but a new *definition* of what God is – an image change that's all, nothing that a bit of cosmetic surgery cannot fix.

—— 246 ——

Just being himself. – Existing is good and not-existing is bad. That should have answered Hamlet's question, but how was he to know? Hamlet was not a theologian (possibly a non-existent Danish prince – in which case he was bad) but why should he have kept abreast of the latest in scriptural exegis? 'And God saw everything that he had made, and behold, it was very good' (Gen. 1:31). This told the exegete that existence was in itself a good thing, much to be admired. By extrapolation, when God reveals to Moses that the divine name is 'I AM THAT I AM' (Exod. 3:14), a theologian will help himself to the view that God does not only 'exist', but that he must also be 'good' – an interpretation which inevitably leads to an exaltation of 'being', to a wild condemnation of 'non-being' and to a wholly misleading concept of 'good'. From such an argument too springs the erroneous syllogism: 'If Being is good and God is good, God must be "Being".'

'Wait a minute, God must be what?'

'God is Being.'

'Being what? You can't just be "being", you've got to be "something".'

'No, no, you don't understand. God is Being-itself.'

'Well if God is Being-itself, let's dispense with the word "God", for we already have a word for Being itself and that's "being".'

'Yes, but when I talk about God as being Being I don't mean "being" in the normal dictionary sense. You see God is unique, so the word has a slightly shifted meaning when applied to him. What I am trying to say is that God is the ultimate reality behind all things. He is the power that sustains all being, yours, mine, the whole lot. Everything that exists owes its existence to its "being" and Being is, as I say God.'

'So what exactly is Being?'

'I've told you, it's God.'

'You're just being perverse. Why take the one thing which nobody is sure exists and call it "being". That chair is more obviously "being" than God is, at least I can see it and feel it; and anyway, what about the Bible? We were taught that God is someone who speaks to people, who appears in visions, who sends a fish to swallow a prophet, who talks from inside a burning bush. Why should Being-itself be concerned if the Israelites reach the Promised Land or not? Did Being-itself wipe out humanity with a flood? Did Abraham circumcise his penis as a sign of his covenant with Being-itself?'

'You have asked too many questions and you're getting crude.'

'You have read too many books by that daft theologian Paul Tillich.'

'Yes, I suppose I have.'

—— 247 ——

Why hold on? – If the God of the Bible really is such a cruel swine, such an embarrassment to the doctrines of love and truth, why not junk him altogether? Christians give two reasons for holding on to the Old Testament. The first is that these books predict and promise things about Jesus Christ. Biblical scholars and many Christians now agree that this is not accurate, that the New Testament gospels were written to make it look as though Jesus' coming had been foretold by the older scriptures. For instance when Jesus ordered his disciples to fetch a colt for his ride into Jerusalem (Luke 19:30) this was supposed to fulfil the prophecy of Zechariah (9:9), 'Behold thy king cometh unto thee having salvation, lowly riding upon an ass and upon the colt of a foal of an ass.' With many such examples it is held that the Evangelists invented the stories in order for it to look like a case of divine prophecy.

The gospel writers of the second century certainly knew their scriptures; Matthew pointed to twenty examples of scriptural fulfilment, Luke to twenty-five. In order to persuade Jews to join the new cult of Christianity, they had to show that the Messiah, who was promised by the Hebrew Bible, had indeed materialised in the form of Jesus 'Christ'. There can be little doubt as to what end the gospels were written or which way around the New Testament prophecies occurred. But for those Christians who fervently believe in the Old Testament prophecies, an important question remains: Is it still worth holding on to the Old Testament (for the sake of the prophecies) when keeping it means continuing with the brutal, embarrassing Old Testament God of Israel?

But there is another reason why Christians need to retain the Old Testament which has nothing to do with prophecy. Christianity teaches that Christ was the saviour, he came down to the world to show people how they might be saved from the stigma of original sin. Because of Adam's behaviour God is displeased with the lot of us. By adhering to the doctrines of Jesus, it is believed that God will overlook the inherited disgrace of a chosen few, granting them happiness at a future date. Because of this Christianity *needs* the story of Adam and Eve and the doctrine of original sin more than Judaism or Islam do; for if Adam had not taken the apple, or worse still if Adam had never existed, Jesus' whole *raison d'être* would disappear in a puff of smoke. If mankind had not been tainted by Adam's petty misdemeanour, none of us would need to be saved, and would hence see no point in a saviour. This simple fact chains the Christian to the whole Bible not just his beloved New Testament, and the God of Israel has to come along for the ride.

—— 248 ——

Paul. – From the Christian point of view God made himself understandable to human beings through Jesus Christ and it is therefore towards Christ that one should look in order to understand God and to attain personal salvation. There is a danger in this scheme that the God who showed himself to Moses will become redundant; and if he does become redundant what do Christians suppose he was doing talking to Moses in the first place? Paul was aware of this problem from the outset, but was cautious. As a Jew, he had been drawn to Jesus not just because of the famous epiphany en route to Damascus, but because Christ appeared to be the fulfilment of Jewish prophecy.

Once Paul himself had signed to the new creed, his burning desire was to convert the rest of the world to his own radical way of thinking. At first he believed that the conversion of Jews to Christianity would be far easier than the conversion of Gentiles (to understand Jesus' message, after all, you needed to be a Jew, to have been brought up in the scriptural tradition of Messianic expectation) but Paul soon realised he was wrong. To his surprise, many Gentiles were eager to embrace the new religion which very few Jews were. To the non-Jew Christianity offered an attractive package – a sympathetic humanoid God, a miracle-worker, a staunch supporter of the down-trodden, made more vivid by his recent death, and all this was validated by the mystical prophecies of an ancient scripture.

Paul's biggest problem was circumcision. Though a circumcised Jew himself, he was quick to spot that Christianity would gain no converts from outside of Judaism if the first demand on the Gentile fresher was a horrendously painful amputation of the foreskin. After much reflection Paul decided that God's covenant with Abraham, which demanded his people be circumcised, would have to be broken. He talked of 'circumcision of the heart' (a metaphorical term for giving oneself to God) as replacing circumcision of the penis. Paul's ambition was never to dump the God of Israel, but he found time and again that in trying to marry Christianity with Judaism, problems arose and the God of Israel was inevitably compromised.

The Jews were not impressed by Paul's attitude to circumcision, but even less did they like the implication of his teaching that if Christ was the saviour then any hope God had previously given to the Jews via Moses and the prophets was to be superseded by the new message of Jesus. Paul remembered of course that God had promised to be the God of Israel *for ever*, so why should Jews be interested in joining the Christian cult? According to Paul, God will only save those who accede to the message of Christ, but what then is God playing at? It sounds as though he is reneging on his promise to the Jews. And if that is so, why should anyone trust in him?

If God had already saved his people by giving the Law to Moses, what was the point of Jesus? Celsus, mocking Christianity in the second century, asked: 'Well, who is to be believed? Moses or Jesus? Perhaps there is a simpler solution: perhaps when the father sent Jesus he had forgotten the commandments he gave to Moses, and inadvertently condemned his own laws, or perhaps sent his messenger to give notice that he had suspended what he had previously endorsed' (*On the True Doctrine*). When Paul addressed this very problem in his letter to the Romans, he compared the Jews to branches that have been lopped off the divine tree, and the newly converted Christians to new branches that have been grafted on (Rom. 11:16–24). But the reality of what he was saying suggested a new tree trunk altogether.

Paul uprooted the God of Israel without admitting that that was what he had done. He left the Jews to fend for themselves. The Law of Moses had been fulfilled in Christ (Rom. 10:4) and it was time to move on.

— 249 —

Christianity minus the God of Israel. – A generation or so after Paul's death a new Christian leader emerged who almost succeeded in chucking the maverick God of Israel overboard. He was a rich ship owner from Pontus on the Black Sea whose name was Marcion. In 140 CE Marcion came to Rome where he made a large donation to the Christian community there. After a meeting at which he unsuccessfully attempted to redefine the faith, he left Rome in dudgeon, taking his donation back, and set up a rival church which was for three centuries to be as large and as powerful as the Church of Rome.

Marcion's contention was that the God of Israel, as represented by the Old Testament was a wholly imperfect being, yet the Christian schema required God to be perfect. From this, Marcion deduced that the God who created Adam and Eve, the one who threw hailstones at the Israelites in the time of Moses, could not be the same God as the one represented by Jesus.

To get around the problem of Adam and Eve Marcion suggested that the real reason mankind needs Jesus the saviour has nothing to do with original sin, but is due to the fact that the Creator God, who made heaven and earth, was himself imperfect. Jesus' function, according to Marcion, was to rescue mankind from the imperfect creative effort of this Old Testament demiurge.

Marcion went further. When Jesus, the Salvific God, arrived on earth (in the fifteenth year of the Emperor Tiberius) the Creator God refused to recognise him and out of jealousy and irritation had him crucified and sent to Hades.

Jesus' trip to hell has always been a necessary part of Christian doctrine – without it an embarrassing hole appears in the plot. For all those decent old coves like Abraham, Isaac, Jacob and Moses, who happened to have lived long before Jesus was born, had not been baptised as Christians and therefore, according to Christian doctrine, could never have ascended into heaven; they were languishing somewhere down in hell awaiting their salvation. It is for this reason that in the traditional Christian story, Jesus went to hell – to fish these unfortunate goodies out. In Marcion's version, though, traditional Old Testament enemies (the Egyptians, Canaanites, Sodomites etc.) repented to Jesus and were raised from hell, while old friends still loyal to the Creator God (Adam, Noah, Abraham and Moses), suspecting that their God was again leading them into error, refused Jesus' invitation and remained in hell.

One schismatic Mormon sect (The Reorganized Church of Jesus Christ of Latter Day Saints) solves the same problem a different way by teaching that 'the ancient prophets from Adam to Abraham taught and practised the Gospel; they knew Christ and worshipped the Father in his name'. Adam was thus a baptised Christian all along (Gen. 6:67, Inspired Version) and so there was no need for Jesus to visit hell after the crucifixion.

Marcion's 'new Christianity' appealed to those wishing to detach themselves from the cruel God of Jewish scripture; however, it made Marcion many enemies. The Jews accused him of anti-Semitism, while the Christian church in Rome called him 'the wolf from Pontus, first-born of Satan'. None of Marcion's writings have survived destruction, though (as with Celsus) we know a little of what he stood for through the printed refutations of his enemies Epiphanius, Origen and, above all, Tertullian.

Marcion's main concern was to point out the differences between God and Jesus. God he said was vicious and unmerciful, 'fierce and warlike, he conquered the holy land with violence and cruelty; but Christ prohibits all violence and preaches mercy and peace'. Christ said, ' "Let the little children come unto me" ' (Luke 18:16), but God fed little children to the bears (2 Kings 2:24); Christ exhorts his people to leave everything behind and follow him (Mark 6:8); God loads the Israelites with plundered Egyptian jewellery before leading them on their circuitous route to Canaan (Exod. 12:35). Marcion questioned God's motives in high ironic tone, quoted by Epiphanius as saying, 'Good indeed is the god of the law who envied the Canaanites to give to the Israelites their land, houses they had not built, olive trees and fig trees they had not planted' ('Ancorat', III, *Selected Works*).

Marcionite scripture consisted of some of the letters of Paul and the Marcionite gospel (thought to be the gospel of Luke with minor alterations). The whole of the Old Testament was junked. His church admitted women clergy and bishops, but this happy set-up would not remain together for long. Marcionites everywhere were persecuted, burnt, tortured, routed and raped. In the end the Church of Rome was victorious; Christian women were banned from holding office throughout the Christian world and the incongruous God of Israel was put back in at the heart of things.

—— 250 ——

God was originally much nicer. – The prophet Joseph Smith had a direct line to God. While never deviating from his view that the King James Bible was the 'word of God', he nevertheless held that while the original copy had doubtless been perfect, error and corruption had crept into later editions by dint of human error. 'I believe', he said, 'the Bible as it was read when it came from the pen of the original writers. Ignorant translators, careless transcribers, or designing and corrupt priests have committed many errors' (*History of the Church*). This view encouraged Smith to attempt his own edition of the King James Bible which he called The Inspired Version, a version that would, 'by command of God', eradicate all of God's most shameful attributes.

For instance, when God revealed his name to Moses he said (in the King James Version): 'I appeared unto Abraham, unto Isaac and unto Jacob, by the name of God Almighty, but by my name JEHOVAH was I not known to them' (Exod. 6:3). Well, this is not strictly true – in fact it is not true at all. The Bible credits Enoch as being the first to invoke the name Jehovah, a long time before Moses and many generations even before Abraham (Gen. 4:26); nor could God truthfully claim that the name Jehovah was unknown to Abraham as the patriarch himself chose to call the place where God asked him to sacrifice his son, *Jehovah-jireh*, 'as it is said to this day, In the mount of the LORD it shall be seen' (Gen. 22:14). Stories like these make God look foolish, or untrustworthy, or both, but Joseph Smith's Inspired Version put everything right, so that God is freed from blame. Exodus (6:3) in the Inspired Version is thus rendered: 'I appeared unto Abraham, unto Isaac and unto Jacob, by the name of God Almighty, the Lord JEHOVAH. And was not my name known unto them?'

When God repented that he had made mankind (Gen. 6:7) and regretted that he had elected Saul to be king (1 Sam. 15:11), Smith changed the scripture so that it was Noah (not God) who regretted the creation, while God's phrase, 'It repenteth me that I have set up Saul to be king', was newly rendered 'I set up Saul to be a king and *he repenteth not.*' Where God was seen at his most corrupt (for instance, making a prophet tell lies and threatening to kill him for it) God and Smith switched the whole thing around. Thus Ezekiel (14:9), which in the King James Version reads, 'And if the prophet be deceived when he hath spoken a thing, I the LORD have deceived that prophet, and I will stretch out my hand upon him, and will destroy him from the midst of my people Israel,' is fundamentally changed in the inspired Version to get God off the hook: 'And if the prophet be deceived when he hath spoken a thing, I the Lord have not deceived that prophet; therefore I will stretch out my hand upon him, and will destroy him from the midst of my people Israel.'

The Inspired Version was not only dedicated to eradicating God's wilder misdemeanours but also to ensuring that the polytheism of the Old Testament be rendered monotheistic. Thus, 'Thou shalt not revile the gods, nor curse the ruler of thy people' (Exod. 22:27) became, 'Thou shalt not revile against God, nor curse the ruler of thy people.' For all Smith's efforts to clear God's name, the Inspired Version is hardly ever used, not even by the main branch of Mormonism at Salt Lake City.

—— 251 ——

Question of blame. – God's promise to give his people lands which did not properly belong to them, and his instrumental help in Joshua's genocidal conquest of Canaan, offer no comfort to the modern day Palestinian who believes himself to be the victim of an evil persecution justified and encouraged by the mighty God of Israel. As the American theologian R. R. Ruether has observed: 'Prominent rabbis in present-day Israel interpret the ancient commandments to annihilate the Canaanites and the Amalekites as applicable to the Arabs today. Israel's wars against these peoples are holy wars, and the

Israel Defence Forces are sanctified holy warriors' (*Wrath of Jonah*). If the Hebrew Bible is indeed 'the word of God', is God to be held responsible for the present warring conditions of the Middle East? And by the same token, since Christians believe the 'word of God' to reside in the New Testament – in which Jews are dismissed as 'children of the Devil' (1 John 3:10) and the 'synagogue of Satan' (Rev. 2:9 and 3:9) – should God be blamed for the horrors of anti-Semitism?

The simplest solution would be to delete those passages of scripture which fall below our high standards of modern morality, but Marcion did this and look what happened to him. To suggest that God is anything but perfect is blasphemy; to edit, bowdlerise or mistranslate the scriptures is to run the risk of excommunication. Nor is it fair to blame God himself. He cannot be held to account for any of the bloodshed and hatred that religion has caused over the last three millennia for it is not *what* the scriptures say that matters, only *how* they have been interpreted – *cum grano salis* would have saved a lot of lives.

— 252 —

Just analogy. – Jesus asked his followers to pray to 'Our Father, who art in heaven'. Why not 'Our Mother, who art in heaven', 'Our Grandfather, who art in heaven', 'Our Great-Uncle', or 'Our Niece'? By using the word 'father' Jesus must have intended to convey something about man's relationship to God which 'niece', 'great-uncle', 'mother' and 'grandfather' cannot convey. There must be something unique about human biological fathers which Jesus wanted his disciples to acknowledge in their relationship with God. But what is it? What does a father do, or what did fathers do in Jesus' time that made it appropriate for him to use that word 'father' instead of any other?

Did fathers give their sons and daughters lavish playrooms full of wonderful toys and order them not to touch the most wonderful toy therein? Did they send talking snakes to slither up to their children and persuade them to disobey? Did they cast their children out, setting guards on the playroom door so that they could never return? Did they curse their children and grandchildren and all their line for ever? This sort of behaviour has never had anything to do with the normal, human concept of 'father'.

So in what way is God like a human father? Jesus might well have answered that God loves us like a father, he created us like a father and he disciplines us like a father. But Jesus would be wrong; God does not do any of these things like a father does.

'Of course he doesn't, he is God not a father; his love is not human love, for it is divine, it is more perfected. We use the word "love" only because his love is *like* human love, though it is not the same. He did not create us, in the way we create things like pots or poems, we use the word "create" as an analogy for what he really does, which is divine, truly incomprehensible creation. His discipline too is not in the realm of normal human or family discipline, divine displeasure is something quite else. God does not literally punish his sons and daughters like a father does.'

So what are we left with? In the standard sentence, 'God the Father and Creator loves us and punishes us for our sins', nothing actually means anything we think it does. Father is not father, Creator does not mean creator, nor do love and punishment mean love and punishment in their usual senses. It is common religious practice to argue that scripture is not literally true, but is true by virtue of analogy; the God of Israel is not the illiberal ogre he seems to be, say his apologists, provided that you interpret his actions sensitively and do not attempt to take scripture at face value.

But if scripture is the word of God, why should God need to communicate with people by analogy? Why not be literal? One answer suggests that God is deliberately conveying the mystery of his being by avoiding literal explanations; by muddling everybody and talking in riddles (as Jesus did) God has maintained a sense of mystery which is an essential property of successful religion.

This may well be, but even analogy cannot save God from opprobrium. God's behaviour in the Hebrew Bible might be argued away as analogy. 'He did not literally do this or that. Do not misunderstand. These are analogies.' Analogies of what? How can unjust, pernicious and violent behaviour be an analogy for anything nice?

— 253 —

Symbolically true. – A symbol differs from an analogy in that it need not bear the slightest resemblance to its subject. A dove is used to represent the Holy Spirit but, as we know, real doves have nothing in common with holy spirits in either a physical, emotional or any other sense. Elsewhere the dove is suggested as a symbol of peace, sometimes a symbol of love, but there is no reason why doves should not be used to symbolise tummyache, sexual ecstasy, the East Wind, jealousy, hope, the past, incontinence, death, efficiency – it doesn't seem to matter what – for the trouble with symbols is that anything can be said to symbolise anything else; any amount of gibberish can be held to be *symbolically* true. If the Bible's representation of God is symbolically true, what is to stop the New York telephone directory from symbolising exactly the same truth?

— 254 —

What about worship? – God is born, so it is said, of human necessity, he is created by a natural, impulsive, unstoppable human desire to thank something or someone for life's little pleasures and prosperities, to offer gratitude for the gift of life itself; to seek help, strength and guidance in times of hardship and to answer some of the imponderable questions of philosophy.

'*Si Dieu n'existait pas, il faudrait l'inventer*,' thought Voltaire: if God did not exist we would have had to invent him. Seeking help and giving thanks is one thing – maybe it is true that human beings are compelled to make a god they can thank, a god that will shield them and offer an explanation for all the mysteries of the universe. But what about worship? Are human beings born with a burning desire to do that too?

According to the American poet and humorist Oliver Wendell Holmes, 'men are idolaters, and want something to look at and kiss and hug, or throw themselves down before; they always did, they always will; and if you don't make it of wood, you must make it of words' (*Poet at the Breakfast Table*, 5). To worship means to offer praise, devotion and adoration which is not the same as giving thanks or seeking help. Oliver Wendell Holmes has confused the different impulses. Most people would not consider 'natural' the desire to kiss and hug anything made of wood, let alone an incorporeal and incomprehensible concept like God.

—— 255 ——

Selfish act. – Even regular worshippers are not always sure what worship is or why and how they are supposed to do it. Does worship require a 'desire to kiss and hug' the object or can something be worshipped just by praising it from a distance? If a person shouts out loud, 'God you are wonderful, marvellous, intelligent, exciting etc.', has he worshipped God, or only flattered him? If there is more to worship than praise, what can it be? Is it necessary that a true worshipper should not just say that he loves God but believe it in his heart as well?

Maybe, but this leads straight away to another inconsistency for if a person believes in his heart that God is supremely wonderful, and if God knows this, what is the point of any outward manifestation of the fact? Why bother to sing hymns, kneel and prostrate if the whole thing can be taken as read from the start?

'Prayer to God', comes the reply, 'is performed as a duty both to please God *et pour encourager les autres*. Religion does not work if people insist on maintaining their own private relationships with God; it is an act of sharing, and community worship is equally important as private worship.'

In any case most religions do not define worship as just 'praising', or even believing and loving'. Instead they grope for broader explanations. Thus with Don Hustad's Christian Bible definition, he says:

> Worship is the expression of the Christian believer's relationship with God. However, that relationship is complex, since God is at one and the same time our Creator, Redeemer (through Jesus Christ), Sustainer, Indweller (by the Holy Spirit), Friend, and Judge. It helps to remember that we approach God individually as a created one, a redeemed one, a sustained one, an indwelt one, a befriended one, and a judged one. (*Jubilate!*, II)

The Catholic Church sites the first Commandment as God's wish to be worshipped and defines it accordingly:

> To adore is to acknowledge, in respect and absolute submission, the 'nothingness of the creature' who would not exist but for God. To adore God is to praise and exalt him and to humble oneself, confessing with gratitude that he has done great things and holy is his name. The worship of the one God sets man free from turning in on himself, from the slavery of sin and the idolatry of the world. (*Catechism of the Catholic Church*, 2097)

Which means that worship is uniquely beneficial to man; and is of no explicit interest to God. This we could have guessed for God cannot *benefit* from anything; by nature, he is already the supreme expression of all the benefit that there is. He is *perfect*; benefit is a mode of improvement, and perfection cannot be improved. This means that worship, like prayer, is a selfish act – but that cannot be right, can it?

— 256 —

Why do it? – The scriptures uphold the importance of worship: 'Shout joyfully to God, all the earth; Sing the glory of His name; Make His praise glorious. Say to God, "How awesome are Your works! Because of the greatness of Your power Your enemies will give feigned obedience to You"' (Ps. 66:1–4); 'Worship the Lord with reverence, and rejoice with trembling' (Ps. 2:11); 'Praise the Lord alway' (Ps. 117). In the Psalms there is plenty of evidence that ancient people believed worship to be necessary, but the scriptural evidence that God *himself* is calling for it is thin on the ground.

When the devil wished to treat Jesus to a mountain-top panorama of 'all the kingdoms of the world and the glory of them', Jesus responded brusquely, 'Get thee hence Satan: for it is written: Thou shalt worship the Lord thy God' (Matt. 4:10). This is not strictly true. Nowhere is it written, 'Thou shalt worship the Lord thy God'. Jesus must have invented it to avoid having to admire that vista with the devil. Had Satan been more astute he would have challenged Jesus for a source citation. There are commandments to 'fear' God: 'Thou shalt fear the LORD thy God, and serve him, and shalt swear by his name' (Deut. 6:13), but is this what Jesus means by worship?

Jesus may have only intended to say, 'Thou shalt *respect* the Lord thy God', as elsewhere he had used the word 'worship' to mean *respect* such as when he exhorted people to watch their table manners: 'Thou shalt have worship in the presence of them that sit at meat with thee' (Luke 14:10). When a man vows to the woman in the marriage service from the Book of Common Prayer he is asked to pledge, 'With my body I do thee worship, and with all my worldly goods I thee bestow', obviously implying a different form of worship to that given by Muslims to God at Mecca.

Perhaps the most famous call to prayer is the appeal in Deuteronomy: 'And it shall come to pass, if ye shall hearken diligently unto my commandments which I command you this day, to love the LORD your God, and to serve him with all your heart and with all your soul' (Deut. 11:13), an echo of the first Commandment: 'You shall love the Lord your God with all your heart, with all your soul and with all your mind.'

Most churches refer to these passages as the firmest evidence that God desires to be worshipped, but still the precise definition of what worship entails is missing. People may feel that they love their children or spouse with 'all their heart, with all their soul and with all their mind', so dutiful worshippers need to know how their love for God is supposed to differ from this. We don't need incense to love our families; though scent is sometimes helpful on a spouse.

— 257 —

Apotheosis. – 'GOD! GOD!'

'Here I AM, sitting high in the seventh *hekhalot* of the seventh heaven, resting my back portion on a golden throne, and my brassy feet among the clouds. A river of fire flows beneath my chair, my hair is white and woolly, my bowels are troubled, my breasts bursting with milk. And what a racket! Millions of heavenly choirs are singing my praises. It is worse than a beehive in here.

'In days gone by Abraham was my friend. He circumcised his flesh for me; I fixed his wife's fertility problem; I made her laugh and spiced up her sex-life when she was ninety years old. I ate with them at Mamre too – griddle cakes and veal – quite delicious! I played a prank and Isaac nearly died.

'But now even Abraham has become a bore – fauning, sycophantic, flattering. Here he comes now. See how he trembles and grovels as he makes his way towards me. And who is that with him there? Egh! it's Iaoel. The one who makes them all learn the same old poem that he wrote more than a million years ago, "Eternal one, Mighty One, Holy

El . . ." I must have heard it a billion times. He's prodding Abraham
to start. Just listen to this—'

> Eternal one, Mighty One, Holy El, God autocrat,
> self-originate, incorruptible, immaculate.
> unbegotten, spotless, immortal,
> self-perfected, self-devised,
> without mother, without father, ungenerated,
> exalted, fiery,
> just, lover of men, benevolent, compassionate, bountiful,
> jealous over me, patient one, most merciful.
> Eli, eternal, mighty one, holy, *Sabaoth*, most glorious El, El,
>   El, El, El,
> you are he my soul has loved, my protector,
> eternal, fiery, shining, light-giving,
> thunder-voiced, lightning visioned, many-eyed,
> receiving the petitions of those who honour you
> and turning away from the petitions of those who restrain you,
> by the restraint of their provocations. (*Apoc. Abr.* 17:8–20)

'Wake up! Wake up! Put on your strength, O arm of God. Wake up!
as you did long ago in days gone by. Was it not you who hacked the
raging monster in half, who ran the dragon through? Was it not you
who dried up the sea, the waters of the great abyss, who made the sea
bed into a safe pass for the redeemed?' (Isa. 51:9–10).

'Ah yes, I did all those things, but long ago. I sent hornets to sting
the Hittite too and put haemorrhoids up the Philistines' backsides. I
wiped the Jebusites off the face of the earth, and the Moabites and
the Amalekites too for that matter (though they were tough). Israel
thought I was on her side, but I killed more of them than any –
destroyed them in their thousands, dropping them into the earth,
rotting their flesh with plagues, starving them even to death. I fed
them to the wild beasts and let their sons and daughters be hacked
to pieces by the swords of their enemies.

'I saw the lady drop a millstone on Abimelech's head and watched as a tent peg skewered Sisera, I laughed when Job was eaten through with worms and received the sacrifice of Jepthah's daughter. I remember also when the children teased Elisha; it was I who sent fierce bears to tear them limb from limb.

'And now they want me back. I promised them I would return at some stage to establish a new kingdom on earth. But look at them now, feverishly trying to compute the day of my coming; they think they can calculate it from things I have said; but I haven't said a word.

'And why should I return to the sons of Adam? None of them believes in me properly any more. Not like they used to; for now they say that I did not wipe the Jebusite off the map, that I did not send the hornet and the haemorrhoid. What can they mean by this? That I, El Elyon, El Sabaoth, creator of all their vile bodies, am but nothing?

'That is it, they worship me as NOTHING now, swearing that I cannot be seen, but Adam saw me and he did not worship. Noah saw me too, as did all the patriarchs. They bowed, they annointed their stones and sacrificed lambs but that was "acknowledgement", not "worship". They "worship" me now and will continue to "worship" until they are sick of it, until they force me to disappear into a cloud of their own unknowing.

'But here I am for the moment at least; secret, unseen, unheard, imagined only, perhaps glorious, maybe radiant, in trumpets and singing, mid marble palaces, sapphire pavements, rivers of fire and factories for the milling of manna:

EHYEH ASHER EHYEH;
Transcendent GOD,
He that IS THAT HE IS;
He that will fail your lofty fantasy,
For "Love" can never drive the sun and the other stars,
And what you cannot speak about, you must pass over in silence.'

BIBLIOGRAPHY

I Primary sources

The Bible
Versions used at unboundbible.com:
New American Standard
American Standard
Basic English Bible
Darby Version
Douay-Rheims Bible
King James Bible
Latin Vulgate
Webster's Bible
World English Bible
Weymouth New Testament
Young's Literal
Inspired Version, tr. Joseph Smith (1833)
The New Jerusalem Bible (London, 1985)
New Revised Standard Version (London, 1998)
The People's Bible, tr. Sidney Brichto (London, 2000 –)
Revised Version (Oxford, 1926)

The Qur'an
English translations:
Arthur J. Arberry (London, 1955)
George Sale (1734)

The Book of Mormon (Salt Lake City, 1830)

A Companion for the Festivals and Fasts of the Church of England (London, 1717)

The Dead Sea Scrolls, ed. Geza Vermes (Harmondsworth, 1962)

Doctrine and Covenants (Salt Lake City, 1835)

Enuma Elish, tr. A. S. Heidel in *The Babylonian Genesis: The Story of Creation* (Chicago, 1946)

The Mishnah, tr. J. Neusner (Yale, 1988)

New Testament Apocrypha, ed. Wilhelm Schneemelcher (2 vols, Cambridge, 1991)

Old Testament Pseudepigrapha, ed. James H. Charlesworth (2 vols, New York, 1983)

A Pearl of Great Price, ed. Franklin D. Richards (1851)

Toldoth Jesu, tr. G. R. S. Meade (1903), from the German translation of Samuel Krauss (Berlin, 1902)

Aelred of Rievaulx, *Spiritual Friendship*, tr. Mary Laker (Washington, 1974)

Anon, *Denis Hid Divinity* and *The Cloud of Unknowing*, tr. Justin McCann (London, 1924)

Anselm, *Meditations upon the Passion of Our Lord* (London, 1751)

Augustine of Hippo, *Confessions*, tr. E. B. Pusey (London, 1907)

Bernard of Clairvaux, *St Bernard's Sermons on the Canticle of Canticles*, tr. A priest of Mount Mellory (Dublin, 1920)

Catherine of Siena, *The Dialogue*, tr. Algar Thorvold (London, 1896)

Caussade, Jean-Pierre de, *Spiritual Counsels*, included in *Abandonment to Divine Providence*, ed. J Ramiere (Exeter, 1925)

Celsus, *On the True Doctrine*, tr. R. Joseph Hoffmann (Oxford, 1987)

Dionysius the Pseudo-Areopagite, *The Celestial Hierarchy*, Dean Colet tr. J. H. Lupton (London, 1869)

John of Ruysbroeck, *The Adornment of the Spiritual Marriage*, tr. C. A. Wynshenk (London, 1916)

Josephus, *Whiston's Josephus*, tr. William Whiston (London, 1737)

Julian of Norwich, Revelations of Divine Love, ed. Grace Warrack (London, 1914)

Leon, Luis de, *De los nombres de Cristo,* tr. A Benedictine of Stanbrook (London, 1926)

Lucian, *Alexander the False Prophet,* tr. A. M. Marmon (Harvard, 1925)

Mechthild of Hackborn, *Select Revelations of St Mechthild,* tr. A secular priest (London, 1875)

Nicholas of Cusa, *The Vision of God,* tr. Emma Gurney Salter (London, 1928)

Pascal, Blaise, *Pensées,* tr. W. F. Trotter (New York, 1910)

Plato, *Complete Works,* ed. John M. Cooper (Indianapolis, 1997)

Tauler, Johannes, *Meditations on the Life and Passion of Our Lord Jesus Christ,* tr. A secular priest (London, 1875)

Teresa of Avila, *The Life of St Teresa of Jesus,* tr. David Lewis (London, 1916)

Tertullian, The Writings of Quintus Sept. Flor. Tertullianus (3 vols, Edinburgh, 1870)

II Secondary texts

Abelson, J., *The Immanence of God in Rabbinical Literature* (London, 1912)

Albright, William Foxwell, *Yahweh and the Gods of Canaan* (London, 1969)

Allen, Warner, *The Timeless Moment* (London, 1946)

Andrae, Tor, *Mohammed: The Man and his Faith,* tr. T. Menzel (London, 1936)

Aqiba, *Alphabet of Aqiba* (first to second century CE)

Aquinas, Thomas, *De regime principum,* tr. Gerald Phelan (New York, 1938)

Aquinas, Thomas, *Summa Theologiae,* ed. Timothy McDermott (London, 1989)

Arberry, Arthur, *Sufism: An Account of the Mystics of Islam* (London, 1950)

Armstrong, Karen, *A History of God* (London, 1993)

Armstrong, Karen, *Muhammad: A Western Attempt to Understand Islam* (London, 1991)

Armstrong, Karen, *The Battle for God* (New York, 2000)

Assman, Jan, *Moses the Egyptian* (London, 1997)

Augustine, *Enchiridion*, tr. Albert C. Outler (*http://www.iclnet.org*)

Augustine, *Of the City of God*, tr. John Healey (2 vols, London, 1945)

Augustine, *Treatises on Various Subjects*, ed. Royle Ferrari (New York, 1952)

Ayer, A. J. and others, *What I Believe* (London, 1966)

Baillie, John, *The Sense of the Presence of God* (London, 1962)

Bainton, Roland, *The Mediaeval Church* (London, 1962)

Bainton, Roland, *The Penguin History of Christianity* (London, 1967)

Bartlett, John, *The Bible, Faith and Evidence* (London, 1990)

Becker, J., *Messianic Expectation in the Old Testament* (Edinburgh, 1980)

Beckwith F. J. and Parrish, S. E., *The Mormon Concept of God* (Lempeter, 1991)

Berger, Peter (ed.), *The Rumour of Angels* (New York, 1981)

Bernheim, Pierre-Antoine James, *Brother of Jesus* (London, 1997)

Blenkinsopp, Joseph, *A History of Prophecy in Israel* (London, 1994)

Blunt, John, *Dictionary of Historical and Doctrinal Theology* (London, 1870)

Boethius, *The Consolation of Philosophy*, tr. V. E. Watts (Harmondsworth, 1969)

Breasted, J. H., *The Development of Religion and Thought in Ancient Egypt* (New York, 1912)

Brichto, Herbert Chanan, *The Names of God* (New York, 1998)

Brooke, J. H., *Science and Religion* (Cambridge, 1991)

Buber, Martin, *I and Thou*, tr. Ronald Gregor Smith (New York, 2000)

Buckley, M., *At the Origins of Modern Atheism* (Yale, 1987)

Butler, Alban, *Lives of the Saints* (London, 1756–59)

Cantor, Norman, *History of the Jews* (London, 1994)

Carter, Sydney, 'It was on a Friday Morning', *Hymn Quest*, (London, 2000)

Catechism of the Catholic Church (ET: Geoffrey Chapman, London, 1994)

Cerny, J., *Ancient Egyptian Religion* (London, 1952)

Christian Faith: Doctrinal Documents of the Catholic Church, ed. J. Neuner and J. Dupuis (London, 1992)

Cohn, Norman, *Cosmos, Chaos and the World to Come* (Yale, 1993)

Cohn, Norman, *The Pursuit of the Millennium* (Yale, 1995)

Cosslett, Tess, *Science and Religion: Some Historical Perspectives* (Cambridge, 1984)

Dante, Alighieri, *The Divine Comedy*, tr. Charles S. Singleton (Princeton, 1973)

Day, J., *God's Conflict with the Dragon of the Sea* (Cambridge, 1985)

Dictionary of the Bible ed. James Hastings (5 vols, Edinburgh, 1927)

Diderot, Denis, *Pensées Philosophiques*, tr. John Hope Mason (London, 1982)

Duffy, Eamon, *The Stripping of the Altars: Traditional Religion in England 1400–1580* (Yale, 1992)

Eilberg-Schwartz, Howard, *God's Phallus* (Boston, 1994)

Eliade, Mircea, *The Quest: History and Meaning in Religion*, tr. W. J. Trask (Chicago, 1969)

Embodied Perspective, ed. Howard Eilberg-Schwartz (Albany, 1992)

Epiphanius, *Selected Works*, tr. P. R. Amidon (Oxford, 1990)

Esposito, John L., *Oxford History of Islam* (Oxford, 1999)

Evelyn, John, *Diaries and Miscellaneous Writings* (5 vols, London, 1906)

Gabriel, Josipovici, *The Book of God: A Response to the Bible* (New Haven, 1998)

Gibbon, Edward, *History of the Decline and Fall of the Roman Empire* (London, 1776–88)

Gottmann, Julius, *Philosophies of Judaism* (London, 1967)

Graves, Kersey, *The Bible of Bibles* (Cincinnati, 1879)

Graves, Kersey, *The World's Sixteen Crucified Saviors* (New York, 1875)

Gray, John, *The Biblical Doctrine of the Reign of God* (Edinburgh, 1979)

Hardy, A. Lister, *The Biology of God* (London, 1975)

Henry, Matthew, *Exposition of the Old and New Testament* (London, 1710)

Henry, Matthew, *Shorter Catechism* (Belfast, 1845)

Hick, John H., *Evil and the God of Love* (London, 1966)

Hick, John H., *Philosophy of Religion* (Englewood, 1963)

Holmes, Oliver Wendell *Poet at the Breakfast Table* (Boston, 1872)

Hornung, E., *Conceptions of God in Ancient Egypt: The One and the Many* (Cornell, 1982)

Hume, David, *Dialogues Concerning Natural Religion* (London, 1779)

Hunter, Michael and Wootton, David (eds), *Atheism from the Reformation to the Enlightenment* (Oxford, 1992)

Hustad, Donald P., *Jubilate! Church Music in the Evangelical Tradition* (New York, 1952)

Ifrah, Georges, *The Universal History of Numbers* (tr. David Bellos, Sophie Wood, E. F. Harding and Ian Monk) (London, 1999)

Irving, Washington, *Life of Mahomet* (New York, 1849)

D'Israel, Isaac, *Curiosities of Literature* (London, 1791)

Jacobs, Louis, *The Jewish Religion* (Oxford, 1995)

Jacobs, Louis, (ed.), *The Jewish Mystics* (London, 1976)

James, William, *The Varieties of Religious Experience* (London, 1901)

Janowitz, Naomi, 'God's Body', *People of the Body: Jews and Judaism from an Embodied Perspective*, ed. Howard Eilberg-Schwartz (Albany, 1992)

Johnson, Paul, *A History of Christianity* (London, 1976)

Johnson, Paul, *A History of the Jews* (London, 1987)

Johnson, Paul, *The Quest for God* (London, 1996)

Kant, Immanuel, *Critique of Practical Reason*, tr. Lewis White Beck (New York, 1994)

Kaufmann, Walter, *Critique of Religion and Philosophy* (Princeton, 1958)

Kaufmann, Walter, *Nietzsche: Philosopher, Psychologist, Antichrist* (Princeton, 1968)

Kaufmann, Yehezkel, *The Religion of Israel from its Beginnings to the Babylonian Exile*, tr. Moshe Greenberg (London, 1961)

Kennedy, Ludovic, *All in the Mind: A Farewell to God* (London, 1999)

Kramer, S. N., *Sumerian Mythology* (Philadelphia, 1944)

Küng, Hans, *Does God Exist? An Answer for Today*, tr. Edward Quinn (London, 1978)

Lane-Fox, Robin, *Pagans and Christians in the Mediterranean World* (London, 1986)

Lane-Fox, Robin, *The Unauthorised Version: Truth and Fiction in the Bible* (London, 1991)

Lecky, W. E. H., *History of European Morals* (London, 1869)

Lewis, C. S., *Mere Christianity* (London, 1952)

Luther, Martin, *Works Volume 12*

Mackie, J. L., *Evil and Omnipotence in the Philosophy of Religion*, ed. Basil Mitchell (Oxford, 1978)

Macquarrie, John, *Principles of Christian Theology* (London, 1955)

Macquarrie, John, *Thinking about God* (London, 1975)

Maimonides, Moses, *The Guide of the Perplexed*, tr. M. Friedländer (New York, 1956)

Marmonstein, A., *The Old Rabbinic Doctrine of God* (London, 1927)

McGinn, Bernard, *The Foundations of Mysticism* (London, 1992)

Miles, Jack, *Christ: A Crisis in the Life of God* (London, 2001)

Miles, Jack, *God: A Biography* (New York, 1995)

Miller, P. D., *The Divine Warrior in Early Israel* (Cambridge, MA, 1973)

Milton, John, *Paradise Lost* (London, 1667)

Mirk, John, *Mirk's Festival: A collection of Homilies by Johannes Mirkus*, ed. T. Erbe (1905)

de Montfaucon, Bernard, *Antiquity Explained and Represented in Sculptures* (10 vols, London, 1721)

Newton, Isaac, *Newton's Philosophy of Nature*, ed. H. S. Thayer (New York, 1953)

Nietzsche, Friedrich, *Works*, ed. Oscar Levy (18 vols, London, 1905–10)

Nicholson, E. W., *God and His People* (Oxford, 1986)

Nicholson, Reynold A., *The Mystics of Islam* (London, 1914)

Ochs, Carol, *Behind the Sex of God* (Boston, 1977)

Otto, Rudolf, *The Idea of the Holy*, tr. John Harvey (Oxford, 1923)

The Oxford Companion to the Bible ed. Bruce Metzger and Michael Coogan (Oxford, 1993)

The Oxford Dictionary of the Christian Church ed. F. L. Cross and E. A. Livingstone (3rd Edition, Oxford, 1997)

The Oxford Dictionary of World Religions ed. John Bowker (Oxford, 1997)

Pagels, Elaine, *The Origin of Satan* (New York, 1995)

Paine, Thomas, *The Age of Reason* (Paris, 1794)

Paley, William, *Natural Theology* (London, 1802)

Pannikar, Raimondo, *The Trinity and the Religious Experience of Man* (Berkeley, 1977)

Pelikan, Jaruslav, *The Christian Tradition: A History of the Development of Doctrine* (Chicago, 1971–82)

Raisanen, Heikki, *Marcion, Muhammad and the Mahatma* (London, 1997)

Redford, D. B., *Egypt, Canaan and Israel in Ancient Times* (Princeton, 1992)

Richmond, James, *Theology and Metaphysics* (London, 1970)

Robinson, John, *Exploration into God* (London, 1967)

Robinson, John, *Honest to God* (London, 1963)

Ruether, Rosemary Radford, *Wrath of Jonah* (New York, 1969)

Russell, Bertrand, *History of Western Philosophy* (London, 1946)

Russell, Bertrand, *Marriage and Morals* (London, 1929)

Russell, Bertrand, *Unpopular Essays* (London, 1950)

Russell, Bertrand, *Why I am not a Christian* (London, 1957)

Sartre, Jean-Paul, *The Devil and the Good Lord*, tr. Lloyd Alexander (New York, 1995)

Schmidt, Wilhelm, *The Origin of the Idea of God* (London, 1912)

Schopenhauer, Arthur, *Essays and Aphorisms*, tr. R. J. Hollingdale (Harmondsworth, 1970)

Scott, George Ryley, *Phallic Worship* (London, 1966)

Scruton, Roger, *The Philosopher on Dover Beach: Essays* (Manchester, 1990)

Smart, Ninian, *The Philosophy of Religion* (London, 1979)

Smith, George, *The Chaldean Account of Genesis* (London, 1876)

Smith, Joseph, *Essentials in Church History* (Salt Lake City, 1964)

Smith, Mark S., *The Early History of God: Yahweh and Other Deities in Ancient Israel* (San Francisco, 1990)

Smith, Sydney, *Works* (3 vols, London, 1848)

Soggin, J. A., *A History of Israel* (London, 1984)

Swinburne, Richard, *Is there a God?* (Oxford, 1996)

Swinburne, Richard, *The Coherence of Theism* (Oxford, 1977)

Tillich, Paul, *Systematic Theology* (3 vols, Chicago, 1959–64)

Trible, Phyllis, *God and the Rhetoric of Sexuality* (Philadelphia, 1983)

Van Seters, John, *The Pentateuch: A Social-Science Commentary* (Sheffield, 1999)

Voltaire, *Philosophical Dictionary*, tr. Theodore Besterman (Harmondsworth, 1985)

Walker, D. P., *The Decline of Hell* (London, 1963)

Walsch, Neale Donald, *Conversations with God* (New York, 1995)

Ward, Keith, *The Concept of God* (New York, 1974)

Waugh, Alexander, *Time: From Micro-seconds to Millennia, a Search for the Right Time* (London, 1999)

Waugh, Evelyn, *The Loved One* (London, 1948)

Wilmhurst, W. L., 'Contemplations', *The Two and the One*, Mirea Eliade, tr. J. M. Cohen (Chicago, 1965)

Wilson, A. N., *God's Funeral* (London, 1999)

Wilson, A. N., *How Can We Know?* (London, 1985)

Wilson, A. N., *Jesus* (London, 1992)

Wilson, A. N., *Paul: The Mind of the Apostle* (London, 1997)

Wittgenstein, Ludwig, *Tractatus Logico-Philosophicus*, tr. C. K. Odgen (London, 1990)

Zuhur-u'd-din Ahmad, *Mystic Tendencies in Islam* (Lahore, 1991)

LIST OF ABBREVIATIONS

Apoc. Abr.	*Apocalypse of Abraham*
Apoc. Adam	*Apocalypse of Adam*
Apoc. Sed.	*Apocalypse of Sedrach*
Apoc. Pet.	*Apocalypse of Peter*
Apoc. Shem.	*Apocalypse of Shem*
Bar.	Baruch
2 Bar.	2 Baruch
Cop. Gos. Thom.	*The Coptic Gospel of Thomas*
Chron.	Chronicles
Col.	Colossians
Cor.	Corinthians
Dan.	Daniel
Deut.	Deuteronomy
Eccles.	Ecclesiastes
1 En.	*Ethiopic Apocalypse of Enoch*
2 En.	*Slavonic Apocalypse of Enoch*
3 En.	*Hebrew Apocalypse of Enoch*
Eph.	Ephesians
Esd.	Esdras
Esth.	Esther
Exod.	Exodus
Ezek.	Ezekiel
Gk. Apoc. Ezra	*Greek Apocalypse of Ezra*
Gal.	Galatians
Gen.	Genesis

Gos. Phil.	*Gospel of Philip*
Hell. Syn. Pr.	*Hellenistic Synagogal Prayers*
Hab.	Habakkuk
Hag.	Haggai
Heb.	Hebrews
Hos.	Hosea
Isa.	Isaiah
I.S. Thom.	*Infancy Story of Thomas*
Jos. Asen.	*Joseph and Aseneth*
Jer.	Jeremiah
Judg.	Judges
Jas.	James
Jon.	Jonah
Josh.	Joshua
Jub.	*Jubilees*
LAE	*Life of Adam and Eve*
Lam.	Lamentations
Lev.	Leviticus
Lad. Jac.	*Ladder of Jacob*
Liv. Proph.	*Lives of the Prophets*
Macc.	Maccabees
Mart. and Asc. Isa.	*The Martyrdom and Ascension of Isaiah*
Mal.	Malachi
Matt.	Gospel of Matthew
Mic.	Micah
Nah.	Nahum
Neh.	Nehemiah
Num.	Numbers
Obad.	Obadiah
Odes Sol.	*Odes of Solomon*
Ps.-Philo	*Pseudo-Philo*
Pr. Jac.	*Prayer of Jacob*
Pet.	Peter
Phil.	Philippians

Prot. Jas.	*The Protevangelium of James*
Prov.	Proverbs
Ps.	Psalms
Ques. Ezra	*Questions of Ezra*
Rev.	Revelation
Rom.	Romans
Sam.	Samuel
Sec. Gos. Mark	*Secret Gospel of Mark*
Sir.	Ecclesiasticus/Sirach
Sib. Or.	*Sibylline Oracles*
Test. of Levi	*The Testament of Levi*
Thess.	Thessalonians
Tim.	Timothy
T. Job	*Testament of Job*
Tob.	Tobit
T. Sol.	*Testament of Solomon*
Tit.	Titus
Wisd. of Sol.	Wisdom of Solomon
Zech.	Zechariah
Zeph.	Zephaniah

INDEX

333